Performance at the Limit

Can you imagine your organisation as a Ferrari or a McLaren, a Toyota or a Force India? Your management team as a pit crew? Your sales force as the race team and your marketing and research department as the design studio creating a Formula 1 car?

Formula 1 has an estimated turnover of $4 billion, employs 50,000 people in more than 30 countries and has a foothold in every major and developing economy. With performance as the central focus of every organisation, *Performance at the Limit* uses the case of Formula 1 motorsport as an example of how business can achieve optimal performance in highly competitive environments where dealing with change effectively is paramount. This second edition builds on the success of the first and contains a wealth of new material, including many more interviews with Formula 1 drivers and other key executives active in the sport.

MARK JENKINS is Professor of Business Strategy at Cranfield School of Management. He has twenty-one years' experience as a teacher and consultant in the areas of competitive strategy, knowledge management and innovation. He has undertaken research on the performance of Formula 1 teams since 1997.

KEN PASTERNAK delivers seminars for executives and advises banks and businesses in the areas of leadership and management, organisation development and teamwork. Based in Helsinki, his activities are focused in the US and Europe, plus the CIS and other emerging economies. Previously, he worked for Citibank and the European Bank for Reconstruction and Development.

RICHARD WEST has held senior commercial roles with the McLaren, Williams and Arrows Formula 1 teams and the Jaguar Sportscar team. Having raised in excess of $165 million of commercial sponsorship, today he works as an international keynote speaker and facilitator and runs a management training company that uses Formula 1 as a central theme.

Performance at the Limit

Business Lessons from Formula 1
Motor Racing

2nd edition

MARK JENKINS

KEN PASTERNAK

RICHARD WEST

CAMBRIDGE
UNIVERSITY PRESS

CAMBRIDGE UNIVERSITY PRESS
Cambridge, New York, Melbourne, Madrid, Cape Town, Singapore, São Paulo, Delhi

Cambridge University Press
The Edinburgh Building, Cambridge CB2 8RU, UK

Published in the United States of America by Cambridge University Press, New York

www.cambridge.org
Information on this title: www.cambridge.org/9780521449632

© Mark Jenkins, Ken Pasternak and Richard West 2005, 2009

First edition published 2005
Second edition 2009

Printed in the United Kingdom at the University Press, Cambridge

A catalogue record for this publication is available from the British Library

Library of Congress Cataloguing in Publication data
Jenkins, Mark.
    Performance at the limit : business lessons from Formula 1 motor racing /
    Mark Jenkins, Ken Pasternak, Richard West. – 2nd ed.
        p.   cm.
    Includes bibliographical references and index.
    ISBN 978-0-521-44963-2 (hardback)   1. Performance technology.
    2. Industrial management.   3. Grand Prix racing–Management.   I. Pasternak,
    Ken, 1951–   II. West, Richard.   III. Title.
    HF5549.5.P37J46 2009
    658.4–dc22   2009007295

ISBN 978-0-521-44963-2 hardback

Contents

Figures

Tables

Plates

Acknowledgements

As with the first edition of *Performance at the Limit*, one of the hardest parts of writing the second edition has been to know where to start saying thank you to the many people who have contributed to its content.

Formula 1, both as a sport and a business, takes huge commitment and unrelenting effort in all areas. Despite these pressures, everyone we have spoken to gave freely of their time, experience and knowledge to assist us in the creation of this book. We would like to express our gratitude to all those who have supported this project and trust the reader will bear with us in recognising the people by name, as without their time and contributions *Performance at the Limit*, both first and second editions, would never have been written.

Firstly, and without whom our research could not have been undertaken so thoroughly, our sincere thanks go to Formula 1 supremo Bernie Ecclestone for allowing us unrestricted access to round 4 of the FIA Formula 1 World Championship, the Formula 1 Gran Premio De España Telefónica at Barcelona in April 2008. His positive response to our request meant we were able to meet and talk to some of the great names in the sport and business of Grand Prix racing, with many of the interviews with key people taking place over that weekend.

Equally, *Performance at the Limit* could not have been published without the continued commitment of our publishers, Cambridge University Press. Paula Parish has worked with us on the second edition and our thanks go to her. We are also indebted to Margaret Hamer for transcribing a considerable number of the interviews and for working on some of the figures, and Nardine Collier for preparing the index. Additionally, our thanks go to Charly Salonius-Pasternak for proofreading and commenting on the manuscript, and also to Angela Thompson for her additional work on a number of key transcripts.

To Nahrendhra Mohar and Jane Gorard, formerly with BBC World, we offer our sincere thanks for their tireless support and for using the original version of *Performance at the Limit* as the inspiration for an eight-part global television series 'Formula for Success', and also for the professional manner in which Ian Sollars and the entire crew of TV production company Sunset + Vine conducted themselves in producing the series using the authors' many contacts.

In terms of our specific thanks to the Formula 1 and motorsport community, Max Mosley as the President of the sport's governing body, the FIA, responded in detail to the authors in writing and gave us some concise and insightful views of the challenges facing Formula 1. Our thanks go to Tony Purnell of the FIA who also shared his thoughts with us.

Flavio Briatore, the Managing Director of the Renault F1 team, gave us an amazingly frank and entertaining overview of what it takes to successfully operate a Formula 1 team and a diverse range of additional businesses, including his involvement with football club QPR. Special thanks must also go to Patrizia Spinelli, Renault F1's Communications Manager; John Mardle, Operations Director; and James Gilbride, Account Manager, for their continuous supply of facts, figures, materials and arrangements.

Ferrari made us incredibly welcome both trackside and at our second visit to the factory at Maranello in Italy. Stefano Domenicali, as Jean Todt's successor in the key Ferrari role, was forthright with his views and comments on teamwork and the importance of every role in the team structure, but none of this would have been possible without the assistance we received from Luca Colajanni. His tireless efforts assisted us by providing a unique insight into the business and sporting affairs of the 'prancing horse'.

Christian Horner of Red Bull Racing added a fresh approach to our questions. As one of the new breed of younger team principals in Formula 1, his views were open, honest and clear. In addition, we were warmly welcomed into the 'Red Bull Energy Station' during the Barcelona weekend. It was fascinating to see how such a facility has formed a central meeting point for members of all of the teams, the media, television crews and the like, all catered for, all welcomed and all being made aware of the Red Bull lifestyle commitment to Formula 1.

Regarded by many as the sport's top technical man and leading tactician, Honda's Team Principal Ross Brawn gave us an incredible insight into life at Honda and his comparisons with his time at Ferrari and the challenges he faces today. His views on the integration of various working groups spread out across the globe and why revitalising Honda's racing efforts are part of a three-year plan make fascinating reading.

A driver's schedule today both on and away from the track is gruelling in terms of time allocation. It is therefore particularly satisfying to be able to thank McLaren's Heikki Kovalainen, Red Bull's Mark Webber, WilliamsF1's Nico Rosberg and Ferrari's Felipe Massa for their contributions. Our thanks also go to the manager of Kimi Raikkonen and Jenson Button, David Robertson, for his frank views of driver management today, and to Jukka Mildh who was our conduit to Nico Rosberg. Our thanks also go to former Grand Prix driver and now driver manager and TV commentator Martin Brundle who added some valuable insights into the world of a current-day driver.

Driver fitness now plays a vital role in achieving performance at the limit. It was therefore very helpful to be able to spend considerable time with Aki Hintsa, McLaren's Team Physician, and to discuss his role in keeping the team's drivers and key staff in top condition.

Sir Jackie Stewart's views are as valid today as they were at the start of his career in the 1960s. A former World Champion, Team Principal, pundit, TV commentator and today a highly successful international businessman and corporate ambassador for The Royal Bank of Scotland Group, the words of 'JYS' are always worth reading and the authors' thanks go to him for his time and commitment to the many questions put to him.

From a business perspective, John Hogan, senior consultant to Just Marketing and Vodafone, gave us his views of the changing face of Formula 1 as a business and Peter Digby, Managing Director of Xtrac transmission technology, inputted greatly as to the ever-changing requirements of a first-class engineering supplier.

From the sponsors' perspective, Isabelle M. Conner, Chief Marketing Officer for ING's Corporate Communications and Affairs, gave us a truly unique insight and a range of personal guidelines that anyone wishing to enact a sponsorship programme should heed. Her view of how to 'attack' a new opportunity was simple yet clear and concise and our thanks are also extended to her for supplying us with a range of data and materials that aided our research greatly.

The authors noticed tremendous improvements since 2005 in the increase in the numbers of journalists, photographers and TV crews present and also the ways in which the teams look after and assist them in their quest for information. Very special thanks go to journalist David Tremayne who gave freely of his views and time. Chief Operating Officer (COO) Alex Burns and Head of Marketing Scott Garrett of WilliamsF1 provided us with major inputs, as did John Howett of Toyota F1 with assistance from Alastair Moffitt. Ian Phillips of Force India and Jim Wright of Toro Rosso also add greatly to this book through their comments as two of the longest-serving commercial men in the business.

For the first version of *Performance at the Limit*, the authors also interviewed Sir John Allison, John Barnard, Paul Edwards, Bernard Ferguson, Patrick Head, Eddie Jordan, Paul Jordan, Paolo Martinelli, Raoul Pinnell, David Richards, Dickie Stanford, Paul Stoddart, Pat Symonds, Jean Todt, John Walton, Sir Frank Williams and Hiroshi Yasukawa. Their words are in some cases still quoted and for those where they are not, we recognise and appreciate their original contributions and the value of their comments in our research process.

The authors hope and trust that we have correctly identified everyone's inputs and contributions; however, last but definitely not least, to our enduringly supportive wives, Sandra, Harriet and Denise, thank you for your commitment and understanding during the long hours our research, writing and production has demanded of us ... and of course the odd visit to a race, or test session, and the various factory visits that have made writing this second edition such a pleasure!

Mark Jenkins, Ken Pasternak and Richard West
Ampthill, Helsinki and Dartford

Note on the reference system

A numbered list of all sources used is given in the References section at the end of the book. Where these sources are quoted from or referred to in the main text a superscript numeral cross-refers to the relevant numbered source.

The Grand Prix experience

In April 2004, the authors attended the San Marino Grand Prix at Imola in San Marino, Italy to interview a number of the leading protagonists of the Formula 1 world for the first edition of *Performance at the Limit*.

Four book print runs and four years later, in April 2008, we once more entered the Formula 1 paddock with invitations to interview sixteen individuals over just two and a half days; there was no time to waste!

The ability to gain access to Formula 1 must never be underestimated and, as we described at the time of writing our first book, there are in reality two types of Grand Prix world – the outer and the inner – and nothing has changed in this respect!

The outer world of the circuit is comprised of the public grandstands, vending areas, programme sellers, campsites, huge parking areas and tens of thousands of people hoping to take a picture or obtain an autograph of their favourite driver or personality.

The inner world is the paddock which exists within an area controlled by the electronic security pass issued by FOM (Formula One Management). Access is gained via a microchip sealed within the plastic FOM access pass when swiped across a reader at the automated entrance gates.

This is the inner sanctum of Formula 1, a place for the teams, drivers and the movers and shakers of the sport. In simple terms it means no pass, then no entry, as access to the Formula 1 paddock is highly restricted. Almost strangely, this 'exclusivity' is what sponsors, guests and VIPs expect. It is a place where deals are cut, won and lost. It is the world of international sporting power brokers and businessmen and -women.

The paddock is where the Bridgestone tyre company's stock of racing tyres and fitting facilities are based, the teams' racing car transporters and the multipurpose race hospitality areas and team working areas all congregate. It is also where the increased number of FIA[1] vehicles and personnel that oversee the technical and safety rules of the sport operate from within their distinctive blue and gold facilities.

Passing through the electronically activated security gates, the first-time visitor is greeted by the sight of a range of immaculate articulated trucks, vans and vehicles in the various teams' colours and designs. These are the 'workhorses' that bring pit equipment, spares, bodywork, fuel and countless other items of equipment to each of the European Grand Prix.

These vehicles are specifically designed and manufactured not just as transportation for the racing cars and their spare parts, but also as mobile workshops, data management suites and meeting and briefing rooms. Once in position they are adorned with extremely tall telemetry and radio communication masts and throughout the weekend are endlessly polished and cleaned by the 'truckies' who drive them to and from events.

The scale of 'the show' is simply enormous and the logistics of this are astonishing. For non-European races each team moves about 8 tonnes of sea freight on top of the 30 tonnes of air freight for the cars and the garages.[2] Throughout the European season, this fleet of trucks, vans and mobile hospitality areas makes its way from race to race on a weekly basis. For the 'long haul' international races, the entire contents (although not the units themselves) and much more besides is flown, as described below.

When watching a 'long haul' Grand Prix such as Brazil or Australia, just consider for one moment that in terms of actual content, everything you see before you, in addition to all of the equipment as yet unseen in the garages and main paddock area, has to be packed, boxed and transported to a central airport, then flown across the world in a fleet of air freighters, then be unloaded, customs cleared and then transported to the circuit for use before being reloaded and then sent back to the teams' individual HQs!

One of the most striking visual things to have changed in just four years since our visit to Imola is the size of the teams' combined hospitality, guest and media units or hospitality centres. The McLaren centre (nicknamed 'Saturn 5' by one of the long-term Formula 1 hands!) and the 'Red Bull Energy Station', stand out as high-tech, mobile architectural wonders with their smoked glass and tubular steel exteriors, but upon gaining entry, the quality of the fittings, the food and drink service and the politeness and efficiency of the staff would put many top restaurants and hotels to shame.

They also feature meeting rooms, media offices and private areas for engineers and VIPs to discuss confidential matters; they are in effect extensions of the teams' home base facilities.

The positioning of these units, racing car transporters and mobile workshops is closely overseen by an FOM representative. In Formula 1, image and performance go hand in hand. Such is the attention to detail in paddock layout, that it is possible to run a measure along the front of the trucks and motorhomes and find them millimetre perfect.

Only one unit stands clear of this line by several metres and it is the ever-present, but discrete silver and dark grey coach with its darkly tinted windows belonging to Formula 1 ringmaster Bernie Ecclestone, where countless people wait patiently for an audience with motor-sport's most powerful man.

The window overlooking the paddock walkway is oval, almost a tinted eye when looked at carefully, and it is clear to the onlooker that at all times Bernie is aware of who is in his paddock.

The way the media is handled by the teams has also changed dramatically for the better. It was very clear that many more of the teams' media personnel have now had formal training – some are ex-journalists themselves – and that they are sympathetic to the demands of the press and their team drivers and senior staff accordingly. With sponsors and manufacturers demanding greater returns, it is clear to see every effort is being made to meet their demands.

When first entering the paddock, the visitor is confronted by a truly astounding sight. Backed up to the pit garage complex are the racing teams' transporters. Above the garage complex at most venues are several floors of VIP boxes, administration offices and the media centre. And above them is the rooftop paddock club where several thousand VIPs are hosted by the teams, sponsors and manufacturers involved in Formula 1.

Step inside the teams' garages and you enter another world completely. Painted and in some cases tiled floors, complete wall-to-wall panelling featuring images, the teams' names and sponsors, digital clocks, plasma screens and weekend timetables all topped off with custom-made overhead gantries carrying heat, light, power, compressed air – it is simply a workshop created for a weekend to the very highest standards, always mindful that the world's media and TV watch on.

While all of this carries the 'i' word – image – the teams themselves are of course there to race. In among the deal-brokering, VIP and sponsor tours and endless meetings, the drivers, engineers and mechanics have to concentrate upon practice, qualifying and the actual race meeting, and their schedule is another work of art within a clearly defined timetable, as seen in Figure 1.

Spanish GP 2008 – 25–27th April 2008

Friday 25th April

Paddock Club: 145 pax - Garage Times: 09:00 – 09:45, 12:00 – 13:30, 16:00 – 18:00

08:45	Paddock Club opens
08:45 – 09:15	Formula BMW Practice session
10:00 – 11:30	*Formula One First practice session*
11:30 – 11:45	*Garage Steve Nielsen Interview*
11:55 – 12:25	GP2 Practice session
12:00	*Paddock Club Lunch*
12:30	*Paddock Club Lucas Di Grassi Appearance*
12:50 – 13:10	Formula BMW Qualifying session
13:10 – 13:50	*Formula One Paddock Club pit lane walk*
13:45 – 14:00	Garage Pit link
14:00 – 15:30	*Formula One Second practice session*
16:00 – 16:30	GP2 Qualifying session
17:00 – 17:45	Porsche Mobil 1 Supercup Practice session
18:00	Paddock Club closes

- Please note this timetable may be subject to amendments

Saturday 26th April

Paddock club: 156 pax - Garage Times: 08:30 – 10:30, 12:30 – 13:30, 15:15 – 17:30

09:15	Paddock Club opens
09:30 – 10:00	Formula BMW First race
10:00 – 10:45	*Formula One Paddock Club pit lane walk*

Figure 1 Timetable for Spanish Grand Prix, 25–27 April 2008.
Source: Team Renault F1.

11:00 – 12:00	*Formula One Third practice session*
12:00 – 12:15	*Garage Steve Nielsen Interview*
12:00	*Paddock Club Lunch*
12:25 – 13:10	Porsche Mobil 1 Supercup Qualifying session
12:45	*Renault Suite Lucas Di Grassi Appearance*
13:00	*Paddock Club Nelson Piquet Appearance*
13:15 – 13:50	*Formula One Paddock Club pit lane walk*
13:45 – 14:00	Garage Pit link
14:00 – 15:00	*Formula One Qualifying session*
15:05	*Paddock Club Lucas Di Grassi Appearance*
16:00 – 17:20	GP2 First race (39 laps)
17:30	Paddock Club closes

- Please note this timetable may be subject to amendments

Sunday 27th April

Paddock Club: 166 pax - Garage Times: 08:30 – 12:30

08:30	Paddock Club opens
08:00 – 09:15	*Formula One Paddock Club pit lane walk*
09:15 – 09:45	Formula BMW Second race
10:30 – 11:20	GP2 Second race (26 laps)
10:50	*Renault Suite Nelson Piquet Appearance*
11:05	*Total Suite Nelson Piquet Appearance*
11:20	*Bridgestone Suite Nelson Piquet Appearance*
11:15	*Paddock Club Fernando Alonso Appearance*
12:00	*Paddock Club Lunch – First course*
11:45 – 12:20	Porsche Mobil 1 Supercup First race (14 laps)
12:20	*Paddock Club Lucas Di Grassi Appearance*
12:30 – 13:15	*Formula One Paddock Club pit lane walk*
12:30	Formula One Drivers Track Parade
13:15	*Paddock Club Lunch – Second course and desert*
13:30	*Garage Pat Symonds Interview*
14:00	*Formula One Spanish Grand Prix 2008 (66 laps)*
17:00	Paddock Club closes

- Please note this timetable may be subject to amendments

Figure 1 *(cont.)*

As the weekend progresses, the pressures increase. Friday is a time for circulating the paddock, searching out specific people and journalists, catching up on the latest 'word' on the street.

Come Saturday, and the mechanics, tyre fitters, engineers and drivers can be seen moving from motorhome to garage, garage to media meetings, back to motorhome for lunch and, if required, a massage. There is practice and there is qualifying – the need for pole position (the front of the starting grid) occupies everyone's minds and at today's meeting at the Circuit de Catalunya it is a Ferrari and Renault front row – the Spanish fans can be heard above the engine noise as Alonso steps from his R30 Renault car at the end of qualifying!

The paddock is now alive with journalists. The top three qualifiers, Kimi Raikkonen (Ferrari) on pole followed by Fernando Alonso (Renault F1) and Felipe Massa (Ferrari), walk out from the press suite and into a corral of photographers, TV cameras and journalists with their arms extended, holding voice recorders. Each of the drivers makes his way around the inside perimeter of the circle, accompanied by a PR person from their team, answering questions about their performance, the car and their expectations for the race on the following day.

For the drivers and team principals, assisted by their marketing and PR teams, Saturday evenings usually mean official sponsor dinners, guest appearances and drink parties. While sometimes onerous, all recognise the importance of these events and undertake them professionally.

Sunday of course is the longest and most important day. Arrive early enough and you will see the first people (motorhome staff) arriving and opening up their various 'HQs' for the day ahead. Shortly after, engineers, mechanics, team managers and drivers arrive (the team principals are never far behind!). Suddenly, the paddock is abuzz, the 'truckies' are giving the race transporters one final polish, the drivers, now focused, still stop and smile for photographs and autographs, the journalists continue to search for one more quote and Bernie Ecclestone can be seen frequently going from motorhome to motorhome ensuring the show runs faultlessly.

Amidst the noise, energy, sights, smells and sounds, one becomes increasingly aware of the crowd, the paying public who for hours have driven, camped, walked to see their favourite stars in action. On this day the grandstands are full of – what else? – Fernando Alonso supporters.

There is a sea of colours representing his Renault team and all around there are banners and chants spurring their Spanish hero on.

As at all circuits, the fans wait with air horns, flags, fireworks and banners and thirty minutes before the start of the race, when the pit lane officially opens, they begin to cheer. Earlier in the day, the drivers must complete a lap of the circuit on the back of a flatbed articulated trailer or in open-top cars. They wave and the crowds cheer them, but this is nothing compared to the noise of the engines and the combined sound of the crowd as they wave them out with just minutes to go before the start of yet another Grand Prix ...

Exactly on the appointed minute, the cars are flagged off on their final warm-up lap to complete one lap under controlled conditions, the pole sitter leads them all round, each car zigzagging around the circuit to warm up its tyres, to form up for the grid where seconds later the five red lights come on in sequence, go out as one and the Spanish Grand Prix is under way.

The paddock is now quiet, almost empty; everyone is focused on the track and pit lane but one thing never changes, the deadline for the next race. Teams of motorhome workers have already begun to pack the items that are no longer required; some people, their work already done, are leaving the circuit to avoid the queues at the end of the day.

The authors, with their interviews complete, head for the airport and, by the time they arrive, the news is filtering though from the Formula 1 Gran Premio De España Telefónica 2008 – it is a Ferrari one/two finish with Alonso retiring due to engine failure. It's a disappointing day for Alonso (and his fans) as he packs up and heads for home, but in just two short weeks it's off to Turkey and another Grand Prix ... the show goes on!

1 | Introduction

Since publishing the first edition of *Performance at the Limit* in 2005, the authors have introduced concepts from the book to thousands of executives and business-school students, Formula 1 enthusiasts and, more interestingly, non-fans through our speaking engagements, teaching assignments and Pit Stop Challenge events.

The BBC introduced these concepts to an even wider audience, numbering in the millions worldwide, by airing 'Formula for Success', an eight-part television series on BBC World during the autumn of 2007. Our book served as the inspiration for this well-produced and insightful series. The authors and their insights were featured throughout the production.

The parallels that we explore between Formula 1 and the business world at large seem to resonate with all of these audiences. Our narrative has opened discussion in several important management and business disciplines, has wide international appeal and has proved to be of interest not only to diehard fans of Formula 1, and to our relief has not been perceived as only an exercise in examining 'toys for boys'.

The relevance of our comparisons between the Formula 1 industry and the business environment that corporate executives face day to day lies in the fact that both:

- are highly competitive;
- experience change on a constant basis;
- require continual innovation to stay ahead of the competition;
- rely on sharing of knowledge across functional divides;
- require teamwork to achieve common goals; and finally
- in both the most important measure of success is actual performance.

Much has changed during the five years since we did our original research. Teams have left the arena while new ones have taken their place on the grid. Equally, much younger drivers have entered the sport and, in the case of Lewis Hamilton, exploded onto the scene in his rookie season of 2007. The sport's governing body, the FIA, has, through the Technical and Sporting Regulations, continued to make changes in Formula 1 in an effort to contain the growth of costs, make a statement about becoming more environmentally aware and also to continue to make the sport safer.

In addition, two new racing venues have been added: Valencia, Spain and Singapore in 2008, the former a street race similar to that which takes place in Monaco, and the latter the first night race in Formula 1 history.

Abu Dhabi is already a scheduled addition to the 2009 calendar while South Korea and New Delhi are planned for 2010. Many also hope that a Grand Prix in the US will reappear on the race calendar. Moscow, Mexico City and several other cities are in contention to bring the total number of Formula 1 races to twenty, a number which most participants in the sport believe is the maximum that the infrastructure, budgets and personnel can handle. All these new locations would of course be at the expense of losing some of the more traditional circuits situated in Europe.

To our readers, please note that this is not a book just about the sport of Formula 1. It is not just about racing cars, commercial sponsorship or the politics of motorsport. It is about something which we believe to be far more important and enduring. This book focuses on the problems of sustaining organisational performance in dynamic and competitive environments. We are concerned with how organisations achieve performance levels at the limits of their financial, technological and human potential. It is a book which considers the turbulent ride between outstanding success and humiliating failure and explores the reasons for such outcomes.

To survive and prosper the organisation of today has to be both lean and agile, creative and efficient, effective at recruiting, motivating and retaining the highest calibre of staff, and also able to restructure and redeploy these individuals into teams across a range of challenging tasks and locations. Such demands are accepted as part of the dynamic business environment of today.

However, the ways in which such management challenges are met and addressed are rarely examined in detail. While there is a wide range of work that has considered generic issues such as best practice and performance across many global industries, these often lack the specific insight to help deal with such challenges on a day-to-day basis. In this book we offer a different approach. We do not attempt to distil generic characteristics of performance success across a range of business contexts; this has already been effectively done in a range of management texts such as Peters and Waterman[3] and Collins and Porras.[4] Our agenda is to examine a highly specialised industry in depth. We do so because we believe that this particular industry encapsulates many of the challenges faced by today's managers across many different types of organisation and sector.

Further to the concepts mentioned above, these challenges include: increasing knowledge creation and transfer; working in global and virtual teams; managing across boundaries; enhancing innovation and creativity; accelerating speed to market; effective execution of strategy; creating transformational change and, above all, through all of these challenges, creating sustained levels of performance which competitors are unable to live with. Many of these issues have already been considered in management texts such as Richard D'Aveni's work on hypercompetition[5] and Shona Brown and Kathy Eisenhardt's consideration of fast-paced organisations that are highly adaptable and responsive to change.[6] We are not claiming that the detailed issues we examine provide quick transferable solutions to other organisations, or that we are able to prescribe easy panaceas, but we do believe that the case histories and examples that we examine provide both inspirational and instructional guidance to those seeking to achieve levels of performance – at the limit of possibility.

In this book we draw on accounts of ambition, wealth, enduring relationships and, most of all, levels of passion and commitment which are inspirational to those involved in shaping and managing organisations. In this chapter we first outline some of the key insights we have drawn from our study, we then describe the research process we have adopted and conclude with a statement on the overall purpose of the study.

First, as a preview of our findings, which are developed in detail in Chapter 12, we present the core characteristics of an organisational system (we use this term to emphasise the role of partner organisations in creating performance outcomes) that achieves 'Performance at the Limit'. We do not purport these factors to be necessary or adequate in themselves; however, we found them to be central in the success of Formula 1 teams and the general distinctiveness of the industry.

Characteristics of 'Performance at the Limit'

- *Maintain open and constant communication.* A constant flow of open communication to all in the organisation is critical to ensure that everyone is aware of how things are developing and where potential sources for improvement can be found.
- *Isolate the problem, not the person: the 'no blame' culture.* The readiness of everyone to be open and honest about their mistakes. What is surprising is that this occurs in a context that has its fair share of inflated egos, but there is a widespread recognition that the whole system can only improve when this happens, and this can only be created where the whole organisation is underpinned by a warts-and-all, 'no blame' culture.
- *Build the organisation around informal processes, networks and relationships.* Very often the structure and roles within the organisation will emerge from the particular competences of and relationships between individuals. In this case, rather than creating the structure and fitting individuals into predefined roles, we see the structure emerging from the capabilities of individuals within the organisation, thereby allowing their potential and the performance of the organisation to be maximised.
- *Alignment of goals between individuals, teams and partners.* Alignment at all levels is critical to success. This is both in terms of everyone sharing the same goals, which is perhaps easier in Formula 1 than other situations, but also in terms of everyone understanding how they and the groups they participate in contribute to this performance.
- *Focus, focus, focus.* The successful teams are those which are focused. When teams take their 'eye off the ball' they are vulnerable to competitors who are more committed and more focused.
- *Make quick decisions and learn from the results.* The pressure of Formula 1 is such that the teams have to arrive with a competitive package every two weeks, and sometimes even on consecutive weekends. This puts a premium on fast decision-making and the avoidance of prevarication. Make a decision, live with it, and if it's the wrong one learn from it as quickly as you can and move on.

- *Real gains come at the boundaries.* The critical performance gains occur at the margins, at the boundaries between the various interfaces whether these are component areas of the car, between partner organisations or between different teams.
- *Be realistic about what can be achieved.* This is perhaps not expected in a pressurised environment of this kind. Often teams get ahead of themselves and lose their grip on performance. Change for the sake of change is not embraced here. It has to be realistic change for the sake of performance.
- *Never believe you can keep winning.* Organisations often end up believing their own rhetoric. The key to maintaining success in Formula 1 is to actually disbelieve in the sustainability of your own performance. To feel continually that you could have done it better, and to strive continually for this unattainable goal.
- *Leaders exist at all levels of the organisation.* Success requires a 'portfolio of leaders' all fulfilling and supporting different roles in the system. In effect these teams succeed because there are individuals throughout the organisation who are willing and capable to accept the responsibilities of leadership regardless of their formal authority.
- *Measure everything.* Whether it is a Formula 1 team seeking to get a fraction of a second more speed through superior engineering, or a team sponsor determining whether its investment in the sport has been worthwhile, or a driver trying to optimise his performance, this business is about measuring results and taking appropriate actions based on them.
- *At the edge … not over it.* All organisations can use a bit of internal competition between their individuals and teams in their efforts towards achieving improved performance, but management must be sensitive to the fact that at some point internal frictions, particularly between essential players, can become very distracting, even destructive, to the business as a whole.

The chapters that follow provide both an overview of the dynamics of Formula 1 and also an insight into the ongoing struggle as to how these organisations sustain performance in such a highly competitive and dynamic context.

In Chapter 2 we address the question: why Formula 1? We focus on the reasons why this context is valuable in considering the dynamics of performance. In Chapter 3 we articulate a framework for creating performance using the elements of individuals, teams, partners and the organisation and combine these with the processes of integrating, innovating and transforming. In Chapters 4, 5, 6 and 7 we consider each of the elements of the framework (individuals, teams, partners and organisations) in more detail. This is followed in Chapters 8, 9 and 10 by a consideration of the core processes of integrating, innovating and transforming. Chapter 11 focuses on the nature of performance and how it is achieved 'at the limit'. Finally, in Chapter 12, we reflect on some of the learnings from our study and develop a series of twelve lessons that can be extended from the Formula 1 context.

The research process

The concept for this project first emerged in 2001 when the authors were specifically selected to help design and deliver a management development programme for a leading global law firm, Freshfields Bruckhaus Derringer. Formula 1 was utilised as it provided a stimulating context to consider issues relating to teamwork, project management, client relationships and business dynamics. Our experience in developing this programme led us to focus increasingly on describing, explaining and taking lessons from the sources of performance advantage in Formula 1 motorsport. The idea that Formula 1 provides not only an exciting context but also exemplifies how organisations are able to create and sustain the basis for optimised performance, has led us to develop a more rigorous approach to these questions. The objective of this book is therefore to explore these issues in a more holistic and systematic way than we have been able to do so far, and then to develop a structured basis for both, representing organisational performance and providing a basis for applying the concepts into other contexts.

Our process has involved three distinct stages. The first was to develop the conceptual framework as outlined in Chapter 3, which consists of four key elements (organisation, individuals, teams and partnerships) and three core processes (integrating, innovating and transforming). This was done through a review of published sources that have evaluated the performance of Formula 1 teams. One of the benefits (and challenges) of researching the Formula 1 context is that there is an abundance of published information on the Formula 1 organisations and particular individuals such as drivers, founders and CEOs. A painstaking review of this material enabled us to draw out some of the key aspects of the performance system in Formula 1, which is summarised in Chapter 3. A full list of all published sources used is given in the References section.

The second stage of the process was to identify a number of experienced individuals who were to provide the bedrock of our research. In particular we sought out those who could bring a range of different experiences, either through having worked for differing kinds of Formula 1 organisations or through having worked in other industries. Two examples are the Renault F1 team's Managing Director Flavio Briatore, who formerly ran the US operation of the Benetton clothing company, and Tony Purnell, who founded and built Pi Electronics before selling it to the Ford Motor Company. He then ran Jaguar Racing, and since that team's demise has been acting as an advisor to the FIA. The following outlines some of the organisational characteristics that we endeavoured to represent through our selection of individuals to be interviewed for the book:

1. Exhibited both enhanced and declining performance at different stages in their lifetime;
2. Had undergone a change of leadership and/or ownership;
3. Had created discontinuous innovations which have changed the basis of competition;
4. Illustrated different ownership structures;
5. Illustrated different levels of organisational integration.

In these interviews we were seeking insights into the process and some of the principles which underlie performance. In researching the original book this part of the process was perhaps the most challenging as access to these individuals is normally particularly difficult to obtain; however, through our own efforts and the support of a number of intermediaries and, of course, the individuals themselves, we secured a total of forty-seven interviews. For this second edition we found that access to interviewees (twenty-six new interviews were done) was less difficult; although the fast-paced lives of the people in the sport makes it hard to catch up with them. The legitimacy of our first effort seemed to have opened doors this time around, both to people we had interviewed in 2004 and to new respondents. We are particularly pleased that for this edition we have been able to augment our base of respondents by gaining access to a number of Formula 1 drivers as well. Full details of all the respondents are provided in Appendix C.

The selection of respondents was based on the above criteria, but we also wanted to develop in-depth case insights into particular organisations. This meant that to some extent we used the 'snowball' sampling approach where access to one individual enabled us to identify and contact other relevant individuals.

A further point to our analysis is that, as with Collins and Porras' 'Built to Last'[4], we have also focused on the history and evolution of organisations rather than simply their present-day form. This is because an evolutionary and longitudinal perspective was essential in order to gain a better understanding of the dynamics of performance. We did not therefore simply look at the success stories of those who were at the top of the curve; we considered the way in which such successes were created and formed over time, and also in a number of cases how the success dissolved into failure and the diagnosis of this process.

The final stage of the research involved the detailed analysis of the interview transcripts and the comparison of this data with the range of published materials that we had collated into a full chronological database. We extrapolated some of the key observations and lessons from the data, which are summarised in this chapter and specified in Chapter 12. Our approach to this part of the process was to focus on understanding the details of how these organisations operate, through accounts and anecdotes of specific situations, and also to look for common patterns and themes that emerged. We also sought to pick up on those unexpected, counter-intuitive insights which can add to our understanding of a particular phenomenon or situation. For this second edition we have been able to distil two additional lessons that we have added to the original ten.

It is perhaps worth emphasising that this study does not seek to 'prove' that certain factors create success; nor is it our intention to generalise the issues we observe in Formula 1 beyond this specialist context. The purpose of the data collection is therefore not so much to 'validate' but to 'elaborate' the framework outlined in Chapter 3. In particular we seek to make connections between the processes and elements, for example in terms of the linkage between innovating and performance. A specific focus for us was to understand the inter-related nature of our four elements (individual–team–partners–organisation). The framework was therefore concerned with rich description and aimed to provide a fine-grained understanding of the processes involved in creating and sustaining high performance in one of the most competitive and dynamic contexts possible.

2 | *Why Formula 1 motor racing?*

We have some iconic figures, probably starting with Senna, then Schumacher and now Lewis Hamilton; individuals that transcend Formula 1 and become global stars with the help of the media platform. It has just mushroomed in such a dynamic way. It's because it's got some glitz and glamour, a bit of skulduggery, a bit of everything really.

Martin Brundle, former Formula 1 driver and
now driver manager and commentator

Formula 1 motor racing provides many important ingredients to help us explore the nature of organisational performance. The first is a clear, unambiguous performance outcome – consistently winning races and thereby consistently outperforming the competition. The fundamental importance of this measure of performance, and one which is often overlooked by managers striving to improve their organisations, is that it is concerned with **relative advantage**. The notion of competitive advantage is based on the premise that an organisation's performance is superior relative to all available competition. Formula 1 clearly exhibits this criterion, as a team may make significant performance enhancements to its own car, only to find that it has become inferior to the competition that has made greater advances, and therefore it is the relative rather than absolute pace of improvement that is needed to improve and sustain a competitive position.

All too often managers lose sight of the external relativity of performance and focus too heavily on performance enhancements relative to their own internal benchmarks; in Formula 1 performance benchmarking is always relative to the competition and a team's performance is only as good as the last race. These factors create a context where there is no let-up in the search for both short- and long-term performance gains. In April 2008, McLaren Chief Executive Officer Ron Dennis responded to a question from *Autosport.com's* Jonathan Noble about the early pace of BMW Sauber by underlining the importance in the rate of development during the Formula 1 season rather just the outright pace of a car at the start of the season:

... It is when we get to Europe and the speed of R&D and manufacture starts to make a difference. We'll be very strong and I'm not unduly worried about the future ...

A further aspect that makes Formula 1 a valuable subject for our study is that it integrates all the fundamental resources of organisations: human, financial and technological, and relies on the continual development of knowledge to ensure competitive performance. It is primarily a people-based industry, but also one which requires large sums of cash to fund the technological development and human resources needed to generate superior performance. As we shall explore in later chapters, there are many cases where there is plenty of cash, people and technology and yet these are not integrated in a way that converts such a rich resource base into superior competitive performance.

The longevity of Formula 1 provides us with an important opportunity to consider the long-term implications of performance rather than focusing on those firms which are currently the high performers. This also means that unlike many other performance-based studies we don't have to apply a short-term cross-sectional research approach; we are able to focus on the dynamics of these organisations in terms of their growth characteristics, emergent cultures and the highs and lows of their competitive performance.

The nature of Formula 1 as the pinnacle of motorsport technology allows us to focus on the role of technology in supporting competitive performance. Frequently, technology is seen as an enabler of high performance but also as a huge cost; a potential 'black hole' which can quickly devour an organisation's resources for very little or no increase in performance. Ask most CEOs if they know what kind of return they get on their expenditure on information and communication technologies and the answer will invariably be one of frustration and uncertainty. This is a tension which is particularly evident in Formula 1 where many high-budget teams have been unable to translate their superior technological resources into enhanced performance. Formula 1 provides the ideal context for us to consider this problem.

Formula 1 is a global phenomenon. While in its beginning it was primarily a European Championship (with the Indianapolis 500 in the US also included from 1950–60) it has now become a global spectacle, taking place on five continents across the world; performance therefore has to be seen in a global, rather than local, context. In addition, a shifting axis from west to east can be clearly followed. In 2007 the US Grand Prix was removed from the calendar and in 2008 Singapore hosted its first Grand Prix. 2009 sees the first race in Abu Dhabi, and Grand Prix are planned for India and South Korea, with Dubai and Qatar also lobbying hard.

The global nature of Formula 1 is also exemplified through the ownership of the teams. Despite six out of the ten teams racing in 2008 being located in the UK, only one, WilliamsF1, is wholly British owned. McLaren has a significant ownership based in Bahrain as well as its German and Saudi Arabian investors, and even Ferrari has a small shareholding held outside Italy by the Abu Dhabi government.

A further reason for selecting Formula 1 as a basis for understanding competitive performance is that for these businesses there are no hiding places, as summarised by Toyota's Team Principal John Howett:

I think the very simple thing about Formula 1 is [that] *there's no hiding place and on Saturday you have to qualify and on Sunday you race, and when you work in the real environment everybody tries, I would say, to make excuses for their performance based on, you know, market conditions, etc. etc. But here it's so straightforward – if you finish sixth, you finish sixth; there's no discussion, you've just got to work harder to make the car go quicker.*

Formula 1 provides the perfect 'goldfish bowl' for us to examine the components of performance at the critical levels of organisation:

- the Formula 1 team and its partner organisations;
- teams – the various groups of individuals who among other things create components of the car, coordinate race strategy, and change the wheels and tyres during a race; and
- individuals – looking at how individual employees are able to sustain motivation and develop the skills and competence needed to perform and keep performing at the absolute limit.

While these factors provide a basis for our investigations it is important to be mindful of the limitations of using Formula 1 in this way. Our study is of a very particular and specialised industry. It operates on the basis of a commercial activity to feed a technological system to ultimately create a car to race against the competition. It is therefore less concerned with issues such as customer satisfaction and cost control than other organisations might be, although as we shall see perspectives on the latter are changing. We are mindful of these limitations, but we do believe that the overall benefits of exploring a performance-rich context such as Formula 1 outweigh some of the concerns around its idiosyncratic nature. It is important for managers to look beyond their own contexts not only in order to help them recognise the distinctiveness of their situation, but also to stimulate new ideas and raise challenging questions about their own performance.

Background

Formula 1 is the longest-established motorsport championship series in the world. Its purpose was initially to provide a racing series which allowed different manufacturers to showcase their cars and technology. A fundamental part of Formula 1 is therefore that each team designs and manufactures around six or seven bespoke racing cars each year. There are also several instances where teams design and build their own engines, and this is usually the case with teams who also manufacture road cars such as Ferrari, Honda and Toyota. For this reason, the term 'manufacturer' relates to those who also produce road cars, and the term 'constructor' is used for those who are solely concerned with running a Formula 1 team, such as Red Bull or WilliamsF1. Table 1 provides a summary of some of the distinctive features of Formula 1 in comparison to other internationally recognised race series.

Formula 1 is an 'open-wheel' formula, which means that the chassis of the car is primarily a cockpit for the driver; the wheels of the car are exposed and that, within certain technically specified parameters set out by the FIA, the designers are free to come up with whatever solutions they feel will provide the best race performance. Figure 2 provides a simple schematic to represent the typical layout of a Formula 1 car.

Figure 2 identifies a number of important aspects about the car. The first is the term 'chassis', which refers to the main structure of the

Table 1 *Contrasting Formula 1 with other types of motorsport*

Characteristic	Formula 1	NASCAR	Le Mans & American Le Mans (ALMS)	GP2	Indy Racing League	World Rally Championship
International race locations	Yes	No	Yes	Yes	No	Yes
Cars designed & manufactured by teams	Yes	Yes	Yes	No	No	Yes
Open wheel or full covered bodies	Open	Covered	Covered	Open	Open	Covered
Based on production cars	No	Yes	No (yes in GT class)	No	No	Yes
Type of track	Tarmac circuit	Tarmac oval	Tarmac circuit	Tarmac circuit	Tarmac oval	Tarmac and rough terrain roads
Weather/light conditions	Dry and wet	Dry only	Dry, wet and night	Dry and wet	Dry only	Dry, wet and night

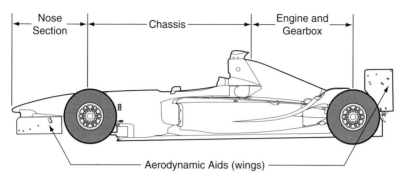

Figure 2 Schematic of Formula 1 car.
Source of car profile: Williams F1.

car. An efficient chassis is critical for the car to achieve the maximum level of grip, thereby maximising cornering speeds. The second is the drive train: a term which comprises the engine and transmission, which is located behind the driver at the rear of the car. These components form part of the main structure and are attached directly to the chassis; the drive train provides the power needed to propel the car around the circuit. The third group of components are the aerodynamic devices, including the complete bodywork, the most important of which are known as 'wings' at the front and rear of the car. These devices, combined with the overall shape of the car, also provide grip, but do so through using aerodynamic principles to create downforce, also known as negative lift. Downforce is created by forward motion in the same way that lift is created in a fixed-wing aircraft, only the wing profiles are in effect reversed, thereby creating negative lift, i.e. suction onto the track surface. A modern-day Formula 1 car creates aerodynamic downforce the equivalent of twice its weight, meaning that in theory it could run upside down on the ceiling of the tunnel in Monaco!

Unlike many other forms of racing these cars are unable to be used on public roads and are not equipped to operate in the dark, although use of floodlit circuits is now being introduced to allow races to take place in the Far East at times suitable for European TV audiences, which is still the main viewing base for Formula 1. They are highly specialised single-seat machines designed to be raced on purpose-built circuits which vary in length from 3 km (Monaco) to 7 km (Spa-Francorchamps, Belgium) with the races covering an overall

Table 2 *Marketing opportunities provided by Formula 1*

THE SPORTS MARKETING LEADER

Formula One is the world's most marketing-friendly sport, as this comparison demonstrates.

Sport	Athletics	Golf	Football	Skiing	Tennis	Yachting	Motorsport
Premier Event	Olympics	PGA Tour	World Cup	World Cup	ATP Tour	America's Cup	Formula 1
Event Frequency	Quadrennial	Annual	Quadrennial	Annual	Annual	Triennial	Annual
Season Duration	1 month	7 months	1 month	4 months	8 months	3 months	8 months
Event Markets	1 country	15 countries	1 country	9 countries	4 countries	1 country	15 countries
Media Coverage	High	Moderate	High	Low	Moderate	Low	High
Spectator Audience	High	Moderate	High	Low	Moderate	Low	High
Weather Dependence	Low	High	Low	High	Moderate	High	Low
Sponsorship Cost	High	High	High	Moderate	High	High	High
Opportunities	Supplier	Participant Event Billboard	Event Billboard Supplier	Participant Event Billboard	Participant Event Billboard	Participant Event Billboard	Participant Event Billboard Supplier

Source: Minardi F1.

16

distance of around 300 km (approximately 180 miles) over ninety minutes. A further important characteristic of Formula 1 is that it is a race championship rather than an individual race such as the Indy 500 or Le Mans 24-hour sportscar event. It therefore takes place over a nine-month period (typically March through to November), with up to twenty races each season.

Formula 1 took over the mantle of Grand Prix racing, which began in France in 1906. The first official season of Formula 1 took place in 1950 with races held in Great Britain (Silverstone), Monaco (Monte Carlo), the US (Indianapolis), Switzerland (Bremgarten), Belgium (Spa-Francorchamps), France (Reims) and Italy (Monza). Although it had all the appearance of a World Championship series, it was in effect a European Championship with the Indianapolis 500 race included, although only Ferrari actually crossed the Atlantic to compete in the American race in 1952. Since 1950 there has been a total of 115 constructors involved in Formula 1, with an average tenure of just under six years (in comparison, the average lifetime of a UK public limited company is around twelve years).

Many great automotive marques have attempted and failed to secure a competitive position in Formula 1; names such as Porsche, Aston Martin and Bugatti were all unable to support their entry into Formula 1 with competitive performances (although Porsche later became a successful engine supplier with the TAG-funded turbo engine, which powered the Championship-winning McLaren cars of 1984 and 1985). Originally a showcase for manufacturers such as Alfa Romeo and Mercedes to demonstrate the prowess of their cars, Formula 1 soon developed into a more specialised activity, with purpose-built single-seat racing cars manufactured by companies such as Ferrari in Italy (which, in contrast to many of its Italian counterparts, introduced road cars to help fund its race activities rather than vice versa) and Cooper and Lotus in the UK.

The spectacle

Formula 1 is the third most watched sport in the world. It is surpassed only by the Olympic Games and World Cup soccer, but unlike both of these events, which take place every four years, it takes place annually. It also enjoys a relatively high frequency of events during the year and also is less dependent on the weather, as suggested by Table 2.

In 2008 eighteen races took place across five continents and in sixteen countries, as shown in Figure 3.

According to the F1 group, the sport's rights holder, more than 588
million people around the world saw at least fifteen minutes of an
F1 broadcast in 2006.[8] For the 2007 Brazilian Grand Prix alone the
global TV audience was 78 million (for the most watched sporting
event in the US, the American Football Super Bowl, this figure was 97
million), but in terms of total 'reach', i.e. the number of people who
watch at least three minutes, the Brazilian Grand Prix drew 152 million viewers while the Super Bowl drew 142 million.[9]

Importantly, Formula 1 has been able to shift from being prima-
rily a European series to one with global appeal and reach. Former
Formula 1 driver and now driver manager and commentator Martin
Brundle said;

*Formula 1 has moved out into other areas of the world where there
are a lot more emerging markets and so the global awareness is much
greater. The Olympics and the World Cup are globally bigger of
course, but they are every four years. F1 events take place approach-
ing twenty times per year and so just the day-to-day awareness of it
has to be so much greater.*

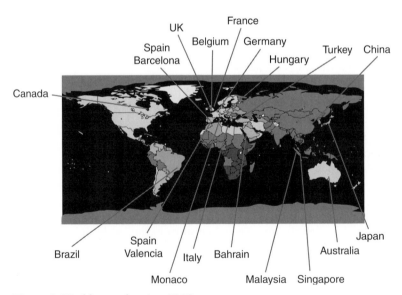

Figure 3 World map showing 2008 races

This attraction provides real commercial benefits for sponsors and allows them to reach a global audience in a way which may not be possible in other sporting formats.

Isabelle M. Conner was a part of the team that brought Dutch bank ING into Formula 1 in 2006:

We had a short list of three: the Olympics, tennis and Formula 1. The Olympics, we decided after further research, was really for brands that were already well known, so that wasn't our case. Tennis was much harder to activate and Formula 1, the more we looked at it the more we saw 850 million fans around the world. The fact that Bernie [Ecclestone – Head of Formula One Management] has brought the sport into people's living rooms in 185 countries; the fact that the sport is growing. How many sports can you talk about where they are growing? And we like the places where they are growing.

During the 2008 season there were ten constructors competing in Formula 1, each of which entered two cars and two drivers per race. Actually, the season had started with eleven teams, but one, Super Aguri, went into receivership in May 2008 due to insufficient funding. Given the need to continually develop their cars the constructors will produce around seven chassis a year and use during the season between 100 to 150 engine 'lives' (a term used to denote the fact that many of these engines are rebuilds rather than brand-new units). With budgets often in excess of $300 million and a workforce of up to 1,000 individuals these are not small organisations, but specialist technology and marketing companies that provide the fundamental part of the glamour and spectacle of the Formula 1 series.

The Grand Prix 'circus' involves around 2,000 people at each race. This number is made up of the racing teams, and a whole range of support organisations from race organisers through the medical teams to the hospitality and marketing operations. However, these 2,000 people are the tip of the iceberg and are supported by an estimated further 10,000 or so back at the various factories and facilities which are part of the Formula 1 industry.

Approximately 150 articulated transporters travel throughout Europe, and when racing at international locations, a similar number of ground freight transport vehicles are used in order to relocate the cars, spare parts and mass of equipment that is required to support

the Formula 1 teams. At the long-haul intercontinental 'flyaway' races
the transporters are left in the home bases of the teams; however, all
of the same relevant equipment has to be packed, containerised and
flown to each of those specific events, where the local ground transport firms take over.

Geoff Simmonds, Renault F1's man in charge of logistics, commented
on the task ahead as his team arrived in Shanghai for the race in 2007:

*We've got 32 tonnes of freight to unpack on the Tuesday, having just
arrived from Japan, then there's the garage to set up, the engineering
suites, the offices for the team, the communications back to base,
the links with the circuit – making sure Flavio [Briatore] has got a
phone line where he wants it – the marketing area, the catering, all
the fridges, the tables and chairs, the cables, the electrics, the hydrau-
lics for the garage. Then there are the cars to unpack, get them built
and fired up so the mechanics can start their work, and it goes on.[10]*

The teams themselves have state-of-the-art design and manufacturing
facilities which deal with a constant pressure to continually improve
and enhance the designs and manufacture of the cars. They use complex networks of high-technology suppliers who are responding to the
demands for new levels of performance from new designs, new materials and new manufacturing approaches. The entire system is fed
by a sophisticated commercial operation, which forges partnerships
based on brand synergies and reciprocal marketing arrangements.
The teams are led by a range of individuals from corporate managers to serial entrepreneurs who live, breathe and sleep the sport, but
for all, most importantly, *winning* is always at the top of the agenda.
Sir Jackie Stewart, three times World Drivers' Champion and former
Team Principal, highlighted how important it is:

*I can tell you how many races I've won, but I haven't the faintest idea
how many times I came second!*

And Dickie Stanford, Test Team Manager at WilliamsF1, reinforced
this drive to be at the top of the podium:

*If we don't win a race there's a problem. We haven't done our job
properly. Somebody, somewhere down the line hasn't done something and we've failed.*

Technological change

Like many dynamic industries Formula 1 has undergone a number of technological shifts over the years which have created new competitors and also destroyed some of the competences of established firms. As with any industry undergoing change these firms either manage to transform themselves or collapse. An illustration of the impact of such changes is provided in Appendix B, which details many of the Formula 1 teams who either collapsed or left the sport from 1950 to 2008. Table 3 shows a summary of some of the key stages in the evolution of Formula 1, with technology shifting from the large powerful Italian cars of the 1950s, through to the light agile British cars of the 1960s, through to the focus on aerodynamic grip which began in the 1970s and has made aerodynamics the central competence for creating performance in Formula 1. It is also interesting to note that in the six Formula 1 seasons for each new decade over the fifty-year period featured in Table 2, Ferrari features strongly in every decade with the exception of the 1980s, an issue we will return to later.

For 2009 major changes will be introduced to Formula 1 in the form of Kinetic Energy Recovery Systems (KERS). Max Mosley, President of the regulatory body for Formula 1, the FIA, was a key driving force behind this new technology entering the regulation. He explained:

I think it very important that Formula 1 should develop technologies which are demonstrably useful in the real world. With the amount of intellectual talent and money that is now deployed by the top Formula 1 teams, it makes a great deal of sense to arrange the formula so that a performance advantage can be derived from doing something which is socially useful. The KERS technology is a good example because, no matter what the means of propulsion of road vehicles in fifty or a hundred years' time, it will still make sense to recycle the energy which would otherwise be lost when the vehicle is slowed.

This hybrid technology uses mechanical or electrical means to capture energy from the car when it is braking that can be reused to help increase speed or acceleration. Formula 1 has always prided itself on being at the forefront of technology and this provides an important opportunity for the racing imperative to add impetus to

Table 3 *Key stages in the evolution of the Formula 1 car*

Year	1950	1960	1970	1980	1990	2000
Top 3 cars	Alfa Romeo (It) Lago–Talbot (Fr) Ferrari (It)	Cooper (UK) Lotus (UK) Ferrari (It)	Lotus (UK) Ferrari (It) March (UK)	Williams (UK) Ligier (Fr) Brabham (UK)	McLaren (UK) Ferrari (It) Benetton (UK)	Ferrari (It) McLaren (UK) Williams (UK)
Typical features	4.5 litre engine, supercharged, in front of driver Tubular frame chassis	2.5 litre engine behind driver Independent suspension	3.0 litre engine Aerodynamic wings 3.0 litre Ford DFV engine (not Ferrari) Monocoque chassis Slick tyres	Ground-effect aerodynamics 1.5 litre turbo charged engines	3.5 litre engine Carbon composite construction Semi-automatic gearbox	3.0 litre engine Launch control Fly-by-wire technology Engine management systems
Approx. horsepower and maximum rpm [49]	400 bhp/ 7,000 rpm	240 bhp/ 8,000 rpm	420 bhp/ 9,000 rpm	600 bhp/ 11,000 rpm (turbos got to around 1,200 bhp in 1988)	600 bhp/ 14,000 rpm	820 bhp/ 19,000 rpm

the development of these important technologies, as underlined by Honda's Ross Brawn:

We're definitely one of the teams that are fully supportive of any environmental or ecological initiatives that can be accelerated through Formula 1; KERS, the Kinetic Energy Recovery System, is a good example. I think there will be other examples in the future – because of course this is the beginning – but Honda are very keen and very supportive because they recognise that Formula 1 is a very intensive environment to generate and develop those technologies. It is possibly more intense than any other environment because it's so competitive. If you identify a technology where you can get lap time the teams will put in the resources, the rate of development is accelerated and this leads to a much faster spin-off into the road cars.

Growth and prosperity

Today Formula 1 is a well-established industry of medium-sized companies, but it is only in recent years that it has achieved this status. In the early 1990s it was still a niche industry of relatively small firms. In 1992 the payroll at Williams F1 included 190 employees; in 2004 this had risen to 493, but by 2008 had only increased to just over 500. There a number of reasons to explain this shift. First, Formula 1 enjoyed a huge growth in TV interest during the early 1990s which made it the most watched sporting series in the world. Second, and partly as a consequence of the increased global exposure of Formula 1, many automotive manufacturers, who had kept their distance (with the notable exceptions of Fiat and Ford), began to get more and more involved.

However, for many it was important to recognise that the unprecedented growth which Formula 1 had enjoyed was unlikely to be sustained. According to Tony Purnell, FIA Advisor:

We've had thirty years of growth but today that growth is flattening off and may well move into decline. What do businesses do when they are in that situation? Well, the classic thing is that if you did nothing, if you stick to the old recipe, you dwindle away and at first the dwindling is denied – perhaps where we are today – and then the dwindling becomes a crisis and you've either got the gumption in the

*business to reinvent itself and leap forward today or you die. That's
the classic life cycle in any business and Formula 1 isn't immune.*

Between 2004 and 2008 one of the major changes has been an
increased focus on limiting the costs of Formula 1. This has been
mainly achieved through regulation relating to the amount of testing
allowed between races (in 2008 restricted to an annual total of 30,000
km) and also through regulations which limit the usage of engines
and gearboxes. In 2004 the teams would be using a new engine and
gearbox for each day of the Grand Prix; in 2008 one engine must last
for two successive Grand Prix weekends and a gearbox for four.

In 2004 the teams would have unlimited testing. In 2008 no
competitor may carry out more than 30,000 km of testing during a
calendar year, tyre sets are limited to 300 per year, teams can use only
one car on each test day, and testing is only permitted at sites that
have been approved by the FIA.

Much of this may seem arbitrary and artificial to those outside
Formula 1. But the imperative is for Formula 1 to take a more strategic view; this includes environmental technologies, but also means it
needs to become far more cost effective, as colourfully summarised
by Flavio Briatore:

*The problem in Formula 1 is that there is no long-term strategy; every
day something new happens and takes priority. Therefore the point is
that we as teams need to get our act together in focusing more on our
offering as a spectacle and as an entertainment business, not just the
continual debate about engineering.*

*With global business conditions as they are at the moment and
therefore the need to control costs, a good example of this is the
enormous growth in staffing.*

*In 1994 and 1995 you had good teams with around 150 people work-
ing in them, and those teams went racing. It was good competitive racing too. Nowadays we have a good race, a bad race, competitive racing,
the same as we had in the 1990s, but with 1,000 people! It means the
product is the same but the cost of the product just in personnel costs
alone is ten times what it was! It really makes no sense.*

*Formula 1 is still dictated by engineering and not entertainment
and without being too contentious, engineers have little clue about
strategy when it comes to entertainment!*

The constant pressure of competition

One of the reasons why Formula 1 provides such an interesting parallel with today's business environment is the constant pressure of competition. Competition can come in many different forms; for Formula 1 a key issue is that standing still means going backwards, such is the pace of development of every constructor. As shown in Figure 4, Formula 1 is constantly improving its performance, despite the fact that regulations are continually formulated in order to keep the speed of the cars within safe limits.

In the 1950 Monaco Grand Prix Juan Manuel Fangio achieved pole position in an Alfa Romeo 158 in a time of 1m 50.2, an average speed of 64.55 miles per hour. In 2004 Jarno Trulli, in a Renault R24, achieved a time of 1m 13.96, representing a speed in excess of 101 mph, underlining the constant pace of development even at a historic road-based circuit which has the slowest speeds of them all. However, by 2008 Trulli's qualifying lap remained the fastest of all time, as various regulations had contained the performance of the car in the interests of more competitive racing and safety.

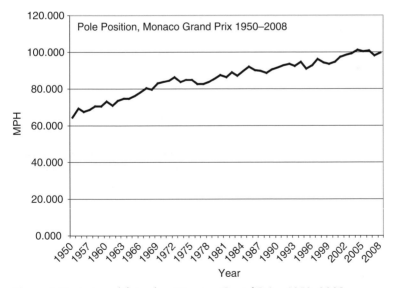

Figure 4 Fastest qualifying lap, Monaco Grand Prix, 1950–2008

Revenue streams

The flow of funds into Formula 1 has moved full circle over the last fifty-eight years. Initially most of the funds were provided by the automotive manufacturers simply by subsidising their own engineering departments to design and build Formula 1 cars. The cars themselves carried very little identification other than the colour schemes used to underline their country of origin: silver Mercedes and Porsche from Germany; red Maseratis, Alfa Romeos and Ferraris from Italy; the light blue Talbots were French and the British racing green Vanwalls and BRMs represented the UK.

The late 1960s saw the advent of commercial sponsorship entering into Formula 1. A major innovator in this regard was Colin Chapman's Lotus team which, in 1968, secured funding from cigarette manufacturer Imperial Tobacco to paint its cars in the colours of its 'Gold Leaf' cigarette brand. During subsequent years tobacco companies became a major source of funding for many teams, with Philip Morris's Marlboro brand proving to be the most enduring. Tobacco companies and other sponsors were funnelling huge amounts of cash into the sport. However, as we look at 2008, the car manufacturers' involvement and investment has come back very strongly. Almost half of the estimated $2.7 billion revenue which flowed into Formula 1 came once again from them, with Japanese manufacturer Honda providing the largest contribution, at $340 million.

The other half of revenue streams of course came from sponsors. A key part of the relationship for the sponsors is that they achieve exposure for their brands on the car; but there are other aspects to the relationship, in particular where the sponsor is also a technology partner, such as the relationship between Ferrari and Shell. Shell not only provides direct cash to support its sponsorship, but also technical support to help develop both the performance of the Ferrari engine, and also its own fuel and lubricant products.

Formula 1 management

The focus of our study is the Formula 1 constructors – the organisations that design, manufacture and then race their purpose-built cars. However, we also need to recognise that as a sporting event, Formula 1 is itself a product which operates in a highly competitive marketplace. This was not always the case; in past years the Formula 1 World Championship was a relatively *ad hoc* affair with the individual race circuits determining the financial conditions for entry and appropriating the advertising and media rights for the event. This all changed in 1972 when the racing car constructors, a typically eclectic and fractious amalgam of organisations, were first represented as a (relatively) cohesive bargaining group by Bernard Charles Ecclestone, an entrepreneur who had formerly raced himself, managed Austrian driver Jochen Rindt in the late 1960s and had purchased the Brabham Formula 1 team in 1970. The Formula One Constructors' Association (FOCA) effectively shifted the balance of power away from the race circuits to the constructors – the teams who raced their cars in the World Championships.

In terms of determining the Championship, points in 2008 were awarded to the top eight finishers in each Grand Prix for both the Drivers' and the Constructors' World Championships, according to the following scale: first place: ten points; second place: eight points; third place: six points; fourth place: five points; fifth place: four points; sixth place: three points; seventh place: two points; and eighth place: one point.

Before long the advertising and media rights for every race in a World Championship became the property of FOCA, with circuits now having to pay for the right to hold a Formula 1 Championship race. The financial gains from these sources were distributed among the teams through the Concorde Agreement (so called because it was signed in Paris at the headquarters of the FIA located at the Place de la Concorde), which specified the basis by which the teams would operate and also the way in which funds were allocated.

This shift of power to the constructors made Ecclestone one of Britain's wealthiest men, and created millionaires out of a number of team owners who had built their businesses up from almost nothing to become successful Formula 1 constructors.

However, the influx of the car manufacturers back into Formula 1 in the 1990s led to concerns that the management company – now called Formula One Management – was too powerful and also that the revenues generated by Formula 1 allegedly were not being fairly distributed to the teams and the circuits, many of which were now requiring significant investment to keep in line with spectator expectations and new safety requirements.

The increasing power of the manufacturers in Formula 1 led to a threatened breakaway series in 2001, but this was averted by an agreement between the manufacturers group (GPWC) and Ecclestone's company SLEC which handled the media rights to Formula 1. In 2006 the venture capital fund CVC partners purchased a 72 per cent stake in the corporate structure that promotes and holds all the media rights for Formula 1. This brought in new finance to Formula 1, but also new pressures. As a successful venture capital operation CVC is not in the business to watch the racing; it requires a sustained return on its investment and therefore will do its best to ensure that the business model evolves in a way that will allow it to achieve its financial objectives.

Interestingly, the previous Concorde agreement expired at the end of December 2007 and has not, at the time of writing, been formally renewed. The basis by which a new agreement is established made for some interesting manoeuvring by all parties throughout 2008 and no doubt will continue into the future.

The task for Ecclestone is therefore to sustain a financial model where the investment required by the teams is realistic and the delivery of the Formula 1 event ensures that there is strong media interest which will draw in the sponsors. Ecclestone's style has always been straightforward and pragmatic. When asked by the authors to comment as to how he saw the major challenges ahead for him, he was characteristically direct:

The biggest challenge is making sure that the participation of the manufacturers is viable and also that the race promoters keep the very high standard expected of them.

3 | *The performance framework*

A Formula 1 team is a highly complex system. It combines many different resources such as human capital, technology, marketing and finance to achieve a performance outcome, hopefully superior to those of its competitors. It is a critical balance between maximising the potential of individual areas and optimising the overall performance to ensure that the integrated effect exceeds the sum of the parts. For many watching the Formula 1 spectacle it is all down to the skill of the driver. In our study we conclude that the driver is an important ingredient, both from the point of view of driving skill and also in influencing the motivation and dynamics of the team. But a driver can never succeed without the support of the organisation and its technology behind him. One only needs to look at situations where the winners of the Formula 1 World Drivers' Championship have moved to other teams following their point of success to illustrate this effect. An example of this is provided in Figure 5.

In 1995, 1996 and 1997 three different drivers won the Drivers' World Championship. Each of these drivers moved to a new team shortly following their Championship success and the subsequent fortunes of each were very different. In 1996 Damon Hill won the Drivers' World Championship but left Williams to join Arrows in 1997, and then in 1998 moved to Jordan, eventually retiring at the end of 1999. Also driving for Williams, Jacques Villeneuve won the title in 1997; he stayed with the team during 1998, but then left to help set up the new British American Racing team (BAR) of which his manager, Craig Pollock, was Managing Director and a major shareholder. However, he was unable to repeat his earlier success and left BAR, retiring from Formula 1 at the end of 2003.

In contrast, Michael Schumacher was Champion with the Benetton team in 1994 and 1995 and then left to join Ferrari. The technical management team at Benetton followed him to Ferrari a year later and three years after that, in 2000, he became World Champion once

29

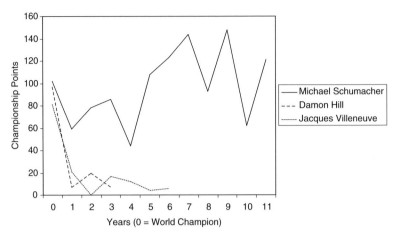

Figure 5 Driver performance following winning the World Drivers' Championship

again. Schumacher's success at Ferrari continued until his retirement at the end of 2006.

Not included in Figure 5 is Fernando Alonso. In 2005 and 2006 he won the Drivers' World Championship driving for Renault F1. The following year, full of confidence, he moved to McLaren and found himself embroiled in an intense struggle with his rookie driving partner, Lewis Hamilton. Alonso was able to stay in contention right up to the last race of the season, but both he and Hamilton ended up losing out to Ferrari's Kimi Raikkonen by one point. Alonso subsequently moved back to the Renault F1 team for 2008, where both the team and he found it very difficult to recapture the old magic for the first part of the season.

The point here is not to explain the demise of some drivers and the success of others, but to illustrate that in the same way that there are many factors that can influence the lack of performance of a driver, such as the design of the car and effectiveness of the race team, there are many factors that explain the apparent success of a driver rather than just driving skills. The driver is therefore one part of a team and in order to sustain success in this highly competitive situation all aspects of the team have to integrate effectively.

It therefore requires **individuals** to be knowledgeable and highly motivated in order to maximise their contribution to the whole system. To achieve success also requires that these individuals work effectively in **teams**, whether they are the pit crew who refuel and change the wheels and tyres of the car in a matter of seconds; or the design team who work to create an aerodynamic component linking in with staff in the wind tunnel and the composites department to create the finished article; or the commercial team who work together to engage a new sponsor, thereby ensuring future funding for the technology. Furthermore, these teams and individuals also have to work with their **partners** at the team and individual level.

This may involve the tyre supplier Bridgestone effectively becoming part of the race team to ensure that the tyre performance is maximised through analysis of wear rates, track temperature and air pressures. It may also involve commercial and technical relationships that allow the team and their partners to benefit. In addition, the system has to work at the **organisation** (or multi-team, cross-functional) level, ensuring that connections are being made between the test team, the race team and the designers to improve the car as effectively as possible, and even where the pit crew are working with the commercial team, to ensure that their most prestigious sponsors get access to the pit garage, but without compromising race performance.

The central framework which we will use as the basis for this study relates to four key elements in the performance system of an organisation: the *organisation* itself, *partner* organisations, *teams* and *individuals,* all working together to produce the outcome of performance.

These four elements are in turn influenced by three dynamic processes which operate continuously across them. These are concerned with: **integrating** – the way in which the organisational system, influenced in large part by its leadership, brings together all of its diverse, but connected activities, providing clarity of purpose and also constantly adjusting the various tensions that need to be balanced to optimise performance; **innovating** – the way in which the system continuously improves and enhances its performance levels; and **transforming** – how the system reconfigures itself in order to create new resources and new performance levels in response to changing conditions and competitive pressures. All of these processes impact on the elements to explain the overall performance outcome, as illustrated in Figure 6. Together they generate the organising framework for the book, which we will now consider in more detail.

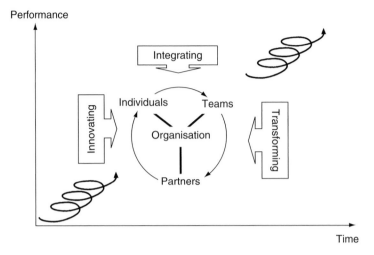

Figure 6 The performance framework

Individuals

For the individuals working in Formula 1 this is their dream job. They have always wanted to be in Formula 1 and have now achieved this; their focus is therefore at one level to maintain this situation, but the highly competitive nature of Formula 1 means that they are constantly striving to both establish their worth and also progress in their careers.

There is a vast range of roles encompassed within Formula 1, from working on leading-edge car design to handling the negotiation of multi-million dollar sponsorship contracts. There is also a huge range of nationalities involved, and not just from those countries which hold Formula 1 races; however, the gender mix is still weighted towards a predominance of male participation. Nevertheless, there are some indications that an already strong female presence in marketing and public relations roles is spreading into the more technical aspects of Formula 1 including aerodynamics and electronics.

Teams

Within Formula 1 the challenges of motivating and coordinating individual talent are central to both creating and sustaining a competitive edge. Employee turnover rates are particularly high in Formula 1; in this context turnover often means staff moving to and being recruited from the competition. This means that, on the whole, Formula 1 teams cannot afford to rely on individual knowledge, but on building a wider social capital that underpins the whole organisation and, perhaps most importantly, by melding individual knowledge into the combined capability of a team.

Teamwork is a central element of the Formula 1 organisation. It is recognised that the performance of the organisation is only as good as its weakest link. Therefore the focus is on ensuring that everyone is up to speed and pulling their weight. In the Formula 1 context we see the team as a small group of individuals who must work together to achieve a clearly defined output.

For example, a team of between twenty-one and twenty-three individuals all have to combine to change all four wheels and tyres and refuel a Formula 1 car in, ideally, less than seven seconds. At this level of performance the team has to work together to a degree of precision unimaginable in most other contexts. This kind of teamwork can be described as 'tightly coupled' in that the team works in a clearly defined context where the smallest change in one individual's performance – such as dropping a wheel nut – will have a major effect on the performance of the whole team. There are some valuable parallels in other industries that have transferred some of the concepts of the pit-stop process into their operations, such as hospitals improving the accuracy of patient hand-offs to and from the operating theatre, or short-haul airlines improving the efficiency and speed of their aircraft turnaround times.

Teams can also be 'loosely coupled', where individuals may be more dispersed, working on other continents, in other timezones and still be required to achieve a set objective within a timeframe. In Formula 1 this may relate to a team of engineers working on a new suspension component, or producing designs, building models and testing them in the team's wind tunnel. Equally it can be the fabrication of components with partner organisations in other countries, testing them on the track in a completely different country and then ultimately installing them on the race car at a Grand Prix perhaps on another continent.

In both contexts, teams have to be able to both function effectively within their predefined tasks and to be responsive to changing situations and adapt to them quickly.

Partners

To achieve the highest levels of performance a Formula 1 constructor can never rely entirely on its own activities. It has to work with
partners. Even when teams are highly resourced and almost obses-
sive about secrecy, the teams are still heavily dependent on external
organisations for component manufacture and supply.

   This is particularly so in the case of tyres. For periods in the history
of Formula 1 there has been a single tyre supplier, and so there has
been no competitive advantage to be gained. However, there have also
been periods when relationships with tyre suppliers became critical in
achieving a performance advantage. For Ferrari in 2002, 2003 and
2004 its relationship with Bridgestone was critical to the performance
advantage that Michael Schumacher was able to utilise en route to
winning the Drivers' World Championships in those years.

   There are of course differing kinds of partners for Formula 1 teams;
these range from technical partners, who provide key products and
technologies, to pure sponsors who have no direct involvement other
than the exposure of their brand on the Formula 1 car.

Organisation

The purpose of the organisation in Formula 1 is very simple. It is a
structure that is designed to generate the revenue streams necessary
to design, manufacture and race the fastest and most reliable car. A
key part of the flexibility and responsiveness of the Formula 1 organisation is attributed to the importance of the informal organisation.
In Formula 1, concepts such as 'grade' and 'structure' are virtually
non-existent. What matters is getting the job done to make the car go
faster and, while there are clear separations between technical disciplines, such as aerodynamics and electronics, to a large extent these are
delineated by parts of the car. A team that works on the gearbox is
defined by this particular component; moreover, the way it integrates
with other areas, such as the engine design, is defined by the component area.

   The fact that technical areas are delineated so clearly allows a
clarity which is perhaps lacking in other organisational contexts. The
hard part is therefore making trade-offs between areas regarding performance, weight and shape, all of which can have major effects on

the other parts of the system. While this is a challenging area for today's Formula 1 teams, it is also where potential sources of competitive advantage are to be found.

Another important point about organisation relates to the core processes that are being undertaken. These almost always cut across functional levels, and without them the organisation is unable to achieve its core tasks. In the context of Formula 1 these processes relate to design and manufacture of the car with all the resultant issues around supply chains and assembly of components. Additional processes revolve around the continuous development and refinement of the car during the racing season, the mechanisms by which sponsors are engaged and brought into the team, and the way in which race strategies are created and executed.

A further aspect of organisation relates to culture. While Formula 1 is a particularly close-knit and incestuous industry, with many employees frequently moving between teams, it is also apparent that each team has a distinct set of values and priorities which often mirror the priorities of its founders or corporate parent and imbue all the activities of the team with shared values and corporate culture. For anyone working within Formula 1 the differentiation between these cultures is very clear. For those looking in from the outside the teams all appear very much the same. Culture is a critical aspect of these organisations; it directly relates to performance and therefore is a key area of exploration for our study.

Integrating

Perhaps an overused term in management, leadership is a descriptor which appears central to both the sustained performance of Formula 1 teams and, perhaps more importantly, to the ability to turnaround failing teams into Grand Prix winners.

The leadership role is fundamentally concerned with integrating; being the 'glue' between the core parts of the operation, which are often in high states of tension. In particular, these relate to the tension between design and manufacturing, between the commercial and technical parts of the business and the tension between the short- and long-term objectives of the organisation. The best leaders in Formula 1 integrate by providing flexibility and clarity for those within the organisation. It is said by many we have interviewed that a Formula 1 team is almost diametrically opposed to the big-business model. Nothing will be achieved through oppressive bureaucracy and burdensome processes. Formula 1 provides some instructive principles for keeping the organisation agile, responsive and fiercely competitive.

Innovating

While cash is certainly the lifeblood of a Formula 1 team, innovation is without doubt the spirit of the team; innovation not for the sake of it, but in search of improved performance in order to make the car go faster. Any team that is unable to sustain a flow of performance-enhancing innovations will quickly find itself at the back of the grid. No team, no matter how small its budget, can afford to stay still when it comes to finding creative ways to improve car performance; and this has engendered some distinctive approaches to innovating within Formula 1.

For example, there are those who have focused on radical new technologies which have disrupted the accepted way in which Formula 1 cars should be built. Such an approach is exemplified by Team Lotus under the leadership of Colin Chapman in the 1960s and 1970s. Others have focused on constantly integrating innovations into their cars, many of which have originated from other teams, but which are combined in highly effective ways to maximise the performance of the car. For example, Patrick Head created the Williams FW14B, one of the most successful Formula 1 cars of all time, through integrating many different ideas from other Formula 1 teams and optimising their performance in one car. Technology is changing but innovation is often about reconfiguring and rearranging ideas from both within and outside the industry.

The kind of organisation that is able to perform at the highest levels with total reliability, but which is also constantly innovating and changing the basis for competition, is the ultimate competitive organisation. Every Formula 1 team has to constantly live with this tension, and how they achieve this provides some important insights into managing the uneasy balance between exploiting today's ideas and exploring those of tomorrow.

Transforming

Change is a constant imperative in any dynamic organisation, so much so that management consultants are now referring to change fatigue and the importance of stability. Undoubtedly, all organisations are finding ways to deal with the problems of constant change; however, for many this is a necessary evil to be countered, and they seek the restoration of stability as the objective of such initiatives. For Formula 1 teams change is a constant pressure they cannot ignore. Nevertheless, today this is at the level of continuous improvement based around their current systems and technologies. This has not always been the case, but it is fair to say that really dramatic change only occurs when teams are performing poorly and when new technologies or new entrants require a more radical response.

There is also the issue of organisational and culture change, where organisations have to reinvent themselves. In Formula 1 few teams have the luxury of being able to do this, unless they have the resources necessary to get them through difficult times, such as the case of Ferrari in the 1980s and early 1990s. Despite many of these firms often being owned by multinational corporations, they are run almost as family businesses. This creates many of the advantages outlined in this chapter but it also creates the kind of inertia which makes radical change especially challenging. It is particularly so when many of the original staff and senior management are still in place – they've seen it all before and therefore provide a potential barrier to the radical change which may be needed to achieve sustained performance.

Performance

Every Formula 1 team wants to win. Despite perceptions from the outside, no-one is going to the race just to make up the numbers. Even the teams at the back of the grid take great pride in the fact that their pit stops can be just as fast as those of the teams at the front. Each team declares that it is its 'will to win' that keeps it going. If they all have an equal desire to win, what then makes the difference? What is important here, as in any organisation, is that there is a clear connection between all the activities which are undertaken and their contribution to performance. However, such connections are difficult to establish in practice. Many managerial initiatives are based on the assumption that there will be a positive impact on performance, but such a relationship is often merely asserted and there is frequently no subsequent effort made to validate this relationship.

In our framework the elements of Individual, Team and Partner are connected to each other to signify the obvious inter-relationships that exist between them. When these components are working in synergy a virtuous circle of activity can exist that allows the collective efforts of all three to drive organisational growth and improved effectiveness. The processes of **Integrating, Transforming** and **Innovating** acting upon the organisation add additional levels of complexity and also create potential conflicts. The spirals in Figure 6 represent the competitive advantages and disadvantages that the interaction between these activities can create for a firm. People or organisations can develop behaviours and momentum that lead to cycles of success or winning streaks. It becomes a virtuous circle involving greater levels of communication and participation. It makes it easier to bond because people respect each other in a group of winners. This frequently occurs in Formula 1, however the circle can also become 'vicious' in the sense that this bonding may manifest itself in terms of arrogance and views of invincibility, which allow new competitors to seize the initiative. It is therefore critical that the cycles of winning are tempered with the ability to challenge and adapt as conditions require. Similarly, if performance deteriorates, then organisations fragment into factions which, in the worst case, pass the blame onto each other, making it increasingly difficult to meld the elements back together. It is all too easy for the virtuous circle to quickly become a vicious one!

Taking all of the above into account we believe that Formula 1 provides one of the few organisational contexts where we can get close to the linkage between individual actions, team outputs, organisational characteristics and performance.

4 | The war for talent: the people of Formula 1

I am a person who is positive inside, so I don't want to reflect any negativity outside, even if we are working in a war.

Stefano Domenicali – Racing Management
General Director, Scuderia Ferrari

Stefano Domenicali is one of a new breed of team principal, having at the end of 2007 formally taken over from Jean Todt as the head of Gestione Sportiva (GS) – Ferrari's Formula 1 operation. In saying the above Domenicali was reflecting on a broader question about his leadership style, but his reference to a 'war' was not by accident, especially as he added:

… that's a word I do not like to use too much, to be honest, as it is done with so many things that are not really part of my lifestyle or character.

The battle on the track is happening alongside the continuing struggle to find, nurture and retain top talent, which is so very much the daily challenge experienced by all businesses. In this chapter we will take a look at the people who populate this sport: the team principals at the top of these organisations, Formula 1 people in general, and Formula 1 drivers. In this second edition we have expanded our examination of drivers, about whom we usually receive the most questions during our speaking and teaching engagements. We will consider their competitive drive and work ethic, physical conditioning, driving skills, ability to work under pressure, and the communication skills required of them in today's racing and commercial environment.

In terms of attracting talent Formula 1 has a special allure. It is perceived as the pinnacle of international motorsport and people working in it, at all levels, believe they are involved in the ultimate racing endeavour. They enjoy a unique opportunity to participate in a global sport and business arena associated with glamour, international travel and the excitement that comes from advanced technologies, powerful engines and high speeds. As one writer put it:

Formula 1 is the archetypal glamorous sport: a heady mix of brilliant and brave drivers, electrifying speed, billionaire backers, debonair celebrities and pioneering design and technology.[11]

Engineers, technicians, mechanics, designers and other specialists find their way into Formula 1 typically from related industries like aeronautics and automobile manufacturing. Some are now even recruited directly out of higher education institutions that cater to motorsports talent development. Suppliers are also tapped for skilled people, as we were told by Peter Digby, Managing Director of Xtrac, a UK-based company that is a leading supplier of high-performance products such as transmissions and gearboxes to all forms of motorsport teams:

Each year I am losing three or four engineers to Formula 1 because we have become the Rolls Royce of training regarding motorsport engineers. If you want a really good engineer, someone who understands assemblies, fits and tolerances and everything else, and how to produce parts at a reasonable cost, we do all of that.

Being a major supplier to ten Formula 1 teams is a two-edged sword, as Digby notes:

Because we supply a lot of teams, if we lost ten guys that would be a problem. Most teams respect this, but not all. I often feel like an employment agency and sometimes feel we should start to charge a finder's fee!

In business life it is usual to be working with people who demonstrate a wide spectrum of personality types and behaviours. This is also true in Formula 1. But a closer examination of the mechanics, technicians, engineers, managers and drivers in the sport reveals certain common characteristics. We have identified several that consistently cut across all Formula 1 teams. Formula 1 people demonstrate:

- Passion and drive;
- Focus and competitiveness;
- Willingness to share knowledge and a desire to improve;
- Entrepreneurial mindset; and
- Attention to detail.

However, before taking a closer look at these, we start with a few comments about the people who lead Formula 1 teams.

Team principals

Team principals sit at the top of every Formula 1 organisation. They are lightning rods for praise, dissent and media gossip. Egos among this group of individuals often run high. This is not a position for someone without a high degree of self-confidence. All team principals are passionate about the sport and work the same long hours as everyone else in their team. Interestingly, people in senior positions at Formula 1 teams typically have not been business school graduates or professional managers. According to Pat Symonds at Renault F1, they have been:

... without exception, people like myself, professional engineers who have been in the business a long while, but not managers. And in common with most Formula 1 teams, we don't have trained managers; you won't find any MBAs here.

Many Formula 1 leaders have been self-made men; sometimes former race drivers or others who have been associated with the motor industry in some way before moving up to Formula 1. They have learned through experience and the 'school of hard knocks', and therefore, they have tended to develop ad hoc practices for managing their organisations. Some can be very detail oriented and, at least in their earlier years, as admitted by most, not very experienced in terms of managing people and external partnerships.

But given new organisational and commercial realities, this has had to change. The teams have grown to the size of major companies. The amount of money at stake has increased significantly over time. Team principals have needed to learn about operating in a different, more professional environment and in some cases, bring in management talent or outside advisors to help provide guidance for their businesses.

A new breed of younger senior leaders has been and is being groomed to take over key positions in Formula 1 organisations. One can also see elements of a strategic approach to change at the top of several organisations. Team principals such as Stefano Domenicali (Ferrari), Christian Horner (Red Bull), Nick Fry (Honda) and Martin Whitmarsh (McLaren) are good examples of well-schooled individuals who have achieved top positions within their teams.

Domenicali's rise to the top came after seventeen years of experience at Ferrari in a variety of positions. He told us:

I was lucky because I have had quite a transversal growth inside the company. I started in administration, moved to human resources, then to sponsorship, followed by organisation and logistics. In the middle of these changes I was also involved in the sporting side as race director for the Mugello track. I was able to see all the different areas of the company.

So how has that prepared him for the most senior position in Ferrari's Formula 1 racing programme?

You need to know everything about the major topics of what running a business means, otherwise you are only focused on the technical side without having understood anything about all the other important things.

While listening to Christian Horner, Team Principal at Red Bull Racing, one can hear the more measured approach of someone who considers himself, first and foremost, a professional manager. For example, he shared his approach to building a successful Formula 1 team:

Invest in people, give them support and the tools to do their job. Don't tell them how to do their job, but give them the right guidance and the right backing and they will deliver for you.

He has also clearly given great thought and weight to creating the right kind of atmosphere that will encourage people to perform at their best:

Within the team there is a steely determination to achieve its objectives. We have a very non-political environment here, a very good team spirit and a group of people pulling together. We've never struggled to recruit people. This is a dynamic team that looks after its employees and rewards success. It's a young team with a goal and a mission. We're pushing very, very hard to try to achieve them.

But even if highly motivated to start with, as well as passionate about what they do, Formula 1 teams, like all businesses, need to be concerned about retaining talent. Historically this industry has seen people at all levels moving across from one team to another. The management of Toyota F1 understands this. John Howett, president of Toyota F1, knowingly or not making a reference to Herzberg's[12] motivational factors, told us:

The salary or benefits package is a hygiene factor, so we retain people primarily by keeping them motivated, involved and by giving them opportunity to grow and develop. We use typical tools that you would find in any well-run business, e.g. job descriptions, performance appraisals, training and development, etc.

Managing people in this industry is not easy. As Pat Symonds points out:

The interesting thing about Formula 1 is they're all rather difficult people to manage because they are self-opinionated, arrogant sort of people in the nicest possible way. To be honest that's what we look for at Renault. We look for people who think laterally, who never accept that something is impossible and who are prepared to work hard. They've got to be team players, while they've got to be individuals. They should be individualistic in their thinking, but team players in their actions.

People who work in Formula 1 are a diverse group, but they exhibit some common characteristics.

Formula 1 people

To summarise, they demonstrate:

- Passion and drive;
- Focus and competitiveness;
- Knowledge sharing;
- Entrepreneurial mindsets; and
- Attention to detail.

Passion and drive

The one word that would encompass the mindset of all the Formula 1 people the authors have interviewed is *passion*; an all-encompassing passion for just about everything that revolves around their participation in this sport. This goes from the people at the top of the organisation, to the mechanics, to the relationship managers dealing with sponsors and their guests on race weekends or test days.

According to Alex Burns, COO at WilliamsF1:

Technical people are delighted to be associated with something at the leading edge of their profession, so there is an inherent motivation for them that says, 'I work for an organisation that is aligned with Formula 1.' It is difficult to measure but there are definite benefits that come from that.

Given the above, it's not surprising to learn that when Frank Williams is hiring new employees he is looking for:

People who have intellect, strength of character, humanity, and a sense of humour, but above all passion.

Although he admits:

... it's not easy to find all of those in one person.

This passion is evident not only in the long hours that are put in, but in the energy with which every task is approached. It overflows into the non-stop discussions about the sport, business and personalities within Formula 1 whether they are on the job or away from the track and factory.

As Stefano Domenicali stated:

We stay together also outside the job as well as at the track. We talk about the 'family spirit' because that's the secret of Ferrari. For us it is normal, but we do find that people coming here from different teams or different realities find it incredible.

We have even heard the use of the word 'love' in reference to the sport and business of Formula 1 from quite a few of the people we interviewed.

Frank Williams told us that:

After all these years we still love what we do. It is a gift when you can work at what you love. There can't be many other businesses where people are truly passionate as they are in Formula 1. I suppose football is one. What did Bill Shankly of Liverpool FC say? 'It's a bit like life and death, but even more important.'

We heard much the same from Flavio Briatore, who became more philosophical:

In your business life and in your career, first you need to choose carefully what you want to do, and whatever it is you choose you need love for what it is you are doing. Quite simply, providing you have that love and that passion for your career, then it is simply a lot of hard work – there is no other way.

One might wonder whether in any industry a survey that asks the question, 'Do you love your job?' would receive as high an affirmative response as it would if the Formula 1 community were polled.

Of all the Formula 1 teams Ferrari holds a special position when one talks about passion. Raoul Pinnell, who was formerly in charge of global marketing at Shell, a major sponsor of Ferrari, told us about the passion associated with Ferrari:

It is just extraordinary and it extends beyond even Formula 1. There are countries in the world in which Shell operates where there has never been a Formula 1 Grand Prix, it's hardly ever on the television, nobody in those countries has ever owned a Ferrari, never seen one in person – but people know Ferrari.

Ross Brawn, former Technical Director at Ferrari during its amazing run of success from 1999 to 2004, told us:

Where Ferrari is different is the sheer passion of the people who work here. If you work at Ferrari and you go home your family ask you about the job, your nephews, nieces, neighbours, everyone asks you what's going on at Ferrari because there's so many people interested in what we do and in supporting what we do.

Ferrari stands out in that it not only garners millions of loyal fans, but also represents the hopes and aspirations of the Italian nation. Seven times World Champion driver Michael Schumacher put it this way:

Driving for Ferrari is more than special; Ferrari is more than a team. In Italy it is kind of a religion. If you win or if you lose, there is a whole country behind you. It took me a while to understand that, and maybe I have learned it the hard way, but now I feel part of that feeling and part of that family.[13]

This enveloping passion extends beyond Ferrari, in fact from all the Formula 1 teams to the millions of fans and supporters who follow the sport on television, through the printed media, online communities and at the track. And it is this passion, translated into brand loyalty, that Formula 1 team sponsors and owners (particularly in the case of the car manufacturers) hope to tap into in order to spur additional product sales.

Matched with their passion, individuals working at all levels in Formula 1 do nothing by half measures. They are, in a word, ***driven*** (and the authors apologise for the obvious pun that cannot be avoided). Some are propelled by the heady excitement of powerful engines and high speeds, some by the leading-edge technology employed, some by the racing competition, and still others by the potential wealth that has accrued to quite a number of successful participants in the sport. No matter the reason for their involvement, anyone working on a Formula 1 team knows only one credo; that is, working flat out in order to push oneself, one's teammates and ultimately their cars to the limit.

According to Jackie Stewart:

The level of driven people in Formula 1 is probably more clear than any other business segment. They work to close-loop procedures because there's a race every two weeks from March until November and there are deadlines to meet. The ability to duck under the fences and make things happen is more clearly obvious than any other business that I know.

Formula 1 people are always being pushed by deadlines, competitive pressures and budget concerns. In Stewart's words:

When you're designing a racing car the design is always running to the limit, the manufacturing is always running to the limit, the number of spares you're going to take to the first race is running to the limit. The people you've got working for you would work, in Melbourne for example, for three nights, non-stop, and work all day. Those people do that, and they would not do that in any other business, so this fever or this allergy that they all have is the same one. It's 'do it yesterday', not ever tomorrow.

Alex Burns highlighted the risk of such a tempestuous pace:

To be honest a number of people are slightly more burnt out than they would have been because they worked over a bank holiday weekend. We know we've used up a little bit of goodwill with our staff in order to make that happen, but they understand. People here all want to be additive to performance and will definitely go the extra mile for something that is a performance gain. They know there is a benefit for it, and the weekend after, when we scored a point at Istanbul [a WilliamsF1 race result in 2008], it makes a difference.

Focus and competitiveness

Successful Formula 1 teams *focus* on maintaining steady improvement and obtaining results. To succeed in Formula 1, according to Jackie Stewart:

it takes a special individual with total commitment and total focus ... nothing like it exists in the corporate world.

From Frank Williams' point of view:

Focus is pretty common among all the top teams. It's partly borne of passion, partly borne of a strong competitive spirit.

Over the years some Formula 1 teams have attempted to expand their brand and move into product areas that would develop additional revenue streams. On this subject, Williams added:

We did not do well with our diversification, and we're glad we're no longer involved. I don't think this is a reflection on a weakness or incompetence of our management, rather than a decision that we do not want to do it. There are other examples of how you can manage diversification successfully. The companies may not all be profitable, but some may feed Formula 1 with specialist services. But for us it's simple, we just focus, we just focus here.

Focus is generally thought to be a positive force in business, but when applied to the wrong strategy or at the expense of the business that can need development, it can be detrimental. Such was the case with Enzo Ferrari's obsession with engines. He believed that motor racing teams lived and died on horse power. It has taken a great deal of effort to change internal mindsets at Ferrari, but that focus had to be re-channelled. While still at Ferrari Ross Brawn explained:

A few years ago it used to be an engine and a chassis. Ferrari was renowned for having very powerful engines, but the chassis was not very good. Today, we would never take that view. It's the car that matters. It's the result of the car on the track that matters and the junction between engine and chassis is seamless. We apply that principle to all areas of the car: electronics, engine, chassis, aerodynamics, structure – it has to be a whole. There is no point in having one area very strong and the other areas weak.

Brawn felt this focus on the integrated package and total control of all the contributing elements was a key factor in its success:

A Ferrari is a Ferrari. It's not an engine, it's not a chassis, it's not an aero package. It's a Ferrari.

Formula 1 people are very **competitive**. They work in highly pressured situations and always under tight deadlines. The very nature of the business is about going faster; improving performance while maintaining consistent quality and reliability. They are constantly measuring themselves against the clock. This pertains not only to performance on the track or changing wheels and tyres in the pit lane, it also relates to making minute but important changes in the chassis, gearbox, engine or electronics so they can reduce lap speeds by a fraction of a second at the next race. Formula 1 people are strongly motivated to improve on each previous performance. Their successes and failures in this sport are on display for everyone to see within the industry and, thanks to the enormous media coverage, on view for hundreds of millions of fans and enthusiasts.

In the words of Flavio Briatore:

Every two weeks you present your balance sheet. Every two weeks people are judging if you have done a good or a bad job.

Stefano Domenicali also sees the very positive aspect of this time pressure represented by the Formula 1 schedule:

Luckily in this job you have the possibility to react after fifteen days so there's not really a year to wait. Match after match you can really show what you are trying to achieve.

Ron Dennis, Team Principal at McLaren-Mercedes, has said:

If you are in Formula 1 and you are not a competitive individual, and I mean anywhere in Formula 1, you are going to struggle and have a tough time. It is a cut-and-thrust business where the rewards for success are massive and the penalties for failure are punitive. When you go into the Grand Prix environment you are constantly trying to outmanoeuvre and out-think your opposition, and I don't mean only in how you are going to run the car in such a way that you win, I am talking about every single aspect of Grand Prix racing: the politics, the sponsorships, the way you portray yourself, how you race, how you look, how you attract investment and how you optimise or shape your performance.[14]

Ian Phillips, now Director of Business Affairs at Force India, has seen and worked with many Formula 1 business leaders. He shared his view of Ron Dennis and Dennis's competitiveness:

I believe that Ron Dennis, next to Bernie [Ecclestone], has done more for raising the bar in Formula 1 than anyone else. He said to me once in the early days, 'I may not be able to beat Ferrari yet, but I sure can make it hurt for them!'

Alex Burns added his view on the subject:

I think what is important about Formula 1 is the strong motivation you get from being associated with something that you really believe matters. These people are here to win; there's a real sense of competition.

Knowledge sharing

Formula 1 is a business that relies on sophisticated engineering techniques, creative design and pioneering use of state-of-the-art materials and electronics. Individual learning is not enough to reach the levels of performance that are required to succeed. Successful Formula 1 teams have therefore become very adept at sharing knowledge across the business and working together. In *MotorSport* magazine (December 2007) Renault F1's Geoff Simmonds commented:

There are so many people relying on each other ... when we take somebody on, he has to be the kind of guy who, when he's finished his own jobs, looks around and sees what he can do to help someone else.

There is no place in Formula 1 for people who guard information closely and are not prepared to share their expertise within the team. Sharing information, especially confidential information, outside the team is another story. During the 2007 season Formula 1 experienced a widely reported alleged breach of business and sporting etiquette, if not illegal sharing of intellectual property, when a senior member of Ferrari was accused of passing information to members of the McLaren-Mercedes team. While court cases regarding individuals involved continue at the time of writing, McLaren was judged by the FIA, ruling body of all motorsport, to have infringed the rules. It was therefore levied with a $100 million fine and lost all of the Constructors' Championship points it had accumulated during 2007.

This unfortunate incident has not in any way dampened the teams' need or desire to ensure that within their organisations appropriate information is shared across functional groups. Without doing so effectively, a Formula 1 team knows it would be putting itself at a competitive disadvantage. So, the search for continual improvement through active, cross-functional communication goes on. This could be anything from the materials used in making components, the aerodynamic designs being tested in wind tunnels and supported by CGI systems that tap into super computers, engine refinements and the fuels and lubricants that are used to drive the engines, to get maximum benefit from the tyres, that as of 2007 are being supplied only by Bridgestone.

Entrepreneurial mindset

While the Formula 1 industry has seen its share of large car manufacturers take positions on the starting grid, the guts of the business are still grounded in individuals who, in fact, act like entrepreneurs. When comparing Formula 1 to other industries Jackie Stewart said:

Formula 1 operates at a faster pace, requires more decisive decision-making, is less well structured, and has little or no bureaucracy. It is very entrepreneurial, very leadership driven and extremely teamwork related.

But as teams have grown to sizes of between 600 and 1,200 employees, maintaining the entrepreneurial spirit has become much harder to do. As a former Team Principal and then advisor to Jaguar Racing, Jackie Stewart has had to caution his colleagues that while they are owned by the Ford Motor Company, they must,

... keep in mind you're a small company where your attention to detail is better and your urgencies are faster. You have to think like you are running the corner business.

With over 525 people in the UK alone, by any standard of any industry the Renault F1 team is a reasonably sized company and additionally there are a further 125–150 people within the engine facility in France. Pat Symonds remarked:

What makes motorsport what it is, is this ability to react, this ability to cut through red tape and just get on with things.

Formula 1 teams have recruited from other industries to fill expertise gaps, but as Symonds points out:

We have always recruited from other industries, particularly aircraft industries. We don't think people need necessarily motorsport experience, but they do need the attitude and mindset that you find in our industry.

While trying to bring in more managerial techniques from large companies, such as formal performance reviews and performance appraisals, Formula 1 teams have attempted to maintain the small-firm feel about them.

Eddie Jordan was one of the more colourful team principals in the days of Jordan F1. He originally entered motor racing as a driver before getting into team management and ownership:

Some people might classify me as a form of entrepreneur, but that is only because I'd probably be unemployable in a regular business.

He recalled discussions with Honda in the late 1980s when they were interested in purchasing his team and suggested putting him under a contract to them:

This gave me a big shock. It meant that I could be hired and fired. Therefore, the only way to guarantee the project is to do it myself and continue myself.

His entrepreneurial nature set the tone for the entire Jordan racing team.

Attention to detail

Formula 1 is a sport where winning and losing is measured in fractions of a second, so it is not surprising that team members pay a great deal of attention to detail. While the lofty vision of a podium finish is crucial for individual and team motivation, day-to-day performance depends on thousands of precise measurements in the wind tunnel, sophisticated aerodynamic and stress simulations on computers, and parts manufactured and assembled to tolerances within thousandths of a millimetre. Every element of design, development, manufacture, assembly and car set-up impacts the fractions of a second that the teams are striving to shave from their lap times. Therefore, focus on detail is paramount.

McLaren-Mercedes' Ron Dennis is renowned for his attention to detail:

I have a view that every single thing in a company is important; the entire spectrum, from how a toilet roll dispenser functions, to who drives our racing cars ... The great companies are those that have the intentions of being the best at everything. And this envelopes the whole environment.[15]

Formula 1 drivers

Our discussion about individuals in Formula 1 would not be complete without taking a look at the people who are the most visible representatives of the sport and the business – the drivers.

Their images appear in advertisements, newsprint and often as items of television news, beyond the sports section. Most drivers have enthusiastic followings that rival those of athletes participating in any sport, anywhere in the world. They are supported by fellow countrymen for sure, but many transcend their own nationalities based on their public personas, real or created by the media.

According to Martin Brundle, former Formula 1 driver and TV commentator:

Drivers, that's really all people want to know about. They want to know what the drivers look like, sound like, how they think, what they are like and what they do when they are not driving. You can offer the media all sorts of key personnel involved with the team, but actually the fans mainly want to know about the drivers.

The authors' experience at training programmes and speaking engagements since the publication of the first edition of this book in 2005 strongly bears this out.

As Sir Jackie Stewart told us:

While the driver doesn't have quite the authority today as he may have had during another period, at the end of the day I still believe that the driver is the captain of the ship. Whatever the CEO might think or the chief engineer might think or the technical director might think, at two o'clock in the afternoon it's only down to one man to interpret what he can get out of that vehicle's dynamics.

In comparison to Sir Jackie's days when drivers were well into their twenties when they started their careers, today it is a different story. According to Martin Brundle:

If you look at the new young stars they are in their late teens, or very early twenties, so the whole thing has moved forward three or four quite critical years. When I first raced in F1 I was twenty-four and was quite young at the time to be a Grand Prix driver. I know in the past there have been some exceptions, but generally speaking the driving age of these guys really getting the job done is just coming down and down and down.

Brundle continued:

Kids are starting at eight years old. By the time they're sixteen they've done literally hundreds of races. So they are experienced, have confidence and race craft, and they are so mature. Most will have had some media training along with a fitness regime and they are more ready for it; they're not as green as we were.

Driver development has taken on a new meaning from Sir Jackie Stewart's day. He told us:

When I was coming into Formula 1 there was an enormous depth of experience and knowledge on the Formula 1 grid. As the young guy I had a great opportunity to learn from others. Today, the young drivers are full of exhilaration and seat-of-the-pants skills, but to succeed you have to have considerable knowledge, depth of knowledge, because first you get experience, then you get knowledge, then you get wisdom, and then you get maturity to go with your wisdom. There are not many that would fit into that last box. When young guys get into Formula 1 I think they genuinely think they know a lot. This is the only sport I know of where there's no coaches.

Sir Jackie warmed to the topic:

Why does Tiger Woods have his coach with him? Why does Federer or Nadal have his? They are the best in the world. It seems racing drivers don't think they need them. Are they so clever? They think they have a higher intellect than any other sportsperson and therefore, we don't need any advice at all and I think that's a big oversight. Tiger Woods' coach didn't win any opens. You don't have to be a World Champion to be a good coach or educator.

We asked Mark Webber about Sir Jackie's assertion. He replied:

You can teach someone up to a point and help them. I'm with Jackie to a degree, but when the lap times change so much due to technology also, it's very difficult.

Martin Brundle supported that view in terms of driver development:

There's another key factor and that is technology on the cars. Before, you needed experience to set a Formula 1 car up. Now you need data. It's a data-driven business and when a team turns up to a race, they have the track mapped to within a few centimetres on a computer software programme. They can run any number of set-ups on a software package with their CFD [Computational Fluid Dynamics] programmes and simulators. With the wind tunnels and aero testing they have packages that can change the aero balance by very small margins, along with corresponding suspension dynamics and weight distribution too. It's not like it used to be – educated trial and error backed up by experience.

Generally, Formula 1 drivers share most of the common characteristics that we have discussed to this point, such as passion, focus, desire to improve and attention to detail. But there are a few other traits that can be associated with them in particular:

- Competitive drive and a healthy work ethic;
- Peak physical conditioning;
- Driving skills and racing intelligence;
- Ability to work effectively under extreme pressure; and
- Communication skills to work effectively within the team and with partners.

Competitive drive and work ethic

While competitive drive is a characteristic that defines all people in this sport it is clear that the man sitting in the cockpit cannot succeed today without a work ethic that pushes his performance, as well as the performance of his team mates, to the limit. During his active days in Formula 1 Eddie Jordan discovered and nurtured the early careers of many successful drivers in what Jordan calls his 'University of Formula 1'. He summed up what he looked for in these young prospects:

I have an old-fashioned way of doing this. I want to see if they have the ****ing fight for it; will they give their last ounce. I get up close and look into their eyes and say, 'Look at me and tell me you ***ing can instead of simply searching for it. Can you find it in yourself? Do you have the ***ing killer instinct, that cures or kills 'em?' I want to hear what they have to say, and very often the language can be very colourful.

In his own equally colourful but more contained way of speaking, David Robertson, Business Manager for 2007 World Champion Kimi Raikkonen, explained his philosophy for what it takes to be a Championship-winning driver:

If you know the top stars, then you know what they're like, they have to have the 'head for what they do'. Their 'head' is all important. It's something that's in the kids' nature, you see the kids, they can't be beaten, they won't be beaten ... if he can do that, I can do that. They never at anytime doubt themselves – these are the ones that have the chance to make it to the top.

Mark Webber, driver for Red Bull Racing, said in a May 2008 BBC Sports interview that he believes:

All Formula 1 drivers are talented, but the really great ones have an incredible feel for what they need to do, how to have the car on the limit ... It's not something you can usually see, but it's that one to two percent difference.

But along with competitive drive the best drivers must also have a sound work ethic. Their services are not just required on race day. Drivers put in gruelling sessions on test tracks, participate in meetings with designers and engineers and attend innumerable sponsor events. The best do this with a natural grace and aplomb that inspires and builds confidence in everyone else on the team.

As WilliamsF1 driver, Nico Rosberg, told us:

I try to be respectful to everyone in the team. I want to show them that I appreciate all the effort they put into the job for me. I think this is the most important thing. To go with this I occasionally invite them for drinks or play soccer with them to continue building our relationships.

Peak physical conditioning

It may not be obvious to those who do not follow the sport, but Formula 1 drivers must be highly conditioned athletes. A Formula 1 racing car can accelerate from 0 to 180 kilometres per hour (110 miles per hour) and back to 0 in less than six seconds. This can put a driver under 5 gs of force under braking. So drivers must be as fit as fighter pilots. Therefore, gone are the days when drivers played hard into the night and then hopped into their cars for races the next day. In the 1970s and 1980s there were World Champions who smoked and drank considerably, but that would not be considered feasible or appropriate now. All the Formula 1 drivers today benefit from personal trainers, carefully crafted diets and scheduled rest and relaxation periods.

During a race, given the considerable levels of stress and heat, drivers can lose a great quantity of bodily fluids. They are schooled in how to hydrate themselves correctly before a race and they also have the ability to drink fluids during a race through an electronically controlled tube fitted into their crash helmets. What has become apparent during the last twenty years is how much leaner the drivers have become. Mansell, Hill, Cheever and Warwick, for example, were all tall, well-built men. Today, drivers are smaller, lighter and certainly in terms of their well-developed cardiovascular systems, in much better condition to withstand the cumulative stresses of an eighteen-, nineteen- or even twenty-race season.

Brad Spurgeon, who covers Formula 1 for the *International Herald Tribune*, wrote in an article in April 1996 that Erwin Göllner, a Formula 1 physiotherapist, had said that:

A race driver must be born with the sense of speed inside him, but he may not be born with the physical strength and condition necessary for driving a Formula 1 car. That must be developed through hard work and a program of exercise.

Further in Spurgeon's article he wrote about another Formula 1 trainer at that time, Pierre Cometet. As an osteopath, a physiotherapist and an expert in ergonomics Cometet worked closely with driver Ukyo Katayama who drove for the Tyrrell team. Cometet was quoted as saying:

I've noticed that for many drivers, the higher they move up the hierarchy the more anxious they become, the more stressed-out and nervous. This then becomes a major obstacle to continued success.

Today, one team has taken the conditioning of its drivers (along with other team members) to the next level. We spoke with Aki Hintsa, Team Physician for McLaren-Mercedes and the architect of the 'McLaren Lab Program'. Hintsa is a practising orthopaedic surgeon, has been a senior executive on the business side of medical administration and also a missionary doctor in Ethiopia. He has had experience with world-class athletes from many sporting fields, including track and field, where he has worked with some of the world's best. According to Hintsa:

It was not easy to build up the programme because the environment is very challenging in Formula 1. In track and field athletes are competing at the highest level, but Formula 1 is much more complicated. In both there are stress and health problems, but in the Formula 1 package comes jet lag given the constant travel, demanding nutritional issues and the constant pressure from the media and public interest. It is almost impossible for the drivers to live a normal life anymore.

The McLaren Lab Training Program that Hintsa developed is a framework within which the team members can measure their physical and mental fitness and develop their overall physiological performance. Certainly different teams take their own approaches to training that can build up the physical conditioning and capabilities of drivers and other team members. The McLaren Lab Program is unique in the systematic and consistent approach it takes for measuring five elements of development, including cardiovascular fitness; biodynamical factors, e.g. musculoskeletal balance, flexibility and strength; nutrition; mental energy and general health. Everything gets measured and followed, goals are set for each individual, and follow-up is recorded with all other data so a complete picture of before, during and after can be seen and analysed.

According to Hintsa:

We are following more than 150 different physiological and mental parameters; we have baseline tests and in all those tests we measure number and scales.

Heikki Kovalainen joined the McLaren-Mercedes team in 2007 after his rookie year driving for the Renault F1 team. What was it like for him to be indoctrinated into this new approach to development? According to Hintsa:

He had some examinations, some tests. I knew him from earlier days and of course because we are both Finnish, it was easy to communicate with him. We started from scratch, zero point with him. We had to change everything, how he trained and his way of thinking. Everything.

We asked Hintsa if Kovalainen was satisfied with the changes. He said:

In other teams they are doing it differently, but I believe he has been satisfied with this new philosophy of training and performance. You have to ask him.

So we did. Kovalainen told us:

It's a very thorough programme and process. I think the biggest difference is in how complex the programme is, how thorough it is. You know it is based on facts and numbers, pictures and graphs; rather than a fitness test and how you feel. Rather than only doing fitness tests, we do a lot of body scans. We check the bones, we check the muscle, we check blood, joints, we do spine scans, just very thorough things that give you a clear picture and the results of which can help you.

And yes, Kovalainen told us:

I feel physically stronger, I feel easier in the car.

This was a particularly poignant comment, as on the day following this interview, during the 2008 Spanish Grand Prix, Kovalainen experienced a wheel failure that caused his car to plough head-on into a tyre barrier at 240 kilometers per hour (150 miles per hour). The crash lasted 100 milliseconds, which is apparently three or four times longer than a typical crash. Kovalainen's body experienced a force twenty-six times that of gravity or one g more than a fighter pilot would experience strapped to an ejector seat. In retrospect it was therefore good news for him that the McLaren Lab was doing something right and, remarkably, he was able to come away from the incident virtually unscathed and ready to drive in the next Grand Prix two weeks later.

Driving skills and racing intelligence

A driver's on-track skills are honed through countless experiences during testing and races as they work their way through the various racing levels up to Formula 1. In reply to our question about getting advice to improve his driving performance, Nico Rosberg told us:

Only you yourself can improve when driving the car by analysing what you can do better.

Some drivers are natural talents, but all need grooming because the skill requirements to drive in Formula 1 are a cut above any other car-racing formula.

Eddie Jordan said:

The gap between all of the formulae and that of Formula 1 is so immense, it's huge, it's a chasm. With all the razzmatazz and all the bits and pieces and the gizmos on the car it is mind blowing what the driver has to do.

Suffice it to say, being able to drive an 800 hp Formula 1 car while dealing with all the technologies that Jordan refers to, and while maintaining control at the limit, takes fast reactions, exceptional coordination and strong nerve.

One often talks about drivers who are 'quick' or 'fast', and the teams see many young prospects who might be able, over time, to move up to Formula 1. McLaren's Team Principal, Ron Dennis, has said that speed is something that can be detected based on data, but it takes something more to develop drivers who can reach the top level:

Detecting speed is a science, as technology allows teams to study optimal sleep patterns, heart rates and the driving skills of cornering, braking and acceleration. But nurturing a fast, young driver is, by contrast, an art.[16]

One thing that makes a top driver stand out is his racing intelligence. Drivers have a remarkable ability to memorise each turn and elevation on every one of the Formula 1 racing circuits. After driving for up to two hours drivers can recall every gear change or other chassis or engine adjustment made at any given moment during a race. While making split-second decisions guiding their car around the track drivers must also be thinking about race tactics, wear on their tyres, car handling and also dealing with unexpected situations. When Jenson Button achieved his first podium finish for the BAR-Honda team at the Malaysian Grand Prix in 2004 he revealed afterwards that he had suffered oil spikes during the early laps. This meant he had to repeatedly reset the oil pump during the race by pressing the pump button ten times in quick succession. Sometimes, he commented later, this was necessary more than once during a lap:

A driver makes thousands of decisions every single lap he's out there and he lives or dies by them, literally.[17]

The top drivers take in a vast amount of data, compartmentalise it and then use the appropriate information when required. They retain everything and can bring forward remembered experiences and references to avoid problems and difficult circumstances. Being able to keep these memories on tap, ready for use, is a skill great drivers must develop.

Those hoping to become top level Formula 1 drivers eventually learn the importance of continually upgrading their knowledge and skills.

Finland's Kimi Raikkonen has remarked:

You never stop learning, I guess. I don't think you get much faster as you get more experienced, but you do get better. You learn to adapt to changing conditions. You learn to get the best out of your tyres as they degrade. And you learn to be more consistent. You learn to make fewer mistakes.[18]

Ability to work under extreme pressure

We asked Mark Webber what was the best piece of advice he has been given as a driver. His reply reinforced an element from Raikkonen's comments:

On track I would have to refer to a friend of mine, Mick Doohan, who races motor bikes [authors' note: Mick Doohan is a former Grand Prix motorcycle racing champion]. It's such a big word and is so important in many sports – 'consistency' – is so important, it's relentless at any level. It is absolutely imperative that you consistently deliver week in and week out. And this is the ultimate test of us drivers. So, Mick was big on not having any weak circuits, not having any favourites. You have to like them all, it's your job.

The need for consistent results has perhaps been present in the sport since its inception, but the continual pressure on drivers due to media attention has escalated in recent years to a fever pitch. As Martin Brundle says:

It's a twelve-hour day now being a Grand Prix driver. The amount of meetings they are in regarding car set-up, tyre choice, engine parameters and race strategy is immense. David Coulthard [Coulthard decided to retire from Formula 1 at the end of 2008 at the age of thirty-seven, after a fourteen-year career] is a good friend, and I also do his contracts. His schedule for any given Grand Prix day is incredible, and with media slots filling any voids they are full on through a GP weekend. Then as soon as they finish the race they'll be off testing somewhere or a team media appearance. So with winter testing they are on a merry-go-round that doesn't stop year round.

We had first-hand experience of this hectic schedule when we tried to organise interviews with drivers at both Grand Prix and test dates. In addition to their team test or race driving commitments they are being ferried between sessions with the media, sponsors, fans, celebrities and race authorities by harried minders. One of our interview time slots was lost just because the driver could not fit us in and still be able to eat lunch.

Given such demands on their time, it is amazing that most drivers remain level-headed and approachable (to the extent one can reach them). Martin Brundle replied to a hypothesis that today's drivers are so wealthy they tend to be arrogant:

I don't find Formula 1 drivers by and large arrogant at all. I find them down-to-earth people, which they are: they've two legs, two arms, just like other people. It's just that they happen to be good at driving racing cars. But they are under a lot of pressure; as the budgets get bigger the demands on them become difficult to handle while performing mentally and physically at the highest level. Imagine driving for a $400 million team consisting of 1,000 people and you are paid $20 million. That is an enormous opportunity and yet pressure for a 25-year-old to handle while also juggling the technical, commercial and media demands inevitably upon him.

Pressure on drivers can also build from within the team and there is no better example than the McLaren-Mercedes team experience in 2007. Two new drivers were paired up: two-time World Champion Fernando Alonso and rookie Formula 1 driver, Lewis Hamilton. What unfolded was totally unpredicted. Hamilton's impact on the sport was immediate. During his first nine races he appeared on the podium nine times. As those who follow Formula 1 know, there ensued not only a close battle for the Drivers' Championship between these two and Ferrari's Kimi Raikkonen, but also a rivalry that sometimes appeared quite bitter was played out in the media. After the turmoil and disappointments during the year, Alonso returned to the Renault F1 team for the 2008 season. When coupled with 'Spygate' the amount of pressure that was bearing on both McLaren drivers was enormous.

How do top drivers deal with the pressure? David Robertson, who not only manages Kim Raikkonen but also Jenson Button, told us:

If you ask me to do something under the pressure they experience, the nerves would crack me up so I would become slower on the track. But with them it's like a plus, a bonus to have some little bits of nerve. It makes them raise their game as opposed to being lowered. Nine out of ten people would do the opposite.

Communication skills

The driver's ability to communicate his views and insights is crucial. Much like the language divide that often exists between information technologists and commercial specialists, drivers and engineers have to get to know how each other speaks. Pat Symonds recalls:

We often laugh about a driver who'll come in and say, 'There's no grip at all out there.' Of course the engineer says, 'Well, how did you get out of the garage, then?'

Symonds added:

You don't need a driver to be an engineer, but you do need him to be clear, logical and relatively verbose, without going on too much.

Internally, communication between driver and his support team is crucial. Feedback from drivers during test days about a new aerodynamic component, for example, provides them with the live, on-the-track performance knowledge that will validate the thousands of readings that have been taken in simulators and wind tunnels. On the test runs and qualifying laps that lead to race day, it is the driver's input that enables the all-important set-up of the car to be just right for when the five red lights go out to start the race.

Along with this internal team technical preparation, communication becomes vital with regard to the driver's mental preparation. As driver Heikki Kovalainen said:

We talk to our specialists in sports psychology and mental preparation. We have made mental maps of many people, especially people who I work with – my engineers, my trainers, the close people around me and with whom I am all the time communicating on a day-to-day basis. Also from that side we have very clear results, you know, how we can improve that communication, how we can become better and not just when I am driving. We have certain processes to do before I go to the car. We try to stay on the high level all the time rather than have one good day; we try to make sure that we realise when mental energy is not strong enough and then try to get it back to a level before the race starts.

External to the racing team, today's Formula 1 driver also needs to be what one might call 'sponsor-friendly', that is, schooled in the art of public relations and the business of marketing. They, in fact, spend far more time touring around the world at the behest of their sponsors and performing public relations duties, than actually driving in racing competitions. An increasing number of drivers are masters at this task and they truly give superior value to their sponsors and other supporters. For many younger drivers this is a steep learning experience. In July 2008, Lewis Hamilton was asked whether he had realised the extent of the sponsorship side when he first got into Formula 1 the previous year. He replied:

When you are coming through the ranks, you have absolutely no comprehension of what it takes to be a top Formula 1 driver. You have no idea, because all you do until that point is train and race, train and race. Then you get here and it's all so new, and you really have to get on top of it. ... You just have to be on top of it the whole time.[19]

However, some drivers are better at this than others. Lewis Hamilton, Nico Rosberg and Jenson Button are three that come to mind who are very comfortable in front of cameras and audiences. Kimi Raikkonen is famously less so. But his manager David Robertson does not seem to be too worried about this:

I'm a firm believer in you get them (i.e. drivers) not to worry about anything else but their driving. It's the most important thing they do. The biggest thing is that they are not judged on anything but their driving! Everybody loves a winner – winning teams and drivers always find it easier to get sponsorship than the ones at the back of the grid. All sponsors want their product or brand associated with winning.

Raikkonen himself has said:

I like the racing and the other stuff is not always the best thing. Everyone in F1 is here because they love racing and driving, but when there are too many things that you don't enjoy or too many things you don't want, it is time to go away.[20]

Of course, after saying this in June 2008 the media reported aggressively that Raikkonen was contemplating retirement after having won the Drivers' Championship the previous year.

How does WilliamsF1's Nico Rosberg deal with the constant whirl of events away from the track itself? Interestingly, he deferred to his father, Keke Rosberg, who himself had won the Drivers' Championship in 1982 while also driving for Williams:

Outside of the car especially my father has given me a lot of advice. He has always said that it is not enough to be a good driver because here are twenty-two drivers in F1 who are good. But you need to do a better job in setting up the car to your likings, in talking to the media, in doing PR events for the team, etc. so as to increase your value as a driver and really get the best out of your job.

However, it was Ferrari's Head of Motorsport Press, Luca Colajanni, who brought us back to the bottom line as far as performance is concerned:

In the end, communication of Ferrari – especially in Formula 1 – the only measure you can apply are the results. They tell you nice things about you if you win; if you don't win, whatever job you do, they will complain.

Plate 1 Nigel Mansell loses a wheel in the pit lane at Estoril in Portugal as a result of a misunderstood visual communication during a pit stop.
Source: Sporting Pictures

What if you could focus on the things that *really matter?*

75 million people around the world can, because at ING we cut through
the complexities of managing your money. We believe that saving,
investing and preparing for your future should just be... easier.

BANKING · INVESTMENTS · LIFE INSURANCE · RETIREMENT SERVICES

WWW.ING.COM

Plate 2 ING exploits its Formula 1 sponsorship programme across a wide
range of media.
Source: ING Corporate Communications and Affairs

Plate 3 Formula 1 ringmaster Bernie Ecclestone keeps a watchful 'eye' on all proceedings in the paddock from his strategically situated motorhome.
Source: the authors

Plate 4 The Red Bull Energy Station – a Grand Prix weekend home for all Formula 1 team members, media and other guests.
Source: Red Bull Racing

Plate 5 The Ferrari pit-stop crew in action. Notice the use of innovative light signal rather than the usual lollipop man.
Source: Ferrari SPA

Plate 6a Mark Webber, driver for Red Bull Racing, chatting with author Richard West in the Red Bull Energy Station.
Source: the authors

Plate 6b McLaren-Mercedes driver, Heikki Kovalainen, with author Ken Pasternak in the team motorhome.
Source: the authors

Plate 7a Ross Brawn, Team Principal of the Honda Racing F1 team, talking to the authors.
Source: the authors

Plate 7b Mario Theissen, Team Principal of BMW Sauber F1 team, speaking with authors Mark Jenkins and Ken Pasternak in his motorhome office.
Source: the authors

Plate 7c David Robertson, Manager of drivers Kimi Raikkonen and Jenson Button, sharing his thoughts with authors Ken Pasternak and Mark Jenkins in the Ferrari motorhome.
Source: the authors

Plate 8 The WilliamsF1 team ensure the wheels and tyres are meticulously cleaned and inspected after each session.
Source: the authors

5 | *Winning through teamwork*

Formula 1 is entirely teamwork related; there's almost a dependency on teamwork.

> Sir Jackie Stewart, former Triple World Drivers'
> Champion and former Formula 1 Team Principal

Formula 1 – a team sport

At the end of every Grand Prix television broadcast viewers can watch a post-race press conference, where the three podium finishers are sitting behind a table, the winner in the centre with the second-place finisher seated to his right and the third-place finisher to his left. Sporting their sponsors' caps and watches with their overalls closed to the neck, they towel sweat from their brows and pour themselves drinks from a pitcher containing an unidentified orange-coloured liquid. In turn they answer questions about the race from an off-screen interviewer. After doing so, the drivers whose native tongues are something other than English make a short comment in their own language to their fans at home. Invariably, the driver graciously pays tribute to the many contributors within the team who had made it possible for him to finish in the top three.

And rightly so. Formula 1 drivers know they would not be racing week after week without the extraordinary efforts of the entire team. While the driver is seemingly alone as he navigates the circuit, Formula 1 is a team sport and the skills of the best driver cannot guarantee victory without a well-coordinated and efficiently executing team behind him.

Our research has determined that Formula 1 teams exhibit several key traits that foster the type of teamwork that is required to win races. Team members within their functional units share a clear, *common goal*: work at *building trust* between each other, are willing to *learn* and *collaborate*; *communicate* openly within a *no-blame culture* that has been established by the senior leadership of the organisation.

Before discussing these characteristics we will clarify what we mean by 'a team' in the context of this business. Then we will examine, in detail, one crucial Formula 1 team activity that cuts across all of the competitors in this sport equally, the pit stop. All of the traits exhibiting effective teamwork are evident in how a Formula 1 organisation handles its pit stops – changing tyres and wheels, refuelling and sometimes adjustments to or even wholesale replacement of chassis parts – during a race. By convention, the competitors in this business are known as *teams* – the WilliamsF1 *team*, the Red Bull Racing *team* and so on. Certainly the use of this word to describe organisations participating in sports events is not uncommon. But even as the Formula 1 industry has evolved into a multi-billion dollar business, the description of each of its participants as a *team* is significant and the operative word '*team*' conveys something meaningful and powerful.

Unlike a working group which tries to:

... achieve its performance challenge entirely through the combination of individual performances ...

and where:

... no collective work or products or shared leadership is needed[21] ...

Formula 1 organisations are true teams. They understand each others' capabilities and take on complementary roles; they work together toward a common purpose, the achievement for which they hold themselves mutually accountable. They fully recognise that they can only achieve the levels of performance they require by sharing, supporting and learning together.

A Formula 1 team is vitally dependent on the interwoven relationships between people working in functional areas that include design, engineering, mechanics, testing, racing, marketing, finance and logistics. These separate disciplines become further inter-related through a growing number of complicated collaborations with partners outside their own organisations. Since Formula 1 organisations must operate as commercial businesses in a very competitive environment, they must also balance the internal coordination between innovation and control, between cash out and cash in. When Tony Purnell (now an advisor to the FIA), was CEO of Ford's Premier Performance Division that included now defunct Jaguar Racing, he told us:

Motor racing in particular, much like soccer, has got itself into a knot because it's certainly not a sport; it's a business with a sporting element.

This remains as true as ever. It is crucial that the activities within each of the business's distinct departments or disciplines, what we might call sub-teams, must come together throughout the year and, most significantly, at all of the races during the gruelling season.

According to John Howett, at Toyota:

An F1 team is made up of many sub-teams. At Toyota we keep them focused using a process called 'hoshin'.[22] *'It is similar to Management by Objectives, but different. There is a cascade that starts from the top that is a high level target. All group or team targets are aligned to the company's overarching target and to each other. These are circulated so every group can see the whole picture.*

Jackie Stewart has seen the Formula 1 business from perhaps more positions than almost anyone else in the industry. He has sat in the driver's seat as a triple World Champion, in the motorhome as team owner, in boardrooms as a motorsport advisor, and in the broadcast booth bringing Formula 1 to television audiences around the world. According to Stewart, in the quotation that headed this chapter, Formula 1 is:

... entirely teamwork related, almost a dependency on teamwork.

In short, he described the key element on which a Formula 1 team succeeds or fails. He took the team reference further by referring to his associations in the sport as his *family*.

The people that work with us are not just employees. They're part of the family and you've got to build that family up.

The term *family* to describe a Formula 1 team is heard repeatedly in this industry. It conveys a sense that teamwork and working relationships are being taken to a deeper, more personal and meaningful level.

When Raoul Pinnell was Chairman of Shell Brands International and responsible for Shell's successful relationship with Ferrari he shared a story about his own learning experience about the Ferrari racing team family. After joining Shell, Pinnell was charged with negotiating the contract with Ferrari. He flew to Milan where he had organised a meeting with the Ferrari management team:

I had arranged these standard office rooms serving poor coffee and stale sandwiches. During the meeting I banged on about the details of the contract until it ended without result.

Realising there had been a style and cultural disconnect, Pinnell arranged to return to Italy a few weeks later. But this time the Ferrari people offered to organise the venue.

They took me straight to a restaurant and offered me some wine. Normally I don't drink wine at lunch but I realised it would be rude if I did not oblige. They asked me about my family, my friends, my history and my life in general. I kept thinking, 'When are they going to get to business?' I kept checking my watch and thought about my plane departure time. Finally, I mentioned my concern and they said, 'Don't worry; we've got a car ready for you. And now we know you and like you. You are part of the family.' They gave me a big bear hug, we talked and after we agreed certain things in principle, they poured me into a Ferrari for the drive to catch my plane.

Pinnell experienced a clash between his concern for getting the contract negotiated – a more 'Northern European' approach, as he put it – and their relationship focus. But while enduring the initial discomfort of the experience he was also introduced to the Ferrari way of doing business, where in Pinnell's words:

If you are one of the family, we will do things for you, and they expect that this will also work in reverse whether it is in the contract or not.

Perhaps this sense of family that one finds in most Formula 1 teams can be expected, given the constant pressure and tight deadlines under which they operate. Individuals exhibit remarkable commitment to their team and to each other. They are accustomed to pulling together in order to get the job done under difficult circumstances. This element of making it work under adverse conditions adds to the feeling that they are part of a *family*.

The Formula 1 pit stop

No demonstration of teamwork more fully represents the dedication and commitment required in this sport than that which is displayed by the pit-stop crew. Such is the dynamic of the activity that the authors frequently use the Pit-Stop Challenge exercise as part of their client work to improve performance and communication within business teams.

Other than the driver the pit crew are by far the most visible team unit at each race. Their efforts are displayed and replayed in slow motion to be viewed by hundreds of millions on televisions around the world. The successful completion of the pit-stop task is absolutely crucial if a team wants to finish on the podium. According to Jackie Stewart:

Enzo Ferrari knew as a racing driver that you had to have pit signals and you had to have the garage organised. You had to have the pit stops working better because the time that was lost there could never be made up by the driver. Whatever time the driver could gain on the track, it wasn't as much as could be gained changing wheels or putting in fuel.

Just prior to his untimely death in 2004 John Walton headed up the Minardi pit-stop team. Minardi competed in Formula 1 from 1985 to 2005. It was sold to Red Bull in 2006 and now competes as Scuderia Toro Rosso. He told us:

The pit stop plays the major role in the race strategy because a second lost in a pit stop can be the difference between winning and losing a race.

This message has been reinforced time and time again in the years since then. With less passing on the track than many Formula 1 fans would like to see, races are often now won and lost by the pit-stop strategy employed by the team, i.e. when to come in for refuelling and which tyres to use; and by the ability of the driver and his pit team to perform adroitly and with speed.

The pit stop is a very special part of a Formula 1 race. This activity that, at its best, takes place in about seven seconds has been described as:

... a preordained set of manoeuvres that is barely related to the rest of the weekend's efforts calling for complex activities where many discretionary, invisible, coordinated decisions are made in a split second.[23]

The pit stop in its basic form involves changing all four wheels and tyres and adding a pre-measured amount of fuel. Interestingly, it is the regulated flow speed of injecting fuel, 12 litres every second, that determines the total time necessary to complete the pit stop. A Formula 1 pit-stop crew can actually change all four wheels and tyres in less than three seconds. Ironically, this often prompted John Walton to remind his tyre change crew to slow down. He told us:

It's the fuel that dictates the length of the pit stop. The best these guys can do to change the tyres is 2.8–2.9 seconds. It's pretty slick. When we practise it, of course they want to be really quick, but when it comes to the race I often must remind them to 'take it easy, take your time, you've got loads of time', because if we are putting in 52 litres of fuel that takes at least 6½ seconds. We could change the tyres twice during that time.

Taking a closer look at the pit stop reveals the teamwork required to accomplish it successfully. The pit-stop crew's performance in several ways also represents the many team interactions that enable an entire Formula 1 organisation to perform successfully.

Firstly, the scene is set – as shown in Figure 7 a Formula 1 pit stop requires between twenty-one and twenty-three people working in a confined space, not much longer and wider than the car itself, in the pit lane in front of their team garage. This is an extremely hostile environment as other racing cars are passing by on the track at speeds of up to 320 kph (approximately 200 mph) only 15 metres away on the other side of the safety wall, and at 80 kph (50 mph) within the pit lane itself. Earplugs and radio headsets within fire-proof helmets are required because the noise from the engines is deafening. Very often competitor cars are pulling in or out of their pit area at the same time, passing a few centimetres away from the pit crew.

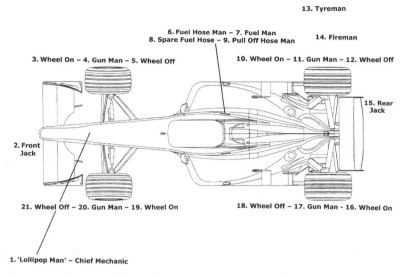

13. Tyreman

6. Fuel Hose Man – 7. Fuel Man
8. Spare Fuel Hose – 9. Pull Off Hose Man

14. Fireman

3. Wheel On – 4. Gun Man – 5. Wheel Off

10. Wheel On – 11. Gun Man – 12. Wheel Off

15. Rear Jack

2. Front Jack

21. Wheel Off – 20. Gun Man – 19. Wheel On

18. Wheel Off – 17. Gun Man - 16. Wheel On

1. 'Lollipop Man' – Chief Mechanic

Figure 7 Schematic of Formula 1 pit stop. Source: WilliamsF1.

The pit crew have been huddled around television monitors in the garage watching the race. They are wearing fire-retardant suits similar to those worn by the drivers, along with helmets and protective gloves. The driver is given a signal three laps before being called in and the pit-stop crew are informed concurrently. The driver is given another alert one lap before coming into the pit lane and he signals back an acknowledgement by pressing the appropriate radio button on his steering wheel – this is received by the pit crew as an audible click. The crew are not permitted into the pit lane in front of the garage until 20–30 seconds before the driver steers the car into the pit-lane entrance. All members of the team then take their carefully scripted positions in front of the garage door. The team members responsible for fitting the new wheels have them ready and in position for fitting the moment the car comes to a stop. Prior to the race, in rehearsal with the drivers, a specific grid was marked with tape or paint markings on the ground. This is a target position for the driver to aim for that will maximise the team's efficiency by aligning the car with the refuelling rig, new wheels and tyres and compressed air-operated wheel-nut guns.

With engines revving at between 7,000 and 19,000 rpm the noise level is extreme, making voice communication within the confines of the helmets very difficult. Each member of the team must know his task, coordinate with others and be ready to communicate his intentions and actions clearly.

The driver pulls into the pit lane, stopping in front of a key crew member holding a front car jack that is used for lifting the front of the car. The jack also carries a simple message that says, 'STOP'. The other members of the crew, looking very much like a team of astronauts in their suits and helmets, jump into action. As the cantilever action of the jack raises the front end of the car, another mechanic places a jack behind the car to raise the rear end in one motion. Three mechanics concentrate on each wheel and tyre. The wheel nut is removed by one using a high-impact air hammer (or air gun). A second team member removes the spent wheel and tyre assembly as soon as the single, central wheel nut is off. He quickly, but carefully, places it to the side so that it cannot roll back and get in the way of the car or any other crew member. The third team member working on that corner puts the new wheel and tyre unit onto the car. Finally the wheel-gun man hammers the wheel nut back onto the axle. At the other three corners of the car the exact same routine is being performed simultaneously.

Meanwhile, three team members wrestle the fuel hose into position. The hose and nozzle weigh almost 40 kilogrammes. The hose is attached to the car by a locking system based on a design borrowed from similar rigs for jet aircraft, so that fuel can be injected into the car at a regulated pressure while the vapour is vented back into the refuelling rig via a central tube fitted within the fuel delivery hose. A third person lays a Perspex shield that is moulded to the shape of the car between the fuel intake slot and the engine mounted in the rear of the car. This prevents any fuel leakage from running into the engine or exhaust system area which at this point is reaching temperatures close to 400°C. Leakage of fuel was in fact the cause of a fire in the pit lane during the German Grand Prix at Hockenheim in 1999. Driving for the Benetton team, Jos Verstappen was fortunate to escape with minor injuries when his car was engulfed in flames during refuelling. The fire was quickly put out by fire extinguishers carried by the mechanics on their belts. Today, every team has one or two people on the fuel team, standing by with fire extinguishers, wearing a self-contained breathing system with their fire-retardant suits.

Additional mechanics also reach into the left and right air intake compartments beside the driver's seating position in order to make sure that no debris has been picked up from the track that could block the air-cooling system. On the other side of the car, another team member cleans the driver's visor.

In real time, all of these activities appear as a blur of movement. However, it is actually a carefully scripted and extremely well-rehearsed performance. When seen in slow motion, it appears very much like a ballet, as each team member performs his task in coordination with the others. The scene has been referred somewhat poetically as a place where:

... task and process unite in a state of flow – a combination of head and heart.[23]

No words are spoken by the mechanics during all of these activities. It is too noisy and happening all too quickly. Non-verbal signals are exaggerated. When a tyre change has been completed the four crew members with air guns either raise their hands high into the air to signal that their tasks are completed or place a coloured gloved hand flat over the top of the tyre surface to indicate they have finished. Unless there is a problem, only one person speaks during this very short period, the team leader. He is responsible for ensuring that all the tasks have been completed as planned. Given the explosiveness, literally, of this highly energised situation, he is also responsible for the safety of the entire pit-stop team and driver. This leader is known as the 'lollipop man', so called because he stands at the front of the car with a round sign on a long pole. The sign says 'STOP' as the driver pulls into position. After the car has been lifted off the ground, he spins the lollipop sign around to show the words 'BRAKES – FIRST GEAR' written on the other side. This reminds the driver to engage the brake and to have the car in first gear so he can depart immediately upon the pit stop's completion. If the brakes are not engaged the rear wheels would spin, making the wheel and tyre change impossible. While this might appear to be an exaggerated, almost unnecessary gesture, given the skill levels of Formula 1 drivers, it is important to recall that at this moment the driver is concentrating on the race situation and he might also be talking in his headset to team engineers who are monitoring the car's performance and to team management providing advice on race strategy.

The lollipop man takes take full and final responsibility for the pit stop as he is the only one with a complete view of all the team members, including the driver, as they complete their tasks on the car. It is up to him to raise his lollipop at the right moment, signalling to the driver that he can accelerate back into the pit lane in order to re-enter the race circuit. This is no small responsibility. Things can go wrong ...

It was the Portuguese Grand Prix at Estoril on 22 September 1991. Nigel Mansell, driving for Williams, was leading the race as he pulled into position for his pit stop and expecting all four wheels and tyres to be changed. Everything seemed to be proceeding according to plan. The lollipop man, watching his crew intently, saw the wheel-gun man on the right-hand rear corner extend his gun into the air, seemingly to signal that his corner was completed. When the lollipop man saw arms raised likewise on the other three corners, he in turn raised his lollipop and Mansell accelerated into the pit lane. However, after travelling only a few meters, Mansell's wheel and tyre assembly came flying off and went rolling down the pit lane. What had happened? It turns out the crew member who had raised his hand on the right rear corner was not signalling that his task was completed. Rather he was leaning across to pick up a spare wheel nut as his had failed during the removal process and had raised his arm to balance himself while doing so! The results for Mansell and the Williams team were devastating; their chance for the Championship was lost as Mansell's car sat idle in the pit lane on three wheels. The regulations do not allow assistance as the active pit lane is considered part of the race track.

On another occasion, at the 1994 San Marino Grand Prix after the accident that would claim Ayrton Senna's life, the race was restarted. One of the slower cars pulled away from the tyre change with the rear jack still hooked under its chassis. As the driver accelerated it flew off, careering into another team's garage, hitting and breaking the arm of one of their mechanics.

During the past few years we have seen a number of pit-stop and pit-lane incidents that have even ended the races of drivers who were in the wrong place at the wrong time. In one 2007 case, a driver departed too early from his standing position in front of the team garage, ignoring the fact that the lollipop was still down. In doing so he pulled the refuelling hose right off the rig and took it with him a few hundred yards down the pit lane. That driver's Formula 1 career came to an abrupt end.

In another incident, in 2008, at the Canadian Grand Prix in Montreal, Lewis Hamilton missed the red light at the end of the pit lane signalling the need to stop and wait for entrance onto the track. The outcome was a crash that ended his race (he drove into the back of a stationary Ferrari), the race of the potential lead driver, Kimi Raikkonen, whom he had hit, and eventually a third driver, Nico Rosberg, in his Williams, who ploughed into the back of Hamilton. Both of the 'guilty' parties were given a penalty at the start of the next race.

A successful pit stop is a strong motivator for the team. It is something that can be felt and curiously, even heard. John Walton told us:

Everybody knows when we've had a good pit stop because you can hear it in all the helmets and radios and earplugs. All the guns sound like there's only one gun. You don't hear the clack, clack, clack of separate guns. It's a great feeling.

The pit-stop team accomplishes the changing of four tyres and adding of fuel in around seven seconds. They do this, typically, two or three times per race for each of their two cars, sometimes even four times, depending upon the race strategy and weather conditions. How can they consistently maintain high performance in such a competitive, highly pressurised environment? What is it that enables these teams to perform successfully week after week?

Our research shows there are several traits necessary for the type of teamwork required by Formula 1 teams to successfully maintain high performance. They are:

- Share a clear, common goal;
- Build trust;
- Collaborate; and
- Communicate openly in a no-blame culture.

Sharing a common goal

For the pit-stop crew a fast and error-free tyre change creates a clear and measurable goal. They know their previous times. They know the times of their competitors. The common purpose – to provide an advantage for their driver – is meaningful and can make a significant difference to the results of the race. Other functional areas of

Formula 1 teams cannot as easily associate their efforts with making as direct an impact on the race. But their efforts to develop new designs, build new components and test them for their reliability gives them clarity of purpose and direction. They know that in the end, it is the sum of all the activities that go into the car and the race performance that will determine success for the whole team.

We asked John Howett how teamwork is built at Toyota and he emphasised clarity of roles to achieve a common objective:

… by clearly defining the targets of the organisation and the group. Clarifying each individual's responsibility of what is expected from them – this is particularly important in teams that operate within a matrix organisation. For example, the engine guys from the engine department may be operating under the leadership of someone from the race team or test team while at the track. Who do they report to and who is in charge? By constantly giving feedback to them identifying what can be done to improve any given situation. Individual, task, team are all important.

Building trust

According to Jackie Stewart the one thing Formula 1 team leaders should never do is:

… compromise their integrity. If you do the right thing you'll always be given credit. It may not come out and you may not hear everybody talk about it, but it's the respect you get for going about your business in an honourable fashion, it's trust … you can't buy it.

Trusting the leader and trusting each other is the glue that integrates the team. It enables open communication and creates an environment for dealing with conflict. It extends from top down, bottom up and literally throughout the organisation. Stewart once again:

Being able to respect the people you are working with, to depend on them, to trust them, to have dependency and trust in somebody that you know is extremely important.

Teams work hard at building trust among team members, getting them to focus on their common goals and aspirations. John Howett told us that Toyota provides an annual budget for non-work-related team building. Other teams do so as well. McLaren-Mercedes has included drivers and engineers within the McLaren Lab Program and especially the annual gathering that takes place in Finland before the start of the season. Aki Hintsa, McLaren team physician:

Once a year we have the drivers, engineers and mechanics together when we all play together, football for example, and we all do fitness tests and have daily routines and training with the drivers. The drivers can see these guys keep pushing hard, trying their best to improve; and the others can see that the drivers are hard workers, real athletes. There develops an understanding that without high-performance teamwork, the drivers will not be able to perform at the optimum level.

McLaren-Mercedes driver Heikki Kovalainen confirmed the significance of this effort to the driver's relationship with his teammates:

It is very important that we have the whole team approach as participants in the McLaren Lab Program especially on the side of communications between the team members. People learn to understand why somebody behaves in a certain way and why I behave like that and then they know how to deal with a situation better. It is not only the drivers who get the benefit.

Collaborating

In the most effective Formula 1 teams roles are clearly defined and individuals know how their jobs inter-relate with others. In order to achieve the speed and consistency discussed earlier, the pit-stop crews, for example, carefully plan out their individual and then coordinated actions beforehand. They review videos of their performance and practice with slow-motion rehearsals. The team looks at every aspect of the pit-stop activity. They consider where better positioning of themselves or their tools, refinement of the equipment being used, or even changing personnel can save fractions of a second. Among these teams there exists a constant thirst for new and better ways to improve. No one is willing to stand on the laurels of past performance.

Pit-stop crews practise throughout the year; they practise at testing and when they arrive at a Grand Prix they practise even more, especially coordinating their activities with the driver's arrival and departure from his spot in front of the garage. Annually, they will do somewhere between 500–600 practice pit stops a year, in order to achieve their remarkable times on a consistent basis. They even practice potential mishaps as well. As we were told by Walton:

We practise getting it wrong. Anything you can think of that may possibly go wrong we try to see how to deal with it. Say you have to change the fuel rig, an air line breaks so there's no power on the gun, a nut flies off down the road, the driver stalls the car and you have to restart, or a wing is knocked off in an accident. We practise them all.

There is a high degree of conformity among Formula 1 team members that enables them to rally around their common culture, helping them create a collaborative atmosphere. Everyone wears matching shirts, trousers, belts, socks and shoes. At the circuit during a race event the pit crew wear matching fire-proof suits during practice, qualifying and the race. Individuals also tend to adopt the jargon and habits of others, driving further cohesion within the team. The team travels to and from the circuits together, work together, live together and eat together. As Geoff Simmonds at Renault F1 stated:

… there's a bond between us – we're all away from home and we look out for each other.[10]

At the same time Formula 1 pit-stop teams are comprised of individuals who are very competitive. This is seen in the way they keep close tabs on the results of other racing team pit-stop crews and also in their continuing efforts to outdo their own past performances. Keeping in mind that each driver has his own group of mechanics and engineers working to get the fastest lap time possible out of his car, there is also a healthy dose of internal competition that usually surfaces as well. Dickie Stanford of WilliamsF1 says:

We want internal competition because that keeps everyone on their toes, but if the team that is working one driver's car is running late,

I'd expect the guys working on the other car to ask if they want a hand.

At Ferrari, Motorsport Press Officer Luca Colajanni acknowledged that between the drivers:

There always has to be some competition because it pushes each of them to improve. But generally we do not have the drivers and the drivers' support teams competing against each other. It's not just propaganda that they say at interviews. They believe in the spirit of the whole team.

Pride and a sense of excellence fuel the quest for high performance even for the teams that are at the back of the grid. John Walton commented:

If you are winning races that's fantastic motivation, the best obviously. If you're down this end [the back of the grid] it's a bit more difficult to be motivated. But one of the things that probably motivates our guys the most is doing a good pit stop and being as good as everybody else at it. In this respect we work as hard as any other team at winning the World Championship.

Communication in a no-blame culture

Constant team practice and discussion about performance provide opportunities for continual review of actions (input) while maintaining a clear focus on the goals (output). It also provides chances for open sharing of views and the retention of knowledge gained from experience.

John Howett said:

Continuous communication, upwards downwards and sideways, is crucial for building effective teamwork.

When he was Team Principal at Ferrari Jean Todt echoed the words of many team leaders when he said:

Communication is the key thing in a company because you have to be seen and you have to explain to people. You have to enable people to participate in what you do.

In October 2007, reflecting on what had been a very difficult but successful year, Todt commented:

The best driver without a great car can't do anything. It's teamwork and we had a good teamwork.[24]

Todt received high praise from David Robertson, Kimi Raikkonen's manager. He stated:

He has the best record in the whole of the sport's history by far. He is a proud man and rightfully so; what he has achieved is incredible. Just one of his many attributes is that he is a good listener. He always said, 'David, if there is anything you feel we are doing wrong, you tell me.' He always had an open door for anyone in the team.

One clear concern we have noted in many interviews is the need to ensure that people do not get undermined by what is reported in the media about the team or themselves. Sitting in his memorabilia-strewn office in Maranello, Luca Colajanni told us more recently:

In our structure at Ferrari there are periodical meetings on different levels: group levels, then the whole team together or the top, say, one hundred. On these occasions the top management can also give hints like 'Don't believe what is written', 'Don't worry, that's not the case.' It can also happen individually if you see that someone is really concerned about what is being reported.

In addition to formal meetings and presentations there is also an informal communication process that takes place within a Formula 1 team. This plays an important role in contributing to an atmosphere of trust and mutual commitment that is vital both for high performance and for sustaining peak performance over a long race season. According to Jackie Stewart:

Communication. Total communication. No hiding behind closed doors. No telling lies. No ... 'Don't tell them that.' Total openness. Total frankness. Total integrity, that's what's required.

Frank Williams emphasised the importance of going around the factory in order to maintain communications in a business that is growing in size and complexity.

We have lots of corridor chats, I'm pretty good at getting around and you always see Patrick [Head] talking to people in the corridor.

Patrick Head also added:

That's the great thing about having the coffee machine in Dickie [Stanford]'s office; it means we talk every morning when I go there for my caffeine fix.

Open communication plays an important role in enabling a Formula 1 team to continually improve performance, especially when things go wrong. Looking back at the Nigel Mansell disaster described earlier, when his wheel and tyre came off in the pit lane, the Williams team actually used the situation to review their procedures and move forward. Dickie Stanford, Test Team Manager, recalled the situation:

We had a wheel-nut failure. So you go back. You talk to the person or the people who were actually using the equipment and we tried to redesign the problem right there. Then we looked at our overall procedures during the pit stop. With the significance of the incident behind us we decided there were a lot of loopholes that we had missed, so we totally rescheduled the way we did a pit stop from the equipment to personnel. We put in different procedures so the car couldn't go without everybody signalling according to a new approach. In those days everybody put their hand up when the wheel was finished, so you had three people putting their hands up at each corner of the car. You got a group of people all squashed within a 5 feet area and it's such a rush when you've all twenty-three putting their hands up.

One person is controlling it and he can't see every one of those twenty-three people. We realised that we only need the guy who does the last job on the wheel to signal to say that he's finished. The lolli-pop man needs only to be able to see the last four men on the wheels, the jack men and the refuelling man.

Stanford continued:

*Individuals doing certain jobs on the car now wear different col-
oured gloves, so the lollipop man is looking for colours rather than
actual people. When the wheels are finished he's looking for four yellow hands because everyone else's gloves in the pit stop are dark. He
is looking for four fluorescent yellow hands, two jack men signalling
to him thumbs up that everything is finished and then the refuelling
man. We even tried putting the refuelling man in yellow overalls to
make him more visible so we could see him, because the fuel always
takes longer than the wheels, but the sponsor's influence put an end
to that.*

Significantly, Stanford concluded the story with the following statement about how the team deals with the stigma of blame:

*We don't hang anyone out to dry. You don't just point a finger at
someone and say they're to blame. That doesn't help because all
you do is create bad feeling. You try to isolate the problem, not the
person.*

An interesting insight into team organisation, communication and
energy flows was offered by Aki Hintsa, Team Physician at McLaren-
Mercedes. In order to come up with his vision for how to address the
physical and mental elements that prepare the drivers and other team
members to perform throughout the gruelling Formula 1 season,
he came up with an original way to describe the inter-relationship
between the drivers and other team members for application in the
McLaren Lab Program:

*The first piece was to define the parameters, the key areas; but how
to create the package in which to apply the activities was more difficult. Then one day it became clear to me. Rather than thinking in
terms of a hierarchy, I thought of our solar system. The driver is at
the centre of the performance package and there are a large number
of support people circulating around him in synchronous order. The
more the driver can give energy and spirit to the system around him,
the better the result. One must also understand that there are people*

circulating around the driver, so-called 'friends' that are just draining energy away; not giving energy back into the system.

The energy that is being drained away can come from outside the team – media, sponsors, personal life – or from inside the team due to conflicts that arise in any family or organisation. We heard from several interviewees that a key role of Formula 1 management is to protect the team from influences that can have a negative impact on performance.

Luca Colajanni sees that protecting the team is an important part of his job:

In the end of the day they are all human beings and they are all affected because they read the newspapers and when they go home and spend some time with their families, sometimes their children say, 'Daddy, they are saying at school that you have done so and so and that next year you will be doing a different job.' We don't want that they can be touched by stupid things that come from the outside ...

6 | *Capability through partnerships*

*Know why you're getting into Formula 1 and ensure you've prop-
erly articulated and communicated these messages throughout your
organisation.*

Isabelle M. Conner,
Chief Marketing Officer, ING Bank

To the 588 million unique viewers who tune into the world's most
watched annual sporting event there is excitement, speed, glamour
and the subtle messaging that 'comes to you from our sponsors'.
Without the flow of cash into teams from the manufacturers and the
range of sponsors, the budgets required to go racing would not be
met. Cash is racing's raw material and affords the teams the latest
and best technologies that money can buy. In 2007 there were 310
Formula 1 sponsors. Of these, ninety-seven companies paid a total
of $834 million to get exposure on Formula 1 cars. Off-car exposure
totalled another $64 million.[8]

However, sponsors do more than supply funds to Formula 1 teams
and in most cases the relationships go much deeper. For this reason
the teams tend to refer to their corporate supporters more often as
'partners' or 'investors' rather than 'sponsors'.

Interestingly, of the ten teams on the grid in 2008, only WilliamsF1
totally relied upon commercial investment for its operation. While the
other teams all have parent companies selling products and services,
WilliamsF1 is purely a racing team. This was summed up by Head of
Marketing, Scott Garrett:

*There are ten teams on the grid of which nine are in business to sell stuff.
Most of them sell cars – Mercedes, BMW, Honda, Toyota, Ferrari and
so on. Two of them sell soft drinks – Red Bull and Toro Rosso – and
one of them sells Indian stuff, either Kingfisher Airlines, Kingfisher
beer. The reason these teams are there is very clear: it's to market other*

*products. They are essentially an outpost of a multinational's market-
ing department, and Formula 1's a pretty good tool for that; it's no
surprise really that they are there for that reason. There's one team on
the grid that doesn't do any of that, that is not owned by anyone else,
is not an arm of anybody's commercial efforts and therefore doesn't
suffer at the whim or vagaries of those enterprises outside of the sport,
and that's Williams. The only reason we exist is to go racing, not to sell
other stuff and that's why we call ourselves the Racing Purists.*

Clearly the financial model has changed in recent years and will
continue to evolve. With changing economic times the teams will be
forced to strive for new and innovative ways in which to obtain their
sponsorship revenues.

As Jim Wright, Head of Sponsorship for Toro Rosso remarked:

*When looking at sponsorship revenues, you can't sell off of a con-
ventional platform especially if there are six or seven teams ahead
of you. You have to provide creative solutions. You have to come up
with ideas and benefits away from the track. You have to be creative.
Of course, sponsors also expect you to be competitive.*

As President of the FIA, Max Mosley also has to consider the element
of funding versus performance. As an international figure with considerable personal business experience he feels strongly that performance
for performance's sake is counter-productive:

*Most Formula 1 teams do care about keeping costs down, but not
at the expense of performance. They all tend to spend whatever
money they can raise. In addition, those teams capable of raising a
big budget generally wish to stay at high expenditure, because the
number of teams able to compete with them is reduced. Only the
very top teams have the top budgets. It would be more difficult for
them if everyone had a lower budget. I think we may eventually succeed in lowering everyone's costs. From a sporting point of view, it
would certainly be better.*

Formula 1 teams have learned that it makes sense to collaborate with
outside firms that have the expertise to meet their exacting specifications and as a means to contain costs. This last point is extremely

important for smaller teams that are operating with more limited budgets, like Force India, a new entrant into Formula 1 during 2008. Ian Phillips, Force India's Director of Business Affairs, also referred back to his early days at Jordan F1 when he stated:

We will not manufacture in-house except for safety-critical parts. I was insistent with Eddie [Jordan] on this in 1991 and I still believe it now. 'In-house' drives up costs massively and I don't believe the money is there to support this. The supply chain today is very good – use it.

But for the moment, the drive for sponsorship funding and technical advantage continues, so in this chapter we examine the main types of partnership and focus on some historical and current examples of different companies that have benefited from working closely with Formula 1 teams.

Types of partnership in Formula 1

In Formula 1 there are four main kinds of partnership:

1) **Suppliers** who provide products and services in return for cash and receive no other direct benefits from their relationship with the Formula 1 team, such as specialist trailer manufacturer JS Fraser (Oxford) Ltd. which provides Formula 1 teams with the articulated vehicles to transport cars and equipment; and hospitality units in which to entertain guests throughout the Championship season.

2) **Technical partnerships** that are focused on the direct provision of products and expertise for building the car in exchange for marketing services to the company, perhaps through limited brand exposure directly on the car or also through access to Formula 1 events. The long-term relationship between Shell and Ferrari would fit into this category.

3) **Corporate partnership** or official suppliers, involving the supply of related products and services in exchange for marketing services and branding; examples of this kind of relationship would be the supply of trucks by German manufacturer MAN to WilliamsF1.

4) **Conventional sponsorship** which involves the supply of funding in exchange for promotion of the sponsor's brand within the team. In the 1970s, '80s and '90s, tobacco companies such as Marlboro, Benson & Hedges and Rothmans were the classic examples of this

kind of partnership. However, since restriction on advertising has caused the virtual demise of tobacco funding in the sport, a wide range of international banks, telecommunication companies, international freight forwarders and a growing range of fast-moving consumer goods (FMCG) companies have stepped in to fill their shoes.

With world businesses rapidly developing in new fields such as finance and telecoms, the departure of one form of revenue was almost seamlessly replaced by emerging multinational companies.

These four categories, between which there are some overlaps, are shown in Figure 8.

The duration of the partnerships vary by category and their nature. Typically, substantial partnerships, such as the supply of engines, will usually be on the basis of renewable five-year contracts. For example the original contract between Williams and BMW ran from the end of 1999 to 2004 and was subsequently renewed to run to the end of 2009; although this terminated early as BMW wished to build its own team in order to benefit fully from its involvement and investment in Formula 1.

Technical partnerships relate to all the key areas and systems of the racing car. These relationships not only provide visibility to the sponsor, but a mutually added value to both the sponsor and the Formula 1 team. For the sponsor this can be a high-performance environment to

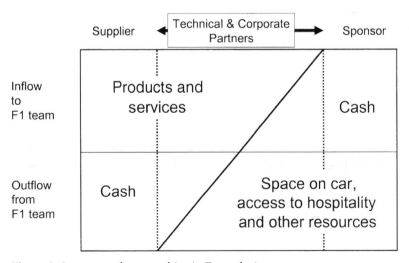

Figure 8 Spectrum of partnerships in Formula 1

Table 4 *Categories of technical partnerships*

Category	Examples
Engine	Toyota (Williams) Renault (Red Bull Racing)
Fuels & Lubricants	Shell (Ferrari) Petrobras (Williams)
Software/Systems/ Processors	SAP (McLaren) Intel (BMW Sauber) MSC Software (Renault)
Instrumentation	TAG Heuer (McLaren) Magnetti Marelli (Ferrari, Toyota, Red Bull Racing, Renault)
Components	SKF (Ferrari) Alcon (Honda)

develop capabilities in areas such as fuels and lubricants, telemetry, and computer systems. For the Formula 1 team it is an opportunity to utilise state-of-the-art technologies. Categories of technical partnerships with some examples are presented in Table 4.

Corporate partnership involves other products and services needed to operate in Formula 1. In value terms, a corporate partner such as Lenovo, which occupied the rear wing of the WilliamsF1 racing cars, spent a reputed $25 million to obtain such space and other sponsors as much as double that amount if the sponsorship gives full naming rights for the team. Examples of these during the 2008 season included the 'ING Renault F1 Team' or 'Vodafone McLaren-Mercedes Team' where the sponsor's name is fully integrated into the team's title. This carries with it major benefits in marketing terms as it adds implied brand 'ownership' of the team which in turn creates valuable image-related benefits in communicating with the consumer. Naming rights give the sponsor special access to the team's assets including driver's time for promotions (within the company or to their clients), factory tours, visits to races and tests, etc. This type of partner is what one might call a Formula 1 team's key customer, as Scott Garrett, Head of Marketing at WilliamsF1 said:

Formula 1 is very good at treating every sponsor as the customer and I guess in this case the definition of customer is he who pays the money.

The fourth category, conventional partnerships, involves the provision of funding in return for enhanced brand awareness and other

Table 5 *Sample corporate partnerships and sponsors in 2008*

Category	Examples
Computer Systems	Lenovo (Williams)
Trucks	Man (Toyota, Williams)
Car hire	Europcar (Ferrari)
Logistics	UPS Direct (Force India)
Communications	Vodafone (McLaren)
Tobacco	Philip Morris (Ferrari)
Financial & Insurance Services	ING (Renault)
Beverages	Nescafe Xpress (McLaren)
Electrical Products	Panasonic (Toyota)
Media	Reuters (Williams)
Watches	Seiko (Honda)
Clothing	Hugo Boss (McLaren)

potential revenue streams. This is the most visible form of partnering in Formula 1. The reasons behind decisions to become such sponsors are, therefore, the focus of the remainder of this chapter. Samples of both of these are illustrated in Table 5.

In addition to sponsors from the fields of finance and telecommunications, increasingly diverse groups of companies are recognising the benefits of investing in Formula 1. A good example of this was the creation of Force India, which entered into Formula 1 in 2008. This team arose from the purchase of SpykerF1 by wealthy businessmen Vijay Mallya and Michiel Mol in October 2007, for €88 million. With the first ever Indian Grand Prix set for 2010 in Delhi, this team is a platform for exposing followers of Formula 1 to this fast-growing country and more specifically, to products offered by Mallya's companies. On the side of the race car the word 'Kingfisher' can be clearly seen. Mallya is Chairman of United Breweries Group, whose flagship product is Kingfisher beer. Mallya's India-based airline also carries the name Kingfisher.

Why this acquisition at this time? According to Mallya:

There is this breed of youngsters in India who are proud of their success – we call them upwardly mobile and aspirational

Indians – they are earning well, they want to show their wealth, they want to show they are different. And that is where we felt, and research showed, that Formula 1 could be absolutely the ideal platform.[25]

But it is also with an eye for what Formula 1 can do for him and his brand internationally that has Mallya excited. In addition to increasing the sales of Kingfisher beer, especially in Europe, Kingfisher Airlines has planned to start international flights in August 2008 and, as Mallya said:

The fact that we have put a large Kingfisher presence on the car is a huge visibility factor in preparation for our international launch.[25]

Another international brand that has made a huge mark on the world of Formula 1 is Red Bull. In 1982 an Austrian entrepreneur, Dietrich Mateschitz, discovered a drink in Thailand that helped cure his jet lag. After several years of adapting the product, the Red Bull energy drink was launched in 1987; five years later it entered its first foreign market (Hungary) and five years after that the US.

By 2007, the company, built solely on this drink, registered sales just over €3 billion, which represents well over 3 billion cans of the product sold in 130 countries. With a keen eye for promoting the young and vibrant brand, Red Bull has been an active supporter of sporting activities and, in November 2005, it took a plunge into Formula 1. It purchased the Jaguar racing team from Ford Motor Company for a reportedly symbolic one dollar, in return for a commitment to invest $400 million in the team over three Grand Prix seasons. This was not its first foray into Formula 1, as Red Bull had been an active sponsor of the Sauber (now BMW Sauber) team prior to becoming an owner in its own right.

In addition to a more and more competitive racing car, Red Bull has brought a completely different approach to exploitation of its ownership of a team and with it it has delivered a large dose of 'fun' to the Formula 1 world.

At Grand Prix, it published and provided free of charge a satirical magazine, *The Red Bulletin*, on each of the four days. It has also tied its brand to Hollywood promotions such as the one for *Star Wars: Episode III* when it had its pit crew dress as imperial storm troopers. As mentioned earlier, in 2007 it introduced the Red Bull Energy

Station into the paddock, an enormous glimmering structure that would put many top restaurants and nightclubs to shame. On offer are food and drinks, omnipresent flat-screen televisions and comfortable seating. It has become the meeting point for journalists, media personnel and others during the Grand Prix weekends. At Monaco the entire energy station structure is floated out into the harbour on giant pontoons!

In 2005, Red Bull purchased the Minardi Formula 1 team and, starting in 2006, has run it under the name Scuderia Toro Rosso (STR). STR operates as a separate team, but shares certain technical resources with the Red Bull team. Mateschitz reportedly wants to see STR sold in the future, thereby ensuring that resources can be fully focused on Red Bull Racing's chances of winning.

Partnerships between organisations can take many different forms to fulfil many different purposes: within Formula 1 these tend to fall into three distinct categories: 1) enhancing market power through brand exposure; 2) leveraging relationships and 3) accessing and developing competences. We consider each of these in further detail.

Partnering to enhance the brand: tobacco

Pure sponsorship arrangements are often directed towards increasing market power by enhancing brand loyalty. For much of Formula 1's recent history tobacco companies were a major source of sponsorship revenue. The first overt sponsorship of a Formula 1 race car, apart from the usual logos of tyre and fuel suppliers, was in 1968, when the rules governing advertising on racing cars were relaxed. The traditional green and yellow Lotus cars appeared in the red, white and gold livery of Imperial Tobacco's Gold Leaf brand, and were renamed 'Gold Leaf Team Lotus', an approach which Lotus owner Colin Chapman had picked up from competing in the Indianapolis 500 where naming the car manufacturer after the title sponsor was commonplace. In fact, before the modern era of the Formula 1 Championship in the 1930s, entrants had included Al Gordon's 'Cocktail Hour Cigarette Special' and Floyd Robert's 'Abels and Fink Special'.[26] In 1972 Lotus took things a stage further with its new car being referred to as 'John Player Special', the name of the cigarette brand, dropping the reference to Lotus all together. This focus on raising funds through sponsorship also increased demands to maximise the available space on the car.

Marlboro and Formula 1

Philip Morris's Marlboro has been one of the most enduring cigarette brands in Formula 1. It was first involved in 1972, when it sponsored the BRM racing team, and in 1973 also supported Frank Williams' embryonic racing team with co-sponsorship from the Iso sports car company, with a team known as Iso–Marlboro. In 1974 the brand moved to McLaren where it was to remain until the end of 1996, a record period of longevity between a constructor and sponsor.

The McLaren racing team was founded by driver Bruce McLaren in 1966. However, he was killed in a testing accident at the Goodwood circuit in the UK in 1970, while driving one of his own CanAm sports cars. This necessitated the team's legal advisor, Teddy Meyer, taking over the running of the organisation. He was assisted by American, Tyler Alexander, who is to this day involved with the McLaren organisation.

McLaren was very successful during the mid-1970s, but its performance deteriorated towards the end of the decade, and Philip Morris instigated a merger between McLaren and Project Four, a Formula 2 team run by former Brabham chief mechanic Ron Dennis, who had started his racing career as a mechanic with Cooper Cars. In 1981 Ron Dennis, with his business partner the late Creighton Brown and technical director John Barnard, all bought a stake in the new company (renamed McLaren International), effectively achieving a management takeover orchestrated by Philip Morris's John Hogan.

Hogan, despite spending thirty years with Philip Morris, has never been a particularly public figure, but his knowledge of the sport and business combined to steer many elements of Formula 1 to the benefit of the Marlboro brand. Hogan also masterminded the Marlboro World Championship Team (MWCT) concept, which not only saw the headline sponsorship with McLaren International, but various levels of branding across many drivers in Formula 1, Formula 3000 and Formula 3. Add in international rallying and world motorcycling and the Marlboro stranglehold of motorsport was almost complete. Throughout the '80s and '90s, the Marlboro brand was synonymous with world motorsport success.

Hogan is now a strategic consultant to both Vodafone (the title sponsor with McLaren) and Just Marketing (the motorsport sponsorship agency). He continues to play a senior and highly respected role within the Formula 1 sponsorship industry.

Red and white McLarens were able to dominate a large part of the 1980s, winning six World Championship Drivers' titles between 1984 and 1991. Aleardo Buzzi, former President, Philip Morris Europe:

We are the number one brand in the world. What we wanted was to promote a particular image of adventure, of courage, of virility. But our sponsorship is not just a matter of commerce; it is a matter of love. We don't just sign a cheque, we support the sport.[15]

In 1988 Marlboro extended its activities to sponsoring drivers directly: both talented newcomers and established drivers. One of its first drivers was the Finn Mika Hakkinen who went on to drive for the McLaren Formula 1 team. Although Marlboro has moved to sponsor Ferrari since then, Hakkinen won the 1998 and 1999 Drivers' World Championships with McLaren. As part of this driver sponsorship programme, drivers would wear Marlboro overalls and would also have their name displayed on the car, within Marlboro's distinctive chevron logo.

Prior to its successes in 1998 and 1999, during the mid-1990s Marlboro had become increasingly concerned with the lack of success at McLaren. Honda, its engine partner, left in 1992 and its star driver, Ayrton Senna, left in 1993. McLaren was struggling to remain competitive. Meanwhile, Ferrari had transformed itself into a high-performing, modern Formula 1 team in the 1990s under the leadership of Luca di Montezemolo. A key part of its strategy had been to recruit the top driver of the time, Michael Schumacher.

This caused deterioration in the relationship between Marlboro and McLaren, which ultimately led to Philip Morris formally withdrawing from its long-term association with McLaren, and beginning a fruitful relationship with Ferrari.

As a result, McLaren CEO Ron Dennis was faced with recruiting a new title sponsor, which he did in the form of the West cigarette brand. Owned by the Reemtsma company, in addition to providing long-term funding, the West brand had one other very important criterion: its black and silver colours mirrored the aspirations of engine supplier Mercedes to create a colour scheme which reflected the Mercedes 'silver arrows' of the '20s and '30s.

Marlboro's growing relationship with Ferrari, the support of its drivers and also the fit between the brand colour schemes of Ferrari and Marlboro, made it a logical move to become the title sponsor for Ferrari in 1997. This was a major shift for Ferrari, which had never used a title sponsor before. Its cars had always been 'blood red' in recognition of the days when Grand Prix racing was a highly nationalistic affair, with cars from each country being recognised by a colour scheme, with the Italian cars of Maserati, Alfa Romeo and Ferrari being blood red. The idea of putting a sponsor's logo and colour scheme all over the car was anathema to Ferrari and its supporters, known as the *tifosi*. However, the fact that the Marlboro branding was also red provided it with an opportunity to create a strong title sponsorship, while at the same time acknowledging the important Italian heritage of Ferrari.

This did require a change in the tone of red being used on the Ferrari cars and many were outraged by this development, as reported by leading Formula 1 journalist David Tremayne:

In 1997 Ferrari changed from its traditional blood red to an orangey hue that did more to reflect the even greater support it was receiving from Marlboro ... But now the Prancing Horse's 1998 livery reflects a tone even closer to the Rocket Red colour of yore, and therefore even more offensive to the eyes of the purists.[26]

However, the relationship with Ferrari has been very successful in terms of the exposure generated for Marlboro. While branding is now limited to purely base colours rather than logos or names in terms of regular coverage, due to global WHO (World Health Organization) restrictions, this relationship continues and still enables the Philip Morris message to be spread throughout the world, via the colour application of the red base scheme for the cars and the distinctive white and black striping 'bar code' in place of actual lettering on the cars.

This thirty-year commitment to the sport is exemplified by the fact that Marlboro was not just putting its name on racing cars, it was working closely with the teams in all aspects of its decision-making. It was also sponsoring track-side advertising and taking title sponsorship of Formula 1 races, even to the extent that the kerbs on some tracks were painted in the red and white colours of the Marlboro brand.

Many of the major sponsorship players in the sport today continue to study the case histories of Marlboro and the methods it

Table 6 *Proportion of revenue provided by categories of partners in Formula 1*

Category	% Share of Sponsorship	
	2004	2008
Car Manufacturers	49%	46%
Beverages	3%	13%
Technology	8%	8%
Tobacco	13%	7%
Oil Companies	9%	6%
Other Automotive	6%	6%
Financial Services	4%	5%
Telecoms	5%	4%
Other	3%	5%

Source: Black Book, Formula 1 2008

used in promoting its involvement with teams, drivers and circuits, to maximise its own involvement. The development of 'alibi advertising' such as branded clothing and fashion accessories, the use of circuit signage and driver and team promotional tours headlined by Marlboro, have all served as examples in the planning of successful exploitation campaigns launched by the Formula 1 sponsors of today.

Partnering to enhance the brand: the automotive manufacturers

Since the proliferation of the 'flying fag packets' of the 1970s, '80s and early '90s the importance of tobacco funding to Formula 1 has reduced to a point where it has virtually disappeared, save for the Marlboro 'bar code' just noted.

In 2004, the tobacco company involvement had declined to less than 15 per cent of the sponsorship inflow to Formula 1 (as shown in Table 6), with the car manufacturers accounting for almost half.

There has been a number of reasons for this: first, the acceptance by the FIA of WHO's Framework Convention on Tobacco Control,

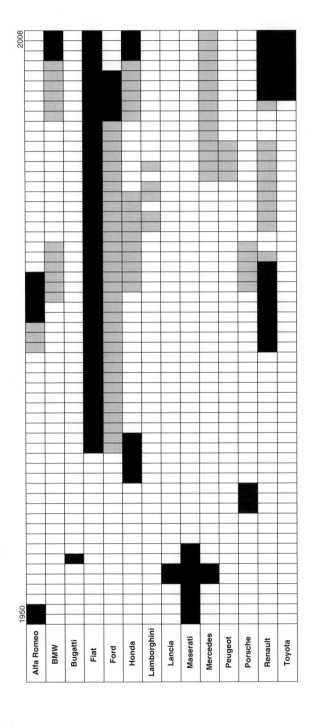

Figure 9 Automotive manufacturer involvement in Formula 1, 1950–2008

which recommended a total ban on all tobacco advertising in motorsport by the end of 2006. This has meant that both teams and tobacco companies took steps to change their sponsorship portfolios in advance of this date.

Second, the competitive nature of the global car market has put greater pressure on the car manufacturers to differentiate themselves from each other. Many of them had noted the significant shifts in market perception that were achieved by Honda and Renault, which were both successful engine suppliers in the 1980s and 1990s. For example, Honda's Type-R 'sub-brand' is underpinned by the Formula 1 programme[27] and during its spell as an engine supplier in the 1990s Renault developed a high-performance version of its Clio (small sports hatch) in collaboration with Williams. These were released as Williams Clio in '1' '2' and '3' versions in the then blue-and-gold colour scheme of the Williams organisation. These cars are still highly prized by car collectors today. In 2008 Renault launched two new Renault Sport high-performance derivatives called the Clio Renault F1 Team R26 and Mégane F1 team R26.

For an automotive manufacturer to differentiate its brand, Formula 1 is an attractive option relative to other advertising expenditures. The automotive manufacturers also have a long history in Formula 1, as summarised in Figure 9, which allows them to draw on racing heritage as a basis for underpinning the brand identities they seek to develop in order to differentiate their products.

Figure 9 shows how, in the early 1950s, a number of manufacturers were involved in Formula 1. In 1954 there were three companies racing their own cars – Lancia, Maserati and Mercedes. However, following a series of major accidents, including a tragedy at the Le Mans 24-hour Sports Car Race in 1955, where eighty spectators were killed when a racing car crashed into the grandstand, by 1959 all three had withdrawn from the sport. Thereafter, for many years Formula 1 was the exclusive domain of the specialist constructor. Growing interest in Formula 1 during the 1990s led to a situation in 2004 where, for the first time in the history of the sport, four of the ten competing teams were fully owned by car manufacturers, in this case by Fiat (Ferrari), Ford (Jaguar), Renault and Toyota. In addition, a number of manufacturers supplied dedicated engine programmes to support established teams such as BMW (Williams), Mercedes (McLaren with Mercedes also taking an equity stake in McLaren), and Honda (BAR) making an all-time high of seven automotive manufacturers involved in 2004.

In 2008 the level of commitment from the manufacturers had increased, with six manufacturer-owned teams and five supported through engines supplied by the manufacturers. However, Honda, wishing to focus fully on its own 'works' team under the direction of new Team Principal Ross Brawn, concluded that it could not continue its level of support of the Super Aguri team and in May 2008 the team entered into receivership. The (wholly or partially) manufacturer-owned teams in 2008 were: BMW, Ferrari, Renault, Mercedes, Toyota and Honda, with the other four teams relying upon engine supply from Ferrari, Renault and Toyota.

There are several reasons for this development: while all automotive manufacturers are driving down production costs, this is common practice and is therefore unlikely to provide any long-term benefit for a manufacturer over its competitors. Sources of advantage in the car industry are more likely to reside in areas such as brand affinities, which clearly Formula 1 can help with. Fans develop a very strong line of communication between themselves and their favourite Formula 1 team. Teams owned by automobile manufacturers clearly hope this bond extends to loyalty in their personal car buying decisions.

Partnering to enhance the brand: financial services

Formula 1 is a continually changing feast of personnel, companies, team ownership and sponsors. In recent years a growing list of financial services firms have become involved including names such as ING, RBS and Santander. What attracts blue-chip companies such as these? ING prepared for its foray into Formula 1 very strategically. The first step was deciding what it wanted from its investment. As Isabelle Conner of ING told us:

You first have to identify what your goal is in an organisation, then determine what opportunities will help you achieve that goal. You have to know what you want before you go out and get it. Our goal was to make ING a household name around the world. Certainly there are a lot of sponsorship, advertising and marketing strategies for doing this. At ING, Formula 1 is at the forefront of each – in a very focused and integrated approach.

We needed something that could give us the reach and the impact fairly quickly. We looked at ten different sports and came up with a shortlist of three: Olympics, tennis and Formula 1. After further research we decided that the Olympics is better for brands that were already well known, so that wasn't our case at the time. Tennis had terrific demographics, but certain elements of the properties were not available for us to activate the way we wanted. Formula 1 clearly had the best opportunities, including a global footprint that resembled ING's business operations, a huge fan base of 850 million television viewers around the world, TV broadcasting rights in 170-plus markets, and the ongoing expansion of the sport. How many sports can you point to that are growing?

While now experienced in the sport, ING came to it with a radical approach from the start. Not since the days of Philip Morris with its Marlboro brand had anyone 'attacked' the sport in such a measured and aggressive manner in terms of building on the Formula 1 association to best effect. As Conner shared with us, more than viewing Formula 1 as a global platform for building its business through brand visibility:

… ING treats Formula 1 as a business: the sponsorship is a means to generate revenue, not cost.

Formula 1 allows it to do this since it helps with:

… building global brand awareness, improving brand perceptions, and driving business that contributes to our bottom line – this makes F1 a core business activity.

As Conner says, for ING, its investment in Formula 1 is paying off in the bottom line. Its research shows that its investment increased new business, enhanced customer relationships and increased global awareness of ING as a bank. Conner illustrated this with the results of a Formula 1 promotion in its home country:

There are many examples of how ING business units around the world are using Formula 1 for sales and marketing initiatives. For example, in the Netherlands, one of our banks targeted 16- to 24-year-olds in

*an F1-themed direct mail campaign, offering the chance to win tick-
ets to a Grand Prix if they responded to a special offer and opened
an online account. More than 14,000 new accounts [were created] in
two weeks, a response rate three times higher than similar campaigns
that didn't use an F1 theme.*

Other financial services firms have also successfully done the same.
The Royal Bank of Scotland Group (RBS) has been actively involved
with the WilliamsF1 team for a number of years. It too, has taken
steps to leverage its investment by displaying not only its logo on
the car and on the drivers' uniforms, but also doing trackside and
winners' podium signage at a number of races and even having the
WilliamsF1 Conference renamed to include RBS in the title. It also
hosts all sorts of client-focused events around Grand Prix weekends,
test days and the like and utilises Formula 1 car simulators and other
Formula 1-based activities as exploitation 'tools'.

One other financial services firm, Santander, joined the Formula 1
world, in 2007. This Spanish bank aligned itself with McLaren for a
reported $20 million annually. According to Juan Manuel Cendoye,
Santander's director of corporate communications:

*A global sponsorship such as the McLaren team in F1 is a way to lev-
erage the single brand in the forty markets where Santander operates
that wasn't possible before.*[8]

Of particular interest to Santander was to make an impact in the
UK, where it had acquired Abbey National bank at the end of 2004.
As an exercise in building brand awareness it concentrated on the
British Grand Prix, with Formula 1-related promotions and signage
at the race circuit. In 2008 it reported that awareness of Santander in
the UK accelerated from 20 per cent to 70 per cent at the end of the
year.[8] That had to be perceived as a useful return on their partnership
investment.

Partnering to enhance the brand: consumer goods

The Dutch company Philips worked closely with Williams in 2007 to
launch two new shaving products for men. One was targeted at the
younger and newer shaver and the other at the slightly older, more

mature shaver with a tougher beard. The two Williams drivers that year fitted the bill perfectly, and according to Scott Garrett the marketing strategy was certainly not an accident.

Nico Rosberg [20 at the time and blond] was right for the new shaver and Mark Webber [28 at the time and dark haired] for the other model. Philips said 'You guys are going to be the personal ambassadors for these products' and of course, Philips paid for those rights.

It was then able to use the drivers in every form of commercial material for each of these products largely in separate campaigns because they were attracting vastly different audiences.

In this successful campaign Philips used the drivers to segment the market. The drivers opened stores; launched products to the trade; launched products to Philips' own employees; were seen in promotional materials; and took part in bespoke promotions, one even offering a successful prize winner the chance to drive a WilliamsF1 car for five laps around the Silverstone track in the UK. There was a fair amount of advertising, according to Garrett, but no more than would have been around a more traditional launch of a product. However, Garrett points out:

The advertising was synergistic because it featured the Williams livery and the assets of the team in each case. It gave it enough creative linkage but also allowed separate targeting and that was smart, very smart.

Partnering to leverage relationships

The trend within Formula 1 has been to move towards increasingly complex and enduring kinds of relationships. Those between a Formula 1 team and its partners involve the flow of cash, goods, services and related benefits such as brand affinity. A key part of this is being able to leverage the synergies between the different relationships of the sponsors. For example, in the 1970s Frank Williams used his sponsor Saudia Airlines, owned by the Saudi royal family, to attract Leyland Trucks which, at the time, was seeking to enter the Saudi and Middle East markets. Through this relationship Leyland was able to sell several hundred heavy duty trucks into this emerging market.

Some thirty years on, the potential for leveraging partnership relationships was not lost on Frank Williams:

BMW deliver a wonderful brand for us, it makes it much easier to open doors.

However, this view from the team was not enough to prevent BMW deciding to go its own way by acquiring the Sauber team. Current Team Principal Mario Theissen had convinced the BMW board that a fully focused team of its own was essential to long-term success. In fact, a measure of success came slightly earlier than expected, when in June 2008 BMW Sauber celebrated with a one–two finish at the Canadian Grand Prix in Montreal, the newly formed team's first victory.

More recently Williams has teamed up with a different kind of partner – a computer manufacturer, Lenovo. WilliamsF1's COO Alex Burns acknowledged that at first the relationship had some trying moments:

I think that Lenovo would be the first to acknowledge that when we first started we did have a problem at a test with a laptop going down when we were starting up the car, which is quite serious.

But as Burns continued, Williams got a taste of the commitment Lenovo had made towards building trust and reliability in their relationship:

What impressed us most was we had the problem on a Tuesday and on Wednesday morning the man arrived in Spain from the States to come and fix the problem. You know, that's pretty exemplary service because a message had gone through the organisation to the top and they'd said fix it immediately; so the right bloke got on a plane straight over the Atlantic. That's pretty impressive for a laptop fault.

That was just the beginning. In addition to laptops, Burns told us it now has a Lenovo super computer onsite, running CFD (computational fluid dynamics) – a computer-based system for simulating and complementing aerodynamic development in the wind tunnel. This onsite supercomputer gives Williams a fourfold increase in capacity over what it had before. In talking about some of the technical processes involved he added:

... that's something that I don't think would have happened if we hadn't been in a technical partnership.

Importantly, it is not just a one-way street; Lenovo has gained as well, and not only in terms of global visibility. As Burns recounted:

I went to a Lenovo European sales event last year after they'd been with us only a few months. Quite a few of their sales guys said to me that one of the things that was important to them about the partnership was it opened up a whole new dialogue with their customers. Normally they'd talk about the computer hardware needs, but now they also talk about how the team did at the weekend. It opens up a whole sort of new emotional contact and allows them to discuss something different with the client. They said it was quite intangible but very, very important for the sales force. They felt the company had made an investment that was allowing them to sell better.

Partnering to improve capability

As the title of this section implies, there are several kinds of partnerships which create improved capability and provide useful learning for both sides of the relationship: Here are some examples:

Honda and product development

An important potential source of advantage for any manufacturer involves speed to market. A key issue for the car companies in particular is the length of time it takes to take a design concept into the showroom. Typically for a manufacturer this process takes around thirty-six months. For a Formula 1 car it takes about twelve months, but can be achieved in less. Many of the process enhancements which Honda was able to demonstrate as a car manufacturer in the 1990s were largely attributable to its policy of engaging teams of engineers in Formula 1 and then moving them back into positions within their mainstream automotive operations.

The learning it had achieved in terms of faster development times was seen to create a step change in the product development process at Honda, and with it a significant improvement in the company's fortunes. However, it is also interesting to note that a number of Formula

1 teams felt that this rotation of personnel disrupted the continuity of their relationship with Honda.

Tyre partnerships and Bridgestone

In 1997 Bridgestone tyres made its first major foray into Formula 1, having previously provided tyres for the, then non-Championship, Japanese Grand Prix of 1976 and 1977. Prior to its entry in 1997 it had in fact been running a Formula 1 test programme since 1989, eight years prior to its actual entry. In its first season Bridgestone supplied a total of five out of the twelve teams: Arrows, Prost, Stewart, Lola and Minardi. For three of these (Prost, Stewart and Lola) it was their first season in Formula 1 and for Lola it never even began, as the team failed to start its first Grand Prix in Australia due to a lack of funds. Having started supplying the smaller midfield teams against the well-established Goodyear Tyre Company, Bridgestone made further inroads in 1998 by supplying two World Championship-winning teams: Benetton and McLaren, making it a total of six teams on Bridgestone tyres.

It was in this season, Bridgestone's second in Formula 1, that McLaren was able to bring Bridgestone its first World Championship. However, things changed significantly for Bridgestone in 1999, when the withdrawal of Goodyear meant that it found itself contractually required to supply the whole Formula 1 grid of eleven teams.

While at one level being the monopoly supplier to Formula 1 is a good thing – the winner will always be using your tyres – on another level the lack of competition means that tyres are no longer a source of competitive advantage and therefore create less interest. At the time, Hiroshi Yasukawa of Bridgestone commented:

Formula 1 has helped us build up international brand awareness for Bridgestone from around 5 per cent to around 35 per cent across Europe. However, when we were sole supplier of tyres awareness went down. No-one was talking about tyres, they were competing on other issues. Now we are competing with Michelin everyone is talking about tyres again.

In 2001 the Michelin tyre company entered Formula 1, first supplying Williams, Benetton, Jaguar, Minardi and Prost, but then in following years adding McLaren (2002) and BAR (2004). This left a situation in 2004 where Bridgestone was effectively supplying the World Champions Ferrari, the old Sauber team that also used Ferrari engines and gearboxes, and two other privateer teams, Jordan and Minardi, that were both using 'customer' Cosworth engines.

This situation brought Ferrari and Bridgestone closer together and allowed them to develop a better understanding of each other's technology, in order to enhance the performance of the total package. According to Hiroshi Yasukawa:

We produce good tyres but if the team doesn't understand how to design the car for the tyres this is just a waste of money and a waste of time. The best way is for everything to be put on one table and it will be discussed.

In 2007 Bridgestone became the sole supplier of tyres to Formula 1. At each of the races it is responsible for supplying teams with two different compounds of tyres, both of which must be used at least once during the race, and sets of rain tyres in the event of inclement weather. But Bridgestone is not resting on its laurels; it is learning from each race and developing new compounds that will make the racing more exciting. For example, in July 2008 it announced that based on feedback from the teams and its own measurements, it is considering changing the two fundamental tyre compounds for 2009 to make them less similar in the hope that the races can be even more competitive.

Ferrari and Shell

Ferrari and Shell have had a very successful partnership. CEO Jean Todt was instrumental in starting up the relationship in the mid-1990s.

Up until 1995 Ferrari had been with Agip [the Italian oil and petroleum company]. *I had contacts in Shell from my past experience* [Todt had been a professional co-driver in the World Rally Championship] *and so we entered into discussions and came to an agreement.*

However, when Raoul Pinnell became Chairman of Brands at Shell in 1997, he felt that the relationship was not all that it could be:

I inherited a sponsorship that had an incomplete partnership approach to it because we had a technical basis for our association and we had a marketing basis for our association. But it didn't appear to me that the objectives were clear, that the activities to exploit benefit from those objectives were in place and there didn't appear to be much data.

Interestingly, one of Pinnell's first actions was to undertake an internal survey within Shell to establish the mood in terms of the value of the partnership with Ferrari:

We did a big management survey, 'Do you think we should be with Ferrari or not?' and we wanted to flush out and understand how a technically driven organisation would respond to rather open-ended questions like that. We were actually a little bit disappointed too many of them just said yes or no without any data.

Pinnell followed on from this initial research to try and establish what the impact of the relationship had been on Shell's customer base:

Around 1999 we did a study and found that 15 per cent of our customers were aware of our association with Ferrari. I considered this to be a challenge. We renegotiated our contract with Ferrari to ensure that we could exploit the relationship as effectively as possible. Now [2004] 27 per cent of our customers are aware of our relationship with Ferrari.

One of the key actions which Pinnell and his team took was to bring the Ferrari brand closer to the Shell product:

We want a brand association; we want a rub-off of the magic and sexiness of the Ferrari brand to a rather neutral brand in terms of its emotional attributes.

But the point that is often forgotten is that the partnership with the Formula 1 team is only the start of the process. Pinnell said:

I think the big learning for me in sponsorship is that everyone assumes that just being placed on a car or on the back of a sports person, customers will somehow make the connection, because they just don't. You have to do lots of other work to help them recognise the link.

A key contribution for Shell was that it was launching a range of differentiated fuels which were positioned to offer the motorist greater levels of power and efficiency, and the relationship with Ferrari would help from both a technological and marketing perspective:

Now much of that work [on the new fuels] has been informed by the work that we have done with Ferrari. The petrol that you use in Formula 1 is very similar to the petrol that you can buy now, so we have had direct technical improvements in working with this terribly demanding partner.

The same applies in the lubricants market, another important area for Shell:

A lot of my work actually is outside of Formula 1 and if I mention a small example to support that – Carrefour in France, ten lubricant brands on the shelf, which one would you buy? Well, we're the only brand that has a little Ferrari shield on our pack of oil that says 'Recommended by Ferrari' – we have given the customer a reason to believe, a reason to purchase our product against everyone else and therefore that's where I spend my time.

It also had a powerful effect with Shell's partners – the petrol stations and their staff:

We gave the staff at the forecourt these red shirts with Ferrari/Shell/ V-Power. It's the first shirt that staff have ever really said, 'Can I keep it, can I take it home?' They get lost, they were 'destroyed in the wash so can I have another one?' This had never happened before and it just shows the kind of impact this can have.

To make the relationship work Shell had to consider not just the strategic and marketing issues between itself and Ferrari, but also other relationship aspects. How they would actually work together 'on the ground':

We've had to think about our own people that interface with Ferrari. I employed a man who works for me who is Colombian, so he exhibits all the Latin skills. He can walk around the Ferrari team and nod, kiss, hug everybody, from the guy who does the tyres to the top guy, with spirit and Latin panache, which is very helpful; and a very good technical guy who is English but again who is smiley and very technically competent so he has public relations skills as well as technical skills. I would call them Relationship Managers on the technical and marketing side that have been critical in the turning around of what we can extract in terms of value. They give you things because of the person dynamic and I have to say that this is a big learning for me.

The other interesting observation made by Pinnell was that he didn't believe that actual performance on the track was the critical factor in Shell's relationship with Ferrari:

I don't actually think winning is everything here. Ferrari transcends even Formula 1. There are countries in the world in which Shell operates where there has never been the Formula 1 Grand Prix, it's hardly ever on the television station, nobody in those countries has ever owned a Ferrari and never seen one, but people know Ferrari! It is a brand phenomenon beyond Formula 1, it's quite unique.

The dynamics of partnerships

If we double the income that we bring in as a result of the partnerships that we develop commercially then there is a very clear correlation between the amount of money and the performance on the track. So we're in no doubt, as commercial people, of the positive effect we can have on performance on the track. In this business success or failure is extremely public and we all feel that pressure; it's not just the driver or the engineer, it's the commercial guys as well. (Scott Garrett, WilliamsF1)

A key part of the partnership process in Formula 1 is its dynamic nature. Partnerships move through different phases which bring different benefits to the parties at different times. Figure 10 shows the potential nature of a partnership lifecycle moving between the stages of initial exploration prior to creation of the partnership through to termination.

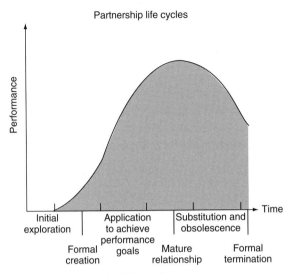

Figure 10 Partnership life cycles

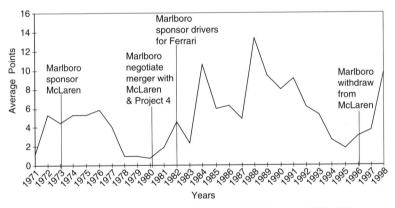

Figure 11 Relationship between Marlboro and McLaren, 1973–97

When these principles are applied to the performance of McLaren through the period of the relationship with Marlboro we can see a similar pattern, as illustrated in Figure 11. When we apply actual performance data we can see how these cycles are reflected in the relationship between these two companies. The initial relationship was founded after Marlboro had tried a number of other teams and linked in to McLaren at a point when it was already well up the performance curve. However, this performance dropped off in the late 1970s and Marlboro played a major role in 'restarting' the partnership lifecycle through the introduction of Ron Dennis and his Project 4 company. This aligned with an unprecedented period of success for both companies during the late 1980s, but moved into decline again in the late 1990s.

Getting the most out of your Formula 1 investment

We asked Isabelle Conner at ING to list some of the key lessons her bank had learned following its first year as a participant in Formula 1. At our meeting she asked if she could think about that for a while. The wait was worth it; so much so that we thought, with her kind permission, we should reproduce her seven points. These are excellent guidelines for any company considering an investment in Formula 1 and resonate with almost every sponsorship and partnership nerve in business today:

1. Know why you're getting into Formula 1 and ensure you've properly articulated and communicated these messages throughout your organisation.
2. While Formula 1 gives sponsors an unsurpassed global platform, it's up to each sponsor to activate and take advantage of all available opportunities. Local business activation is the key to any truly successful sponsorship. Most of it happens away from Grand Prix, via roadshows, showcars, 'feel it' days, sales contests, incentives, etc. ('Feel it' days are part of a Renault/ING programme operating at the Paul Ricard circuit in France where staff, prize winners and incentive trip guests are 'turned into' competitors for a day, culminating in them driving a Formula 1 car).
3. Time is of the essence – the months tick off fast in a Formula 1 calendar year. To maximise your sponsorship's impact, you have to race to activate all aspects of the sponsorship in a compressed timeframe.
4. Negotiate on-track boarding packages for one year, renewable a second year. This gives sponsors more leverage on their on-track visibility year over year.
5. Don't be intimidated by the hundreds of consultants, vendors and agencies that stalk you in the first couple of months via phone and

email to make you aware of their expertise. Choose your partners carefully!

6. Measure and track everything (visibility, awareness, new business, press coverage ...) so you can rectify if need be and also point to tangible results and successes as your sponsorship progresses.

7. Get the press on your side. Reporters love a well-sewn story. If the brief is handled properly, it's free publicity!

7 | *The high-performance organisation*

It's the informal organisation that runs things here. It's the experienced people in the organisation who are empowered to get on and do things.

Alex Burns, COO, WilliamsF1

In this chapter, we will look closely at high-performance organisations in the context of Formula 1 teams by responding to three questions: What business are Formula 1 teams in? Who are their customers? And, most crucially, how do they achieve high performance? This last question enables us to explore the key processes which lead to winning on the track – designing and manufacturing a competitive car, maintaining consistency and reliability, and generating revenue streams so they can keep racing.

What business is a Formula 1 team in?

From one perspective they are in the performance engineering business. They produce a small number of highly specialised vehicles over the space of a year, which they continually develop in order to achieve sustained performance levels. From this point of view, we can understand why the region around Oxford in the UK is referred to as Motorsport Valley, a comparison with Silicon Valley on the west coast of the US, where a local cluster of firms dominate the world in a particular technology, in the latter case micro-processors.[28]

For many on the technical side of Formula 1, it is all about designing cars. John Barnard, former Technical Director at McLaren, Benetton, Ferrari and Arrows said:

It's nice to win but it isn't what gets me going. What gets me going are the technology and the engineering and trying to take another step that perhaps no-one has done.

114

In this case the technology of Formula 1 is 'sticky'; it is located primarily within a fifty-mile radius of Oxford although a number of teams are located well outside this area in Continental Europe. We will elaborate on this later in the chapter.

Who then are the customers of a Formula 1 organisation?

Firstly, it might be useful to consider what product Formula 1 teams are selling. Mark Gallagher, former Jordan and Tyrrell marketer and now Team Principal of Team Ireland in A1 GP, had an interesting view on this when he wrote that Formula 1 teams:

> ...*produce an engineering product yet make their money from selling a service: a marketing service which includes brand exposure for sponsors globally, hospitality, marketing, promotion, PR, endorsements, merchandising and so on.*[29]

So, Formula 1 teams are also in the entertainment and luxury brand business. They produce a spectacle which is both glamorous and exciting, drawing consumers into the atmosphere of the Formula 1 event. Therefore, they provide a platform for all sorts of products and services that seek to enhance the value of their brands through association with this prestigious global series.

The customers of Formula 1 can be defined in two groups. First, the main consumers of the events – the public at large – and second, those firms who provide money or products and services in exchange for brand exposure on the car and access for themselves and their corporate guests to Grand Prix events.

The reality is that Formula 1 teams are in the business of providing a technology-based entertainment. Depending on where you sit, then the business may be more strongly aligned to technology or entertainment. But in the context of Formula 1 both are necessary to define and distinguish it from other race series (see Table 1). Much of the viewing audience is motivated by the excitement of the race and their allegiance to particular drivers, usually one of their fellow countrymen – in 2004 Germany had one of the highest national viewing figures due to the success of Michael Schumacher. In 2007, the year following Schumacher's retirement, viewing figures in Germany dropped; whereas those in Spain and the UK enjoyed strong growth due to the developing rivalry between Fernando Alonso and Lewis Hamilton.

Before discussing how Formula 1 teams achieve high performance we should first explain why Formula 1 constructors exist, and then the different types of business models that prevail.

Why do Formula 1 constructors exist?

If you ask the employees of any Formula 1 team why the team exists, the answer is invariably straightforward – to win races, nothing more, nothing less. But winning races is not a simple business and requires the team to bring together a group of talented individuals with the best technology possible, to design and manufacture a racing car and create the best race team to develop flexible and responsive race strategies to keep them ahead of the competition. The organisation needs to allow specialist expertise to develop but also to balance all the different areas of expertise – aerodynamics, electronics, vehicle dynamics and engine design – in order to optimise overall performance. It needs to engage partner organisations and bring them into the process in a way which ensures both parties are learning and stimulating each other to continually improve. As Martin Brundle commented in a recent interview with *Motorsport*'s Nigel Roebuck:

You go to an outfit like McLaren and you look for the three big light switches so you can flick them on, and say, 'Ah! So that's how they do it!' And you know what, there never is anything. The difference between the top teams is so small, believe me. It's just detail, really – and focus and determination and a winning mentality.[30]

A Formula 1 team run correctly is also a money-making operation. The privately owned teams can only exist if they are able to generate inflows of both cash and products and services, and often do so in highly creative ways involving multiple trading arrangements. However, they are not generally seen as profit-making entities; they exist to keep racing, and with their focus on continually improving performance spend around 40 per cent of their turnover on research and development, which is larger than most companies by a factor of two or three times.

Table 7 *Formula 1 constructors' ownership and engine supply, 2008*

Team	Ownership	Engine manufacture	Exclusive supply of engines	Co-location of engine and chassis
Ferrari	Car manufacturer (Ferrari group which includes Maserati)	Yes	No (also supplied to Force India and Toro Rosso)	Yes
Toyota	Car manufacturer	Yes	No (also supplied to Williams)	Yes
Renault	Car manufacturer	Yes	No (also supplied to Red Bull)	No
McLaren	Car manufacturer (Daimler Chrysler) own 40% of equity	No	Yes (provided by Mercedes Benz High Performance Engines)	No
BMW	Car manufacturer	Yes	Yes	No
Honda	Car manufacturer	Yes	Yes	No
Red Bull	Private	No	No	No
Toro Rosso	Private	No	No	No
WilliamsF1	Private	No	No	No

What are the different types of Formula 1 constructor?

So far we have described Formula 1 constructors in relatively homogenous terms, but they actually take many different forms. Table 7 illustrates some of the different permutations which exist regarding the Formula 1 constructors' ownership and nature of engine supply. A team's strategic objectives, its organisation structure and its corporate culture will all be a function of its ownership.

It can be seen from Table 7 that there are essentially two 'ideal' types of Formula 1 team: manufacturer teams, which are fully owned by a car manufacturer and also make their own engines, Ferrari and Toyota being classic examples of this type, and privately owned teams which are run privately and source their engines from wherever they can secure an advantageous supply; Williams and Red Bull are examples of this type.

The development of manufacturer-owned Formula 1 teams has followed two distinct paths. Either the teams have established themselves as new entrants from scratch – as was the case with Toyota, whose Formula 1 project started in 1999, with its first Grand Prix taking place in 2002 – or they have acquired existing privately owned teams. The Renault F1 team evolved from the acquisition of Benetton in March 2000 for an estimated purchase price of $110 million. This also explains why the Renault engines are still manufactured at a factory at Viry-Chatillon near Paris, whereas all the design and development work and the final assembly takes place at Enstone in north Oxfordshire.

The BMW team originally entered as an engine supplier with the Williams team in 2000, but in 2006 it ended its agreement with the UK-based team and acquired the Sauber team based in Hinwil in Switzerland, to create the BMW Sauber team. Similarly Honda, which had been supplying the BAR team with engines since 2000, made the decision to acquire BAR, and Honda Racing was created in 2005.

The manufacturers each bring different approaches and agendas to Formula 1, as indicated by Honda's Team Principal Ross Brawn:

Honda's involvement in Formula 1 is a little more complex than the majority of teams. The reasons manufacturers are involved in Formula 1 differ. At one end of the scale is the pure marketing approach where principally the teams are involved for exposure. They're in it for brand image. They don't focus on the technical side and don't promote this aspect of Formula 1. They are often the manufacturers who prefer more basic and less challenging technical regulations. Renault would fall into this category and their reasons for being involved are largely marketing. At the other end of the scale, you've got Honda where the marketing and image is important but the engineering challenge and the development of their people in meeting this challenge is very important. Honda want Formula 1 to represent the ultimate form of motor racing challenge and welcome initiatives, particularly environmental initiatives, that can challenge their people. I feel this comes from the spirit and history of Honda. Honda has a large number of board members who have come from a racing and engineering background and in fact our President, Fukui-san, had a deep involvement in the motorbike racing programme in his early career at Honda.

In the case of BMW the technical side is important, but Team Principal Mario Theissen felt it was equally important to create some clear separation between the Formula 1 and road car operations:

The basic guideline when we decided to do a Formula 1 project was to cut it off from the mainstream business, so BMW motorsport and the F1 team are independent in the way that we are free to run the business as we think appropriate. We have the resources required but we are close enough to the big company to tap into the resources if we need something from there, so the corporate research and innovation centre is just a kilometre away from the F1 factory in Munich and we have close links with research and development as well as with prototype production.

Toyota's philosophy on continuous improvement and learning – 'The Toyota Way' – has become a global exemplar of lean technology and how to develop effective approaches to mass production. However, for some, Toyota's philosophy has been one of the reasons why it has, as yet, failed to produce the results to match its significant investment in Formula 1. Leading Formula 1 journalist David Tremayne explains this perspective:

If you look at how much Toyota have been spending – $400 million a year for six years or whatever it is – they haven't got much to show for it, and that's because they've taken the view that the Toyota way – the Japanese way – is the way to do it; well I think events show that's not the greatest way to go about it.

However, Toyota's John Howett brings a very different interpretation to this story:

The Toyota way in F1 is probably misunderstood by most people as it is not seen as relevant in F1 or motorsport. I would suggest this is very wrong.

Howett believes that the reason the Formula 1 team has not been as successful as it might have been is that it has not until recently been applying the principles of the Toyota way:

The Toyota way is about simplicity, common sense and an almost constant learning process, where all the time you are looking at where are we now, where do we want to get to and how do we close that barrier. In very simplistic terms, most European people think about models that are complex and Toyota just brings it down into such simple issues. You see a Toyota production line, it's fundamentally very simple, everything is visualised and it's broken down into things that people can relate to and people can add value to and it's a very quick instant decision-making process. The people have the power to stop the production line because they see an error and then it's fixed. Others are learning from that but I think it's really common sense in many ways, but common sense is often the least common thing you find in life and in business.

But manufacturer teams are not the only ones who entered Formula 1 through acquisition. As referred to earlier, in 2004 Dieter Mateschitz's Red Bull company acquired Jaguar Racing from the Ford Motor Company, allegedly for one dollar, and with a commitment to invest heavily in the team over the next three seasons. This was rather ironic as in 1999 Ford had purchased Stewart Grand Prix for an estimated $120 million. Mateschitz followed this up with the purchase of the Minardi team in 2005, in partnership with former Formula 1 driver Gerhard Berger. Minardi was renamed Toro Rosso.

Since the first edition of this book was published the Jordan team has passed through three different owners under the names Midland, Spyker and, as of 2008, Force India. As discussed earlier Force India is owned by Indian businessman Vijay Mallya who is chairman of United Breweries Group and Kingfisher Airlines. Mallya, who has a long-held interest in motorsport, hopes to capitalise on building interest in Formula 1 in India, leading to a proposed Grand Prix in New Delhi in 2010.

Figures 12 and 13 show two different maps illustrating the location and identity of the Formula 1 chassis and engine facilities. Figure 12 featured in the first edition of this book and shows the situation in 2004, while Figure 13 shows the position in 2008. Whereas the

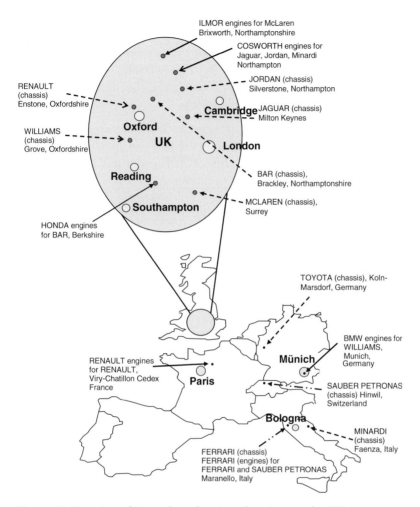

ILMOR engines for McLaren
Brixworth, Northamptonshire

COSWORTH engines for
Jaguar, Jordan, Minardi
Northampton

JORDAN (chassis)
Silverstone, Northampton

RENAULT
(chassis)
Enstone, Oxfordshire

JAGUAR (chassis)
Milton Keynes

Cambridge

Oxford

WILLIAMS
(chassis)
Grove, Oxfordshire

UK

London

BAR (chassis),
Brackley, Northamptonshire

Reading

MCLAREN (chassis),
Surrey

Southampton

HONDA engines
for BAR, Berkshire

TOYOTA (chassis), Koln-
Marsdorf, Germany

RENAULT engines
for RENAULT,
Viry-Chatillon Cedex
France

Münich

BMW engines for
WILLIAMS,
Munich,
Germany

Paris

SAUBER PETRONAS
(chassis) Hinwil,
Switzerland

Bologna

MINARDI
(chassis)
Faenza, Italy

FERRARI (chassis)
FERRARI (engines) for
FERRARI and SAUBER PETRONAS
Maranello, Italy

Figure 12 Location of Formula 1 chassis and engine supply, 2004

location of teams has not changed the ownership has, with manufacturers such as Honda and BMW becoming 'full' constructors, adding
chassis design and manufacture to their engine operations.

As illustrated in Figures 12 and 13, Formula 1 teams are concentrated in two distinct regions – an area to the north, west and south
of London in the UK ('Motorsport Valley') and an area in Northern
Italy around Modena and Bologna, which is heavily based around
Ferrari. There are other teams located outside these areas, such as

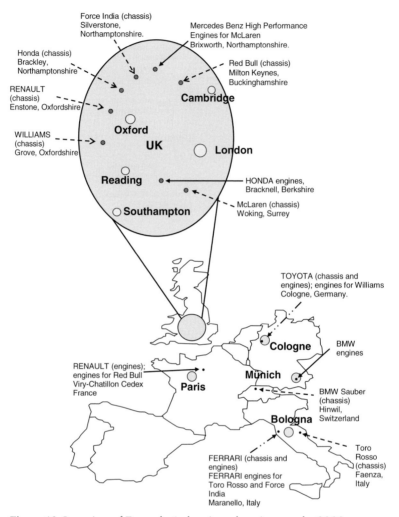

Figure 13 Location of Formula 1 chassis and engine supply, 2008

BMW, based in Munich and Hinwil, and Toyota, based in Cologne. For BMW the two-site arrangement is a function of its acquisition of the Sauber team and means that operations are clearly divided between engine and chassis, as explained by Mario Theissen:

In Hinwil we do the entire chassis and Hinwil takes the lead for track operations so most people at the track are from Hinwil. Munich is the entire power train, so we made a shift in terms of gearbox; we said gearbox is a mechanical part closely linked to the engine. With future power trends like KERS hybrid systems all will be integrated: engine, hybrid components, gearbox and electronics. All this is done in Munich. All the rest is in Hinwil where we have 430 employees, whereas in Munich we have less than 300, bringing the total to about 700.

Toyota came in for much criticism, largely from British journalists, for not locating within Motorsport Valley in the UK as Honda, Renault and Mercedes had done, but for John Howett there are both negatives and positives to this:

On the positive side we have great machine tool capability in Germany, but the area is weak in composites; people tend not to move either way, which is positive and negative [from the UK to Germany and vice versa]. *We have developed our own supplier base; this was tough to start with but we have moulded to each other's needs – they have less baggage from Formula 1 and they are now very loyal even as they are approached by other teams.*

The core processes for winning

During the 1960s and 1970s the Formula 1 teams were very much a collection of individuals working in what could be described as 'micro' organisations of ten to twenty people. In more recent times they have evolved into medium-sized businesses which may have over 1,000 employees. The development of the WilliamsF1 organisation, as one example of this growth, is summarised in Table 8.

In today's situation the nature of the organisation becomes critical to success. Paolo Martinelli, former Engine Director, Ferrari, says:

In the '70s and '80s one strong designer or leader would have been the key to success. But now we have a wider group, we are a different type of organisation. It is about the whole group of people, so it is important that management are able to find the best resources from different parts of the organisation.

In order to win a championship the organisation has to consistently deliver a car and driver to the podium at successive races. This means that the whole organisational package has not only to create a fast

Table 8 *Development of WilliamsF1, 1968–2008*

Year	Employees	Championship Ranking	Key Events
1969	5	8th out of 18 for driver Piers Courage	Frank Williams (Racing Cars) Ltd established with offices in Reading
1977	21	Driver Loris Kessel failed to qualify	Williams Grand Prix Engineering Ltd established at Didcot
1980	62	1st	Driver Alan Jones wins the drivers' title
1986	101	1st	Serious road accident leaves Frank Williams tetraplegic
1987	111	1st	Nelson Piquet wins drivers' title
1990	148	4th	New engine partnership with Renault established
1992	190	1st	Nigel Mansell wins drivers' title, but retires at the end of the year
1994	203	1st	Ayrton Senna dies in accident at Imola. Italian authorities charge Williams management with manslaughter
1997	262	1st	Jacques Villeneuve wins the drivers' championship. BMW confirms that it will re-enter Formula 1 as an engine supplier in 2000 with Williams
2003	475	2nd	BMW renews engine partnership for further five years. Second wind tunnel (60%) completed at Grove facility
2005	493	5th	Partnership with BMW terminated at the end of the year
2007	491	4th	Williams enters into new partnership with Toyota providing engines
2008	540	8th	Williams celebrates its 500th Grand Prix

Table 9 *Key areas of design in a Formula 1 car*

Example Component Areas of the Car (*may involve close collaboration with a partner organisation)	Example Specialist Areas
Chassis	Electronics and Instrumentation
Suspension and Steering	Metallurgy
Engine*	Computational Fluid Dynamics (CFD)
Aerodynamic Package	Finite Element Analysis (FEA)
Fuel*	
Transmission	
Brakes*	
Tyres*	

and reliable car, it has to be adaptable to the changing competitive conditions of a race. It has to make fast decisions, but it also needs to be developing longer-term designs which are going to win races in the future. The core process required to consistently succeed in Formula 1 can usefully be broken down into three areas with very different time spans and organisational requirements:

1) Creation of a competitive Formula 1 car.
2) Consistent race-winning performances.
3) Generation of revenue streams.

We now consider each of these areas in more detail.

Creation of a competitive Formula 1 car

The creation of a Formula 1 car is both a complex and demanding process. It draws on many different technologies from sectors such as aerospace and construction, instrumentation, automotive technology and computer software. It is an amalgam of many different areas, all of which combine to create the optimal racing machine. In a Formula 1 organisation there would typically be structures or groups created around the component areas of the car. Fundamentally there are two aspects to the creation of the car: 1) design and engineering, which involves the evolution of a concept into a detailed design; and 2) manufacture, in which the design is transformed into a car.

Table 10 *Key areas in the manufacture of a Formula 1 car*

Example Areas of Manufacture (*may involve outsourcing)	
Composites	Machining
Electronics*	Fabrication
Models (for use in the wind-tunnel)	Heat Treatment
Components*	Finishing
Quality Control	Casting*

In Table 9 we can see the key areas which are often used to create the design organisation. These relate to the component areas of the car, such as engine and transmission, chassis, suspension and steering and also specialist areas such as electronics and computational fluid dynamics (CFD).The manufacturing process also involves a range of different activities which are used to structure the organisation. These are shown in Table 10.

While ideally these areas should work closely together there is often a distinction drawn between the design office (design and engineering) and the shop floor (manufacturing).

Getting the manufacturing process to work effectively is a critical aspect for any Formula 1 team, and again we see an emphasis on people and informal processes, as well as ensuring that those involved have a strong sense of the 'big picture'. At WilliamsF1 this is achieved by focusing on products rather than processes, as outlined by COO Alex Burns:

We have split the manufacturing facility up into relatively small groups responsible for particular areas of the car, so you are giving people a product focus rather than a process focus. So, rather than saying to somebody, 'You are in charge of laminating', you actually say, 'You are in charge of bringing together the wing'. So someone is responsible for doing that, and the designers and manufacturing people, they all know each other, there is if you like an informal organisation that is based on particular products. You align this and say, 'Right, the challenge for you guys is to get this wing out to Istanbul in time for the race.' They all know exactly what to do, who's going to do what; it's quite well orchestrated.

For Alex Burns, principles such as lean manufacturing provide a very important contribution to the manufacturing process, but also the nature of the Formula 1 challenge means that some of the principles are very different:

What is difficult here is smoothing demand. Classically a lean manufacturer will try and smooth your demand; very difficult to do that here because, if the wind tunnel finds a gain, we want it at the next event and we never know quite exactly when the wind tunnel is going to find a big enough gain that we are going to want to take to an event. So that's quite difficult. It's a constant aerodynamic development programme, most of which doesn't yield performance, but when it does yield performance we need that at the track as soon as possible, because every race that we are faster than our competitors is a relative performance gain.

One issue in the creation of a competitive Formula 1 car is that information from competitors can prove very valuable for competitive advantage and, in some situations, the boundaries of ethical behaviour can be overstepped. This was the case with the 'Spygate' controversy of 2007, mentioned in a previous chapter, where a senior member of the Ferrari team had allegedly passed detailed information to the Chief Designer of McLaren. The exchange only came to light when Ferrari was alerted by the manager of a photocopying shop in Woking in Surrey, England, where apparently an attempt had been made to copy the documents. The subsequent rulings by the FIA meant that other teams are now very careful as to how information on competitors is obtained, as Team Principal of Red Bull Racing, Christian Horner, observes:

It's been a reminder to ourselves and probably every other team in the pit lane just to tighten up their IT policies, employment contracts and policies, just to ensure that the company is protected from rogue information. We literally cannot afford to get involved or could not entertain finding ourselves in a similar position [to McLaren]. Therefore we've taken the steps within the management of the group to say right, let's make sure we don't find ourselves in that position and just reminded each employee. Within a fifty-mile radius of this team we've got five other Grand Prix teams and people move from

*team to team but what they take in their head in experience and kno-
whow is very different from taking drawings and IP from another
team. Sure, Adrian [Newey] came here from McLaren with all his
experience in his head and set about drawing RB3 through his experiences and knowhow, but he didn't bring 380 pages from McLaren
to reference it on, so that's the key distinction I think.*

Consistent race winning performances

The second key area of the organisation concerns the ability to develop
the components and the car as an entire system through testing. As
mentioned earlier, Formula 1 operated a limited testing schedule of a
maximum of 30,000 kilometres per year in 2008 where teams were
only allowed to test on certain days when circuits were available for
testing. This means that testing events are important opportunities to
try out new ideas and components, outside the pressure of a Grand
Prix.

Typically, each Formula 1 team would run a test team of around
fifty people and a race team of around twice this number, but these
numbers continue to vary with annual changes in the regulations. In
each group there would be engineers whose role is to work specifically
with the driver to maximise the set-up of the car and to determine
race strategy. Each car will also have a group of mechanics responsible for working on the car and undertaking pit stops. There are also
'truckies' responsible for driving the transporters and moving equipment around, and also hospitality people who provide catering, often
outsourced through specialist organisations.

A key aspect of the race-winning performance is making sure that
the pace of both solving problems and innovation does not let up during the season. For Alex Burns this means that the time between races
is a critical time for the Williams factory:

*Reliability is a big issue of course; I mean the cars have to be hugely
reliable now, so if we get a reliability problem in a race, more often
than not we will attempt to fix that for the following race. It may
be a faulty sensor that's drifting out of calibration, or just breaking,
that's affecting us. We would try and understand that, do a root-
cause analysis, work with the supplier, get new parts built, or get
parts we've got in stock amended to a new standard, and out to the*

*circuit for the next race. So, that can be challenging at times, to try
and do that in 334 hours. [334 hours is two weeks minus two hours,
typically the time from one race finishing to the next race starting.]*

This approach means that teams have to avoid becoming over-
bureaucratic and thus losing their responsiveness. Burns continues:

*We try to keep it a relatively light touch; quite a lot of the systems
are developed in-house because they are very bespoke to our requirement. Faults would be a good example, where we have written software ourselves that integrates with our intranet system and our email
system so if people are notified of faults automatically, then they are
notified of updates to those faults, those sorts of things. We don't
have a lot of big meetings because they take a lot of time. We try to
keep the number of meetings to a bare minimum, and we have people
who are clear about what their job is and clear that when they are
given a fault it is their responsibility to act on that and act quickly.
People understand the sense of urgency that's required around these
things. Basically a lot of it really depends on having good people
knowing what's required of them and letting them know when they
are not living up to expectations.*

Generation of revenue streams

The third central area within the organisation of a Formula 1 team
is the commercial department whose responsibility it is to attract,
secure and maintain relationships with sponsors and other partners.
More recently this area has also moved into merchandising and other
branding activities.

Typically the structure of the commercial organisation would be
split between business development, which focuses on getting new
sponsors, and account management, which focuses on maintaining
relations with existing sponsors and partners through a variety of
display cars, marketing enhancements and hospitality programmes.

A further and sometimes separate area relates to public relations.
This activity is concerned with optimising the team's communications
with the press and various other stakeholders. It may also involve
the operation of websites and team-related fan clubs. Lifestyle and
mainstream press activation programmes are crucial to this area as

the new breed of sponsors and commercial partners have very clear messages they wish to impart to clients and consumers.

During the 1970s and 1980s, with the predominance of tobacco sponsors, the messaging and branding was relatively non-scientific. Today, PR and press campaigns must reflect fully the clear and subtle messaging of the FMCG, financial and telecommunications companies represented. These well-structured public relations campaigns can also make a considerable impact in terms of differentiating between brands within the same sector.

The informal organisation

It's the informal organisation that runs things here. It's the experienced people in the organisation who are empowered to get on and do things.

When WilliamsF1's COO Alex Burns talks about empowerment in this statement he is not referring to some formal human resources policy, but simply that the informal organisation works because people know who to talk to in order to get something done, without having to work through formal channels and convene meetings. This would take far longer, be detrimental to ongoing innovation efforts, and potentially have a negative impact on production targets.

However, one of the challenges of the organisation is that as the cars become more and more sophisticated, they need more and more specialists to deal with particular areas and as a consequence the organisation gets larger and larger. Burns added:

The problem is as you grow these informal structures break down as you introduce more people and individuals become more specialised.

In the case of WilliamsF1 the focus has therefore been on building clarity into the informal organisation, rather than trying to overlay a functionally correct organisation over the top of it. Alex Burns says:

It's always been that this designer has always done the exhausts, so he goes and talks to Dave who makes the exhausts to sort it all out, who talks to the guy who needs to get the right grade of metal for the manifolds and between them they make it happen and they design the exhaust together, actually produce it together and off it goes and the right quantities go out, so we're trying to make those linkages much more clear and formalise the connections.

A further challenge with the reliance on the informal organisation is that so much of the knowledge and routines are embedded in particular individuals and their relationships. Once again, Alex Burns:

This reliance on the informal makes staff retention critical. It is vital to have experienced staff, people who have been at the sharp end at the track; you then bring them into the factory.

Balancing out the organisation

One key problem is keeping the balance in the hierarchy of the organisation. A Formula 1 team is like any organisation where hierarchies develop and can become dysfunctional. Traditionally in Formula 1 the race team is the 'elite' and those running the test team seen as second-class citizens. Dickie Stanford, Test Team Manager, WilliamsF1:

Ten years ago the test team was like a little dirty group in the corner. Now it's on a par with the race team. We have some people now on the test team who don't want to move on to the race team. At one time the race team were all paid more than the test team and everybody wanted to get on the race team; when I became team manager I looked at the whole thing: the test team actually worked longer hours, so why should they be paid less? So now we made the test team exactly like the race team. We only take people from the test team onto the race team; you have to work on the test team before you move to the race team.

The emphasis in the organisation is therefore to ensure that everyone sees themselves as connected and involved in the ultimate outcome of winning a race.

Making the connections

In order for the Formula 1 organisation to operate effectively management needs to continually connect and balance the many different functional areas and team groupings. For example, when WilliamsF1 is 'on the road' (travelling to and from races) it groups mechanics, truck drivers and hospitality people together in the hotels to avoid creating separate 'tribes'. Former Race Team Manager and now Test Team Manager, Dickie Stanford's approach is that one has to be 'mother' to everyone on the test and race teams:

Not everyone gets on with everyone else so you have to be mother. You have to be mother to around a hundred people when you are racing: have they a problem at home? Have they a problem with one of the other guys – that will snowball quicker than anything else so you have to know everybody.

While historically the technical and marketing sides were kept separate, they are becoming more and more integrated as the teams try to find ways to increase the value of the relationship to their sponsors. Dickie continued:

We also use the testing operation as part of the sponsorship activity, I think we probably now take over a hundred guests a day to some of the tests. It's an opportunity to meet the drivers and see the operation in a more relaxed situation than a race.

The authors attended a test day at Silverstone in 2008 where WilliamsF1 had constructed a huge marquee for the purpose of entertaining actually 300 guests, and with the other teams doing the same, the paddock area gave the impression of a mini Grand Prix.

Such connections are also important between different locations. When moving to the position of Team Principal at Honda Racing, one of the key areas that Ross Brawn identified for development was the relationship between the various sites of the Honda operation:

The potential of Honda, particularly in Japan, is not yet being fulfilled. The lines of communication are not strong enough between the UK and Japan and we are working hard, as a team, to improve the situation. The next stages are to weld together all the various entities of Honda Formula 1 Racing, the F1 facility in Brackley, the engine facility in Bracknell, the research facility in Tochigi. All areas contain highly motivated and skilled technical staff but their efforts are not yet well coordinated and common targets and responsibilities are yet to be defined.

This philosophy mirrors Brawn's approach at Ferrari, where he focused on bringing together the various technical areas of the car to optimise overall performance:

In the next eighteen months or so we are bringing together the two groups based in England into one organisation and we'll develop ways to work as project teams with groups in Japan and groups in the UK. Engineers from the UK are moving to Japan and engineers from Japan are moving to the UK. We are setting up schemes to initiate our Japanese colleagues into Formula 1 as it is very different from their normal environment. We are also sending more and more engineers to the research facility at Tochigi to see where the Formula 1 programme can benefit from the work they are doing there. All the elements need to learn from each other but we have the one common mantra 'One Team'.

8 | *Integrating: effective leadership brings it all together*

The man at the top is the example to the others to follow in the culture or the manner in which business should be done.

Sir Jackie Stewart, former Triple World Drivers' Champion and former Formula 1 Team Principal

We have seen that Formula 1 people are passionate and competitive, and that they also work collaboratively in teams. As in all effective organisations, however, there is a need for individuals who can spur, motivate and inspire their colleagues into action. They do this by creating a harmony within the working environment that enables the separated, but inter-related functions in the business to operate in an integrated manner. This requires a form of leadership that integrates the efforts of strong-willed individuals, so that they can work cohesively towards common objectives.

Given the wide range of personalities in Formula 1, it is not surprising to find differing leadership styles. As one knows from experience the most effective managers are capable of utilising several behavioural styles in order to achieve their goals. The best managers move seamlessly between these styles and use the appropriate ones as situations warrant. It is therefore a little presumptuous to put senior managers into 'cubbyholes' of behaviour. But the fact is that for most managers certain dominant patterns tend to emerge regarding how they deal with their subordinates, peers and bosses within the working environment. Some managers are more low-key than others, some more hands-on than others, and some are more charismatic than others.

No matter the dominant styles they employ, all effective leaders *galvanise* their followers into achieving high performance. Galvanise is defined as '*to arouse to awareness or action, spur*' (the American Heritage Dictionary) or '*to shock or excite into action*' (Compact Oxford English Dictionary). These are precisely the underlying goals of people in leadership roles in Formula 1. They must create awareness within their teams about expectations, competitor capabilities and team mate competencies and limitations. They must spur their teams to higher levels of performance in the design studio, factory, on the test track and at each race.

In the context of integrating all of the diverse activities taking place within a Formula 1 team, the most effective leaders are good at *setting expectations* for the performance they believe can be achieved. They *communicate* these expectations and set goals accordingly. The leader also plays a crucial role in setting the overarching tone for the entire organisation as a *role model*, inspiring loyal followers throughout the organisation. It is also evident that leadership qualities do not reside only in the person at the top of the organisational pyramid, to the extent that some teams are more hierarchical than others. There are leadership roles, perhaps even a requirement for them, given the competitive pressures and tight deadlines in this industry, at *many levels* within a team. Formula 1 leaders stimulate action among their followers by also celebrating successes that are meaningful for their teams. In summary, they create an environment in which individuals can strive for improvement and the overall team can come together to provide a complete package that excels.

It requires only a small stretch of the imagination to consider that Formula 1 leaders are 'stewarding' their teams forward in order to give greater life and vitality to their business's key product, a racing car. A Formula 1 car takes on a life of its own. Each new design and set-up gives the car its own characteristics and peculiarities. The designers, engineers, mechanics and drivers are in some ways working with a living object that requires both stimulation and control.

During the 1970s and early 1980s an entire Formula 1 team was small enough to fit into a unit the size of a single commercial garage. The team leader oversaw the entire operation with a quick walk through the factory (if it could be called that) putting him in touch with all the key people and operations of the business. Teams were run like small, entrepreneurial businesses. If a new component needed to be purchased, the Team Principal would immediately work the phones in order to raise the necessary cash. Decisions were made on a day-to-day, even moment-to-moment basis.

Sponsors in the main were looked upon simply as funding sources. They received an allotted space on the car and/or team uniform and trucks to advertise their product, in return for payment. Technical

suppliers provided their parts and components mainly to place their
company logos on the car and in anticipation of the brand association
that comes with their relationship. Neither of these types of partners was truly integrated into the heart of the Formula 1 team's business activities. These small teams had very limited operating budgets.
Much was done through 'seat of the pants' management. Just surviv-
ing financially and getting a car ready for the next race was the main
goal for most of the teams.

During the past twenty-five years the situation has changed significantly, though staying ahead of the cost of new technology remains
a significant challenge. As the Formula 1 industry has grown in size
and global reach, so too have the racing teams. Along with size has
also come increased complexity. Brand and product sponsors today,
as we have seen, have a greater call on the whole team in order to
leverage their advertising investment. Technical partnerships have
become fully integrated into the teams they support. They play
important roles in the design, development, delivery and installation
of components.

With this complexity and further specialisation the leader's ability to stay on top of the business simply by walking through the
garage has disappeared. As with many growing businesses, the
tendency for separate departments to develop within the organisation, so-called silos or chimneys, has increased. This, in turn, has
required that a new style of leadership and management has had to
emerge to enable Formula 1 teams to cope with the new business
environment.

We have identified several integrating principles, familiar to all
successful businesses, also actively seen in Formula 1. Effective leaders in Formula 1:

- Set appropriate expectations
- Act as integrators, links between different parts of the business
- Focus on results
- Act as role models inspiring with their own determination and
  style
- Are rapid and clear decision-makers
- Protect their work forces from detrimental influences from
  outside
- Are found at all levels in the organisation

Setting expectations

Typically one would expect the leader of an organisation to create the vision that will inspire the team to achieve superior performance. In Formula 1 this is not as difficult a task as it might be in another industry. The image of what success means is visible to all team members throughout the racing season. It includes their driver (or better yet both of the team's drivers) standing on the winners' podium after a race, receiving their trophies and then ceremoniously spraying a magnum of champagne over their fellow drivers on the podium and anyone watching from the pit lane below.

Another representative from the team, perhaps the Technical or Sporting Director, is also on the podium in this vision accepting the constructors' trophy for having finished first, representing the collective efforts of the entire support team working behind the driver.

However, there are teams who are at the back of the grid, without the funding of the larger, wealthier teams. They may be racing a chassis that is not absolute state of the art like their leading competitors, fitted with an engine that is leased from another team's production facilities. These teams have a realistic understanding that their chances to win races or even to attain points in the Championship tables, depend to a degree on factors outside of their control. Sometimes the 'right' conditions, such as inclement weather or mechanical failure or driver error of the front-running competitors, can even out the playing field.

Stefano Domenicali, Team Principal at Ferrari, has no lack of funds to support his team, but he understands the plight of other teams who are not as fortunate:

The reality is that if you have some money you spend it on the car and try to find the performance everywhere you can. If all the money is finished then you're not able to do it, that's the ultimate challenge. I really respect a lot of small teams that have no money or much less than us because it is a different approach to racing. It's a different approach to their job.

Paul Jordan, former Commercial Director of the Minardi racing team, told us at Imola in 2004:

Our motivation is just to be here. We've been going since 1985 and we're the fifth-oldest team. Minardi is the Academy of Formula 1.

We introduce drivers, engineers, commercial people and sponsors to the sport.

In Ross Brawn's words:

I think one of the key things is always to be realistic about what you can achieve. I often think that if you try and achieve too much, you achieve less. It's finding that balance between not turning the organisation upside down and making it collapse, but turning it up a gear so that you react and try to find solutions.

Frank Williams and his partner Patrick Head have demonstrated how shared leadership at the top level of an organisation can work effectively. They co-own and co-lead a business that employs over 500 people. Frank Williams says:

I'm the senior shareholder [70 per cent], *but because I'm very clever, he's* [Patrick Head, 30 per cent] *got the greater amount of work and responsibility, that is to say engineering. I'm mainly business, Formula 1 politics, and money in-money out.*

Williams clearly understands his own boundaries:

I'm not a trained manager; Patrick is actually a better manager than me I think, more logical and structured in his thinking. I'm careful not to manage too many people.

Patrick Head, the technical brains of the partnership, commented on the evolution of their business, in particular his changing role as a leader:

I think fifteen to twenty years ago, Formula 1 was quite different from a lot of normal businesses. Now I don't really think it's that different. We have the same pressures of trying to bring product to market, generating, recognising and nurturing good ideas, keeping each department within the company healthy. To make it work you can't have somebody in a senior position that's protective and defensive.

Integrating groups within the company – providing structure

Head also told us:

A lot of my job as I go round the place is sort of linking. I suppose it is troubleshooting, but also I think I act to a certain degree as a lubricant. I can make sure that if anything is getting jammed I can give it a kick. Equally if I see a programme that is slipping behind and I don't think it is getting the attention that it needs, I get the appropriate people together. I have to keep in touch with what's going on and I do this by talking to people as I move around the factory. I will get feedback as to how things are going and either be able to help move things along myself or get people to talk across departments.

John Howett at Toyota F1 also believes in getting out to where the action is:

If somebody tells you there's a problem, the first thing you should do as a manager is go there and look for yourself because I want to see it, not judge based on what everybody's told me. So many people sit by their desks and say, 'Well, it's the bl**dy idiots in the gearbox shop again, they can't build the gearbox!' When you go there you find it's not that problem, it's actually something else. So, it's all about simplicity and absolute focus on the real issues with very rapid and quick reactions.

Jean Todt, Team Principal at Ferrari from 1993 to 2007, succeeded as an integrator of expertise and talent soon after taking leadership responsibility. He brought all of Ferrari's activities to one location in Italy. He brought in Ross Brawn and Rory Byrne from the World Championship-winning Benetton team on the technology and design side, respectively; and Michael Schumacher with Rubens Barrichello to drive, before changing in his final year to drivers Kimi Raikkonen and Felipe Massa. He retained the best talent from inside the company and created the working environment to support bringing the whole package together. He said:

When I arrived, I analysed the situation. Eventually it was a matter of putting the right people at the right place, something easier to say but more difficult to do. I took power and developed credibility

*with the facts, with real examples, so that slowly people started to
believe that things are moving, that things are changing. There was
no communication in the company. Communication is key. You
have to be seen and to explain to people. You have to get people to
want to participate in what you do.*

Ross Brawn left his position as Technical Director at Ferrari after the
2006 season. He took a year off before being lured back into Formula
1 to become the Team Principal at Honda Racing in 2008. He told us
why he took the challenge:

*I joined Honda because I could see the unfulfilled potential. The
team had the resource, the commitment, but not the results.*

In fact, he felt that Honda:

*... in many ways ... was similar to how Ferrari was when I arrived
there.*

We interviewed Brawn in his motorhome office about five months
into his new job, at the Spanish Grand Prix at Barcelona, and in talking to us he emphasised the importance of integrating the capabilities
that existed within the team:

*What I found at Honda is a lot of very competent people who just
need to be stitched together and that's my priority at the moment.
The potential of Honda, particularly in Japan, is not being utilised.
There's not yet a strong enough understanding and communication
between the two UK-based facilities and our Japan-based facility.
They currently operate as three companies, basically.*

He added:

*In some ways being an engineering-led company means it lacks the
organisation that you need and that's what I am trying to provide.
There's huge enthusiasm and huge resources available. A lot of it is
bottom driven and that means that, often, there's a lack of coordination. In shooting for the target sometimes the means of getting
there is not considered well enough.*

Inevitably, conflict will arise in complex, competitive organisations. Jean Todt of Ferrari told us his approach was to:

... try to take them from the beginning. I keep saying, if you have a cut on the arm and you don't cure it right away, you may have to cut the whole arm off because it gets infected. So if there is a problem, you must open your eyes and not say, 'Let's wait for it to be sorted'; you have to sort it.

We asked John Howett, Toyota F1, whether some conflict within the team was necessary in order to keep a competitive edge. He replied:

Is the Toyota dealer in the next town the competitor or the Ford or VW dealers in your town? F1 people are competitive by nature, but the key is focusing on competing against the other teams as a cohesive unit. Creating healthy competition in the organisation is very good, but conflict can be destructive. So you need to go to the edge, but avoid destructive conflict. That border is very fine and the key is never to lose focus of the primary objective which is to beat the other teams and to win. We encourage transparency and placing the issue on the table.

Focus on results

Frank Williams distils his business focus down to a very powerful and simple question when faced with decisions on expenditure:

Will it make the car go faster?

It is the yardstick against which all key decisions are made at WilliamsF1. This credo is echoed throughout the Formula 1 racing world. Eddie Jordan, the founder of the Jordan F1 team, said:

The philosophy that we use is quite simple; the first thing that gets spent is to make the car quite good. The first priority is speed and the reliability, performance and the rest is chosen ad hoc after that.

Every effort is made at all levels of a Formula 1 organisation to get another fraction of a second out of the car. Winning becomes everything and the intense focus on all aspects of the business to get there, drives the whole process. Frank Williams once again:

In order to make the car go faster, as a rule of thumb, unless it's unaffordable, truly unaffordable, it will be done. We are at war in this business. It really is war. Either you sink or swim. If you drop away from the top three your revenues fall, and when you haven't got the money it makes it even more difficult to get back.

Dickie Stanford, Test Team Manager at WilliamsF1, says:

Nobody remembers second place, sometimes I can't even remember the races we didn't win, they're yesterday, they're history. If we do badly, the entire focus is then on what we did badly, what went wrong and what are we going to do to fix it for the next race. Even if we have a weekend where we finish first and second there are things that go wrong, and we need to identify those and fix them before the next race.

Jackie Stewart says teams have to get the most out of the competencies and innate spirit that exist within the team in order to achieve results:

You've got to use the immense energy that exists in the company, the immense desire to please, to win, to achieve ... this is how we do it, by hook or by crook, we'll get it done ... there's not an 'I can't do it factor,' there always a way to do it.

Given the tightness of budgets, most Formula 1 teams can no longer afford to design and create for the sake of technology itself or just doing something different. Sir John Allison, former Operations Director of the now defunct Jaguar Racing team, told us several years ago:

We don't do anything for change's sake. Everything we do is for a purpose. Nothing is done on a whim. Nothing is done on a guess. Nothing is done on feeling the water, only on the basis of good engineering and good science.

This is certainly even more true today.

Role models

No matter what leadership styles they exhibit, all Formula 1 leaders exude passion and enthusiasm for the sport that becomes infectious to their employees, sponsors and partners. Great leaders inspire their followers to volunteer their skills, knowledge and energy in order to achieve their shared vision.

The story about Frank Williams' return from a crippling accident has been told many times. It serves as an outstanding example of a leader inspiring others through his courage and personal drive. Williams was in a road accident in the South of France in March 1986. His car overturned and he sustained vertebrae damage to his neck. Remarkably, through intensive care and rehabilitation, Williams came back to Formula 1 only four months later to watch his team in the practice sessions at the British Grand Prix at Brands Hatch. He was able to travel with the team to all their races the following year and has missed very few since. Williams is a tetraplegic paralysed from the shoulders down, confined to a wheelchair. Perhaps it is his innate competitiveness, tempered with his personal trials, that fuels Williams' drive for excellence from himself and his team. He said:

I'm truly far more pissed off with myself as a leader if the people downstairs are not adventurous, if they are mediocre. This leads to mediocre racing cars.

As a former World Champion driver and successful Team Principal Jackie Stewart knows the importance of 'walking the talk' for his people. He said:

The man at the top is the example to the others to follow in the culture or the manner in which business should be done.

You need credibility to lead effectively. Stewart once again:

Let's say you've had no experience of running a Formula 1 team and you go down there and meet these old shoes. They're going to find out in two minutes. It doesn't mean to say you're not bright, but you've got to have a shoe that fits the foot, it's not the foot that fits the shoe.

But Stewart is also not just talking about being a figurehead:

You can't be up there in your office. You've got to be in the factory in the morning, in the canteen at lunchtime and you've got to be down there in the afternoon again. They've got to feel you and touch you. It's small, it's dynamic.

Stewart continued:

There were no weeds in my shooting school up at Gleneagles. I would pick up weeds. The staff would think, 'Oh my god, we must have missed those weeds.' I don't care how grand you are or how much you're paid, if there's a weed there, then pick it up. It's all to do with attention to detail, motivating others and if the boss does it, everyone should do it.

Rapid and clear decision-making

Flavio Briatore, Managing Director, Renault F1, says:

In Formula 1 we need everything yesterday. We are no good at looking at things in the long term.

Short timescales, tight deadlines and rapid decision-making have been mentioned by many interviewees as key distinctions about working in Formula 1. Behind every race there are thousands of decisions made at all levels in the teams, and all must be made quickly. Jackie Stewart says:

People in other businesses have it easy, as the company supports them. The decision process is terrible; they are all frightened to make mistakes. If I were frightened to pass cars, I would never have won a race. In a race if I see a gap open up ahead, I have to make a decision. I can't prevaricate. I can't hesitate. I have to decide there and then and generally that's what works here. Formula 1 operates at a faster pace, it requires more decisive decision-making than other businesses.

Flavio Briatore has business interests that go well beyond his role in Formula 1. He admits that Formula 1 takes up 90 per cent of his time, but to also run fashion, restaurant and other businesses he has to use his time efficiently and make quick decisions. How does he do it? Firstly, he said:

Time is very important, and the way you organise your day and your schedule, I don't have time to lose.

Briatore displays an interpersonal style, a connection to people, which one often sees in effective leaders:

For me, when I am talking with someone they are the most important thing in my life at that time. At the moment I talk with you three guys, you're the most important people. In ten minutes there will be someone else, then that person or persons will be the most important person or people. It's always a question of concentrating when you do something and getting the most out of the time spent.

On the other hand, Briatore is not always easy to follow, as driver Mark Webber, who counts Briatore as his manager, has said:

It's not easy to sit down for an hour with him, but it's not easy for anyone to do that with Flavio, and that's part of his mystique.[31]

We had a little taste of that when Briatore told us:

As an entrepreneur you have the target, you have the idea, you have the strategy, after that day by day you need somebody to manage the business. It's about efficiency.

As an example, he went on to say:

I never insist on a meeting of a set time such as one hour. I do however ask my secretary to keep my meetings very tight on time, sometimes just twenty minutes and therefore before I arrive in the office I've already installed discipline into the questions they [my people] will ask me.

Where, how and by whom decisions should be taken is not always clear and straightforward. From BMW's Mario Theissen's point of view:

One important thing is to take decisions at the lowest possible level because that is where the expertise is. Only if there are contradictory arguments does a decision have to be escalated, but then again decided as soon as possible.

However, this should not be taken to mean that Theissen does not stay on top of what matters. As observed by one Formula 1 writer:

Theissen is succeeding in F1 for many reasons. Clearly he is a ruthless and visionary leader, but is also extremely well-organised and takes great care to control every detail of the team's operation.[32]

As described earlier, Ross Brawn had to learn about a new organisation when he entered the Honda Racing F1 team. He discovered a strong need for ensuring that someone is the final authority and can make key decisions:

What I have found is what I had expected in that there was a lack of reference points in the team. And for me that's critical. You need key reference points, people to make decisions and set direction. I found a neutral top management where there wasn't reference points for people to go to, to get a decision. A lot of very good people, but sometimes when the ideas differed there was no good way of resolving the issue and setting a direction.

In defining more effective organisation and decision processes Brawn has also had to deal with the cross-cultural aspects that arise from a team that has bases in both the UK and Japan. This has tested his strong desire to open communication channels within the organisation to get the most out of it:

Sometimes our team in Japan are doing the same project as the team in the UK and they are not talking to each other. Then they all get frustrated because they come up with different solutions and they're not sure which solution to use. That's a gross simplification of what can happen, but that has been happening. So it's my ambition to bring together the different elements within the UK and in Japan. When we achieve this we will have also a competitive advantage none of the other teams enjoy in the facilities, resource and capacity for short, medium and long term projects.

But in terms of decision-making Eddie Jordan's point of view when he was owner and Team Principal of Jordan F1 is characteristically straightforward:

It's very easy to make a decision. We have a very strong policy, the only bad decision is no decision.

Protect their workforce

Flavio Briatore, Managing Director of the Renault F1 team, is THE boss. He does not believe in big organisation structures. Too many managers makes it difficult to have *the same line.* His approach is a very personal one. He believes that the leader must touch everyone to be effective:

You need contact with your people every day. The organisation is big, the logistics are big, everything is big, but we are still a very personal company. There is only room for one leader and the company has to reflect that leader. For me it is about being close to your people.

Coming back to the theme of a Formula 1 team as family, Briatore also commented on his role in protecting his charges:

A team is like a family, you're travelling six to seven months together. You need to protect your people. I try to make them feel secure, you give them the right budgets, the right salaries and make sure their families are happy.

As a leader, protection is also about ensuring your people have the 'space' within which to innovate and produce without distracting influences from outside. Stefano Domenicali takes this part of his role very seriously:

A 100 per cent effort is needed from everyone working here, so you need to cover up the pressure that is coming from the outside. You really need to filter that. So this is really what I have to handle, so they do not have to carry it on their shoulders. They really need to be focused on their jobs and try to be as creative as possible and very professional. But with outside pressure it is very, very difficult.

Leaders at all levels

Leadership in Formula 1 teams is demonstrated not just at the top of the organisation, but at many levels, a notion espoused by Noel Tichy and other experts on the subject about organisations in general.[33] In this fast-paced, entrepreneurial business it is crucial that all employees are willing, capable and encouraged to carry the torch when the appropriate moment arises. Alex Burns, as WilliamsF1's COO, acknowledges the importance of having both the formal structures of a large organisation, but also the informal structures in place, so that communications and project leadership can carry the business forward when faced with tight deadlines:

You just don't have time to run all ideas through an MRP [Manufacturing Resource Planning] system or anything like that. The 'management' role becomes one of problem-solving along the way, rather than 'managing' the process in any formal way.

Such a description of the management process connects with Henry Mintzberg's notion of 'managing exceptionally', where the focus is on dealing with those events and issues which may impact on the process rather than the process itself.[34]

Commenting just two weeks before the team was to ship out the main freight to Melbourne for the Australian Grand Prix, Burns continued:

It's the informal organisation that really takes over at times like these. People in the organisation are empowered to take over because no one individual could get it done.

At WilliamsF1, Patrick Head also encourages empowerment:

I certainly don't want to create an environment where people don't make a move without my say so. Because generally I know enough about what's going on so that no silly things will happen. The biggest thing that holds our organisation back is prevarication. I try to help the process along and hope that those involved reflect on the situation and realise that they could have made certain decisions without me. And maybe next time they will.

As remarked earlier, Mario Theissen is very systematic in his approach to the business. He set out a clear plan for BMW's Board of Directors regarding their full ownership of a Formula 1 team, and manages very strategically. Given the complexity of the business, and the fact that BMW has key operations in two countries, Germany and Switzerland, he has to rely on the capabilities of leaders at all levels of the business. He said:

I spend my time in both places. I have an office in Munich and I have one in Hinwil. In both locations I participate in key meetings. I don't run them myself, however. For instance if we have the power train meeting in Munich, it's run by Markus Duesmann who is in charge of power train. I am present to get all the information and I get close to the people who are making the decisions. I cannot see everybody, every day, but that is the way I try to be involved. Ultimately, I spend about one third of my time at my desk, one third in meetings and one third walking around.

The Formula 1 driver as leader

Given the driver's high profile we would be remiss not to discuss his leadership role within the team. Not all drivers interact with their teams in the same way. Some drivers are actively involved with many aspects of the team's activities. Others restrict their inputs to the on-track performance of the car. In many cases it may be that they are not as integrated into the guts of the engineering equation as one might have imagined. Patrick Head says:

If you had a driver who was all over the technology, he probably wouldn't be a very good driver.

However, there is no denying the fact that the driver plays an important leadership role in a Formula 1 team, both on the track and off. David Richards, former Team Principal at BAR Honda F1, told us:

The role of a great driver is as much outside the car as it is inside the car. In most companies it is clear where the culture and leadership comes from, the MD or Chairman at the top. In a motor-racing team you might think that in a conventional structure it comes from Team Principal. However, a significant, real influence comes from the driver because it is he who people become passionate and emotional about. As a result, they have a far greater role that they can imagine.

Much has been written about the role Michael Schumacher played in Ferrari's successful run between 1999–2004, when it won consecutive Constructors' Championships and Schumacher garnered five of his seven Drivers' World Championships.

While Schumacher was in his last year of driving for Ferrari, Jackie Stewart told us:

The best driver leadership example is unquestionably Ferrari and Schumacher. No matter how good Ross Brawn is, no matter how good Rory Byrne is, no matter how good Jean Todt is, no matter how good other members of their team are, the man who pulled that together was Schumacher. They hadn't won a World Championship in 21 years before he arrived.

Schumacher has been the lightning rod around which Ferrari's success has been built. He catalysed an underperforming team into a modern racing dynasty.

Wearing the bright green colours of his new employer Honda, Ross Brawn more recently recalled:

Undoubtedly at Ferrari we had the benefit of Michael in that he was a natural leader of people, so he could inspire people, he could motivate people and that does make your life easier. There's no doubt that Michael walking around the factory increased motivation.

More specifically we asked Brawn, how did he do that? He replied:

Within the engineering team he always kept a very level head and always respected everybody and always worked with everybody in being part of a team. That was one of the secrets of his success in that he never tried to pull rank within the team. Everyone was his equal and everyone had a contribution to make. If the team determined it was going to go in a particular direction he would give his opinion and even if he didn't agree he would support the final decision. He might come to you afterwards and say you were right or wrong, but he did that in a proper quiet constructive way. Drivers have got to do that.

Speaking about his two drivers at Honda F1, Rubens Barrichello and Jenson Button, Brawn added:

These guys are very good. They work with the team. Gaining trust and mutual respect can be so productive and so positive and yet so corrosive and so negative if it goes the other way. So, it's a very important element of the package.

Leadership roles are played by members of a Formula 1 team at the top, and also throughout the organisation. Given the attention that the media place on the Team Principal and drivers, they may be most visible; but throughout the team, engineers, designers, mechanics and marketing managers must organise processes and motivate their colleagues in order to accomplish complex tasks within tight time-frames. The complexity of meeting short deadlines with high-precision engineering capabilities requires that someone takes responsibility to ensure that all of the work that is being done in separate parts of the organisation, perhaps in diverse locations, gets integrated into the car when the race begins.

9 | Innovating: the drive for continual change

It's a mindset that demands that the company be structured to deliver results quickly, to constantly innovate and also not be afraid to give up on something if it's not working more or less immediately.

Scott Garrett, Head of Marketing, WilliamsF1

Formula 1 is a global motor-racing spectacle where each team relies on technology and the ability to continually innovate, in order to outpace the competition. Innovating is concerned with continuously enhancing performance. It is about creating new opportunities, whether these are related to a product, technology or process. The point of innovating is to create new sources of performance, to find new ways of doing things that may improve both the efficiencies and effectiveness of the organisation.

Innovation in Formula 1 is usually thought of strictly in terms of technology, but the sport has in recent years witnessed remarkably creative ideas in the marketing arena. The impact of Red Bull's involvement in Formula 1, for example, has not just been related to an injection of cash, it has introduced a number of marketing innovations to Formula 1, as described by Team Principal, Christian Horner:

Red Bull has brought a very refreshing appeal back to Formula 1 with the introduction of concepts such as the 'energy station', an open-house facility that is open to any F1 pass holder, which was unheard of previously. We also have some fun initiatives that we have partnered with film promotions, Formula Una [a Formula 1-based beauty contest] *or the Red Bulletin* [a daily newsletter printed during a Grand Prix weekend], *so there's so many initiatives that Red Bull has brought to Formula 1 which I think without which Formula 1 would be a much duller place.*

The ability of any Formula 1 team to innovate is as fundamental as its ability to put a racing car on the grid. It has no option but to continually develop, both its cars and its ways of operating, in order to stay ahead. Chapter 2, Figure 4 shows the speed of the leading qualifying car (pole position) for the Monaco Grand Prix, which has always been held in the luxurious city of Monte Carlo.

From the Alfa Romeo of Juan Manuel Fangio, which took pole position in 1950 at a speed of 64.55 mph, to Jarno Trulli's Renault RS24, which was at the front of the grid in 2004, there is a difference of 36.5 mph. However, it is perhaps surprising to note that this represents a year-on-year improvement of just less than 1 per cent. Many companies today would not be able to survive at such a low rate of performance improvement. Nevertheless there is one factor which helps to explain this overall relatively low figure: regulation.

The regulators of Formula 1 have continually sought to reduce the speed of the cars for reasons of safety and to ensure more equal competition between teams. Speed is a direct factor in creating injuries, hence the regulators' continual efforts to reduce speeds for the sake of safer racing. In contrast to the regulators, the teams themselves are obsessively focused on getting ahead of the competition by building faster cars. They are continually inventive in coming up with ways to make the car go faster; based often on innovations which the regulators have not yet identified. All the design groups in Formula 1 operate on the principle that if the rules don't say you can't do it, then that clearly means you can!

For these reasons Figure 4 has a 'sawtooth' effect, where speeds are increased through innovation, and then reduced through regulation. For example, in the period from 1995 to 1997 innovations in car design meant that the average pole position speed at Monaco increased from 90.8 mph in 1995 to 96.3 mph in 1997. If this rate had been sustained until 2004 the average speed of pole would have been considerably faster.

A further example of the speed of development was provided at the 2006 Brazilian Grand Prix at Interlagos. This was Michael Schumacher's last Formula 1 race before retiring. He finished fourth, but he put in a superb drive through the field after a return to the pits due to a puncture. He also achieved one final record with the fastest lap of the race (at 1 minute, 12.162 seconds). This beat the previous year's record, achieved by Kimi Raikkonen in a McLaren-Mercedes, by just over 0.1 of a second. It says a great deal about the constant pace of improvement in Formula 1 that Schumacher's fastest lap in 2006 was achieved in a car with a 2.4 litre V8 engine, whereas Raikkonen's car in 2005 was equipped with a 3.5 litre V10 engine, which was a much more powerful unit.

So is innovation in Formula 1 different from that in any other kind of company? WilliamsF1's Engineering Director, Patrick Head, thinks not:

Today I don't think there's a lot of difference between a Formula 1 team and any other kind of business. They both have the same pressures of trying to bring product to market, generation of ideas, recognition and nurturing of the good ideas.

So what are some of the pressures and demands of innovating in the context of Formula 1? Two factors emerged from our research: speed to market and the challenge of innovating in organisations which are growing larger and larger.

Speed to market (or the track!)

Whereas there are similarities between Formula 1 and other businesses, there are real differences in terms of the pace and intensity of innovating. The pace of innovation is significantly faster in Formula 1 than other technology industries. Here innovating is a continuous process, with a constant array of design changes and new components being incorporated into the car. This is shown in Figure 14, which was kindly provided by Ferrari. The top part of the figure shows how Ferrari develops its production engines which are used in its high-performance road-going cars. We can see that the total development period for a production engine is 42 months, if we exclude the time for the concept study up to the start of production (SOP). In contrast, during the same period within Formula 1, there have been three new engines designed, built and raced each with three iterations or evolutions (EVO1, 2, 3) of the design. It can also be seen from Figure 14 that within Formula 1 the development process is continuous, meaning that the engine is being both raced and developed simultaneously. For Formula 1 we therefore see a total of nine stages of development compared to the single stage of development for the production engine.

One of the critical aspects of Formula 1 is that it requires all the teams to attend fixed race meetings around the world. Therefore, cars

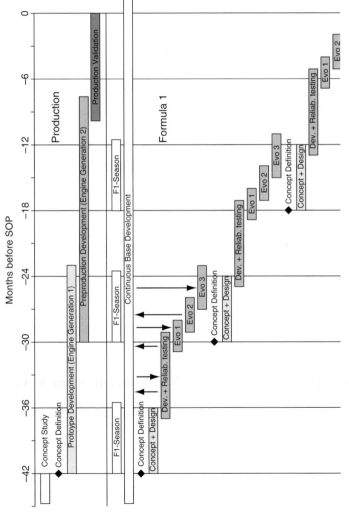

Figure 14 Engine development process at Ferrari, Formula 1 v. production
Source: Ferrari SPA

155

must always be ready to race at each event. Patrick Head, Engineering Director, WilliamsF1:

We are driven very much by specific dates and programmes. That means that with a new component the Chief Designer will know when the design needs to be issued, how long it's going to take to do the design, he'll know roughly how long it will take to manufacture and he can then target a test for the component to be evaluated.

All of these factors require a process in which individuals are familiar not just with the design process, but also the whole manufacture and development cycle; a fact which is underlined by top Formula 1 designer John Barnard:

The key to speed in innovation is being able to integrate the design and manufacture processes. A good designer will go and talk to the fabricators or machinist to find out how the part would be made; it may be that by making some small design changes at this point the part could be easier to manufacture and therefore both quicker to be released and potentially more reliable.

However, Barnard also believes that this means that more traditional management methods such as those used in aerospace are inappropriate for the flexible and responsive context of Formula 1:

The problem is that in a context like aerospace, people can almost determine their own production times, their own lead times. If you sit down and do the project timescale properly you just keep adding on and, 'That'll take this long and then I have to do that and once I've got that done I do this and so on.' You'll end up out here and that's your project lead time. It doesn't happen like that in racing because there's your lead time, there's your project time, that's the race, 'Now you make it fit', and you do whatever that takes.

The ethos of 'doing whatever it takes' means that teams have to go beyond the bounds of their highly pressurised development programmes to stay competitive, as illustrated by WilliamsF1's COO Alex Burns:

In 2008 we were developing a new front wing aimed at Monaco, so it was planned to go to the Ricard test [the Paul Ricard circuit in the

South of France] *and then go on to Monaco; in testing we found a significant performance gain, so we actually rushed one through two weeks earlier to the Turkish Grand Prix, so Nico was racing with that at Istanbul. That call was made on the Sunday of the Spanish Grand Prix* [two weeks before the Turkish Grand Prix], *and we hadn't quite finished designing it at that point, so there's an opportunity to say, 'That's going to give us an advantage at Istanbul therefore can we push it through in nine days in order to get it out to Istanbul in time for the race.'*

A complicating factor is the variability of the different tracks used in Formula 1, which means that innovations are often track-specific. Monza and Monaco are very good examples of this. With the Monza circuit being the fastest circuit in the Championship year a major redesign of bodywork, wings and end plates is required to ensure the minimum of drag on the car while on Monza's super long straights. Likewise the brakes and their cooling require attention with the manufacture and fitting of different-sized cooling ducts and the like. The exact opposite of this requirement is Monaco where due to the confines of this street-based circuit different ratio steering racks have to be fitted to cope with the very tight corners, and aerodynamics are almost the exact opposite of Monza to gain the maximum amount of downforce and therefore grip on the slow corners. Alex Burns bears this out in more detail:

A lot of the aero [aerodynamic] *design work is track-specific. There is an underlying thread of upgrade that goes through the year; you are in a constant state of development but, we'll have a specific package for Monaco, a specific package for Montreal and for Monza. Then you'll have general upgrades that go through for the bulk of the races, so the high downforce races of Barcelona, Magny Cours, Silverstone, Hockenheim; all of these will be relatively similar.*

Another key part of speed to track is the various simulation approaches that are used to predict performance prior to reaching the circuit and therefore it is in simulation technologies that Formula 1 has also made significant progress, as Alex Burns observes:

It is important that our simulation for brake cooling is accurate, so if we go to a circuit and we project the brakes will be at this temperature, we'll be using the same simulation package to predict it for the next races, even though the cooling will be a different package. But if our simulation package isn't correct, we need to correct it, otherwise we are going to have a problem. The brakes might run substantially cooler than we were expecting, that should flag that there's an issue with the simulation and we'd want to fix that before the next event, because you're losing performance by running them too cold and if you're running too hot, you're going to ruin the brakes during the race; you're not going to survive the race. So, you need to get these things right, you need to be accurate with simulations.

Innovating and regulating

There is a continuous battle between the innovation needed to increase speed and performance, and regulation to ensure that there is real competition and that racing is as safe as possible. While in the 1960s, 1970s and 1980s there were many radical innovations, in the 1990s and the 2000s growing levels of regulation have made it increasingly difficult for designers to achieve the 'big breakthrough', as suggested by designer John Barnard:

Formula 1 now is much more a case of detailed development rather than innovation. The rules have boxed it in a lot more from what it used to be. Everybody has more or less found, because of wind tunnels, because of all the testing, all the test facilities that most of these Formula 1 teams have now, they've all ended up being focused down pretty much the same path in the same channel.

However, WilliamsF1's Patrick Head believes that the increasing intensity of regulation has meant that the nature of innovating in Formula 1 is changing rather than disappearing:

I think innovation in terms of bringing in radical new systems like active ride suspension [a hydraulic suspension innovation of the 1990s, now banned] *is much more inhibited by regulation, but new ideas are still needed and the thinking tends to be on a more micro scale. We tend to look at adding a lot of micro-scale innovations together to give a larger overall effect.*

Who gets the benefit?

The history of Formula 1 is littered with innovations where teams have created a step forward in performance, but the innovating team has not always been the one who has enjoyed the most race success as a result of its innovation.

As can be seen from Table 11, often the innovator is not the prime beneficiary of the innovation. While Cooper undoubtedly enjoyed success from its mid-engine layout, it was Colin Chapman of Lotus who took the design to a more refined stage and was able to overtake the Cooper concept on performance. Similarly, while it was Lotus who pioneered the development of the Ford Cosworth DFV engine, which required a different concept in chassis design (the engine formed a structural part of the car), it was Ford's decision to make the engine available to other teams. This meant the performance potential was dispersed across a range of constructors, effectively creating Grand Prix winners out of teams such as Matra, Tyrrell, McLaren and Brabham.

Renault entered Formula 1 in 1978 with a car using a lightweight turbo-charged engine. The regulations at the time stipulated that engines were either 3.0 litre normally aspirated or 1.5 litre turbo-charged. It was generally believed that no-one would be able to build

Table 11 *Who benefits from innovations?*

Innovation	Innovator	Beneficiaries
Mid-engine layout	Cooper	Cooper/Lotus
Cosworth DFV	Lotus	All British constructors
Ground-effect	Lotus	Lotus/Williams
Flat 12 engine	Ferrari	Ferrari
Turbo engine	Renault	Honda
Active suspension	Lotus/Williams	Williams
Six-wheel car	Tyrrell	Tyrrell
Composite monocoque	McLaren	McLaren
Semi-automatic gearbox	Ferrari	Ferrari
Tuned mass damper	Renault	Renault (+McLaren and Ferrari)

a 1.5 litre turbo which would be competitive against the 3.0 litre engines. Renault did so, but in the nine years it raced the turbo engine it failed to win a World Championship. In contrast, Honda which entered with its own turbo-charged engine in 1983, was able to win three World Championships between its entry point and the end of the turbo era at the close of the 1988 season.

But there have also been instances where the innovating team was able to capture much of the value of its ground-breaking work. Ferrari's 'Flat 12' engine was developed originally to be fitted into an aircraft wing, but found its true potential in the Ferrari 312T racing car. The powerful twelve-cylinder format with a low centre of gravity meant that it posed a significant threat to the well-established Ford Cosworth DFV. While there were attempts to copy the Ferrari format, most notably with Alfa Romeo supplying the Brabham team with a Flat 12 engine, these were uncompetitive and Ferrari enjoyed a prolonged period of success before the engine was rendered obsolete by new ground-effect aerodynamics.

These examples raise some important questions about how Formula 1 teams are able to protect their ideas. It did not take the significance of 'Spygate' in 2007 to highlight that secrecy is a big issue in Formula 1, but it is something that Patrick Head believes can be taken too far:

Some Formula 1 teams are so concerned about secrecy and the loss of IP that they literally build physical walls around departments to ensure that if someone leaves from the transmission department, they won't have an idea of what's going on in the suspension department; in contrast we have the view that providing we're progressing and developing it's more positive to have an open internal exchange of information than the risk of losing IP when somebody goes.

From Ferrari's point of view, its location outside of the UK's Motorsport Valley could be a benefit here. Ross Brawn, former Technical Director, Ferrari, said:

If you've got an innovation you're lucky to keep it for three or four months, particularly once it goes out on the circuit. I guess we gain and lose from that because we don't have the grapevine feeding us, but generally I'm happier with the degree of isolation we have.

Another potential concern is the frequent movement of drivers around the teams, but in Patrick Head's view this is not a problem:

Most drivers are only aware of what we're doing on the surface, they know that if they press this button it does that, but they've got no idea of what goes on inside.

Of course, another possibility is that the potency of the innovation is masked by the fact that other aspects of the car perform poorly. Gordon Murray, former Technical Director at Brabham and McLaren, said:

Where we've had a massive innovation and we think we're going to walk it and the driver makes a mistake, the engine fails, you choose the wrong tyres or whatever and you have a series of races where other things go wrong. That happened to us a lot. It can be a bad thing if you cream the first race as everybody panics.

Innovating in public

WilliamsF1's Patrick Head identifies a further key point that, in Formula 1, the success or failure of innovating is a very public one:

You've got to do better and better each year, there is no hiding place if someone's not doing a good job. They can't tuck themselves away, it tends to become visible pretty quickly.

A similar sentiment is expressed by the FIA's Tony Purnell who also combines the point that it is both highly visible and immovable:

In Formula 1 you cannot disguise the truth about your 'product' because you are absolutely exposed to the reality of your situation every two weeks. And that's where Formula 1 is special, it really is.

Formula 1 therefore presents a very particular challenge to the process of innovating: because of the competitive pressures it has to be relentless, but it is also highly visible in terms of the success or failure of the process.

Balancing innovation with growth

Formula 1 teams enjoyed particularly high levels of growth in the period between 1993 and 2003. During this time, the typical number of employees in a Formula 1 team grew from around 100 to 500. This, however, created new problems for how they were going to maintain their flexibility and responsiveness, the essential ingredients of competitiveness.

The nature of technological growth in Formula 1 meant that there was a need for increased specialisation, particularly around the areas of aerodynamics and electronics. This need for increased specialist expertise meant that the process by which a car was designed had changed from essentially a step-by-step linear process to one which now involves many activities occurring in parallel, as summarised by WilliamsF1's Engineering Director Patrick Head:

Probably fifteen years ago the design team would be working on the gearbox for one week and then the next week they'd be designing the rear suspension and then the next week they'd be in the wind tunnel sorting out the aerodynamics; you tended to be involved in every aspect of the car. Today we have specialist areas working in parallel, so we have to deal with the problem of how the transmission, for example, integrates with the rest of the car, how it satisfies the aerodynamic requirements of the diffuser [a structure which manages the airflow under the rear of the car], how it deals with the loadings coming from the rear suspension, etc.

WilliamsF1 dealt with this problem by the senior management now focusing on the integration of these groups:

Fundamentally my job is to ensure that we are producing the quickest car, as opposed to the best transmission or the best rear wing mounting. It's a different way of working and it means that you have to have frequent contact between these groups. We have an open-plan design office and encourage people to liaise with the other departments who have an interest in their work.

The teams had to create structures which were able to bring together these specialists and the necessary equipment, but at the same time ensuring that these groupings did not become ghettos of specialists, detached from other parts of the team. Alex Burns relates some of the steps which have been taken to address this at WilliamsF1:

We're trying to deal with this by creating smaller units and ensuring that we get the interaction between design and manufacturing and align this to the testing and racing operations. I think that once you get above 200 there's a real shift in the culture in a company. You ideally need 50 to 60 people to make things happen quickly. Within these groups you ideally need teams of no more than a dozen, and then ensure that they understand how they fit into the other groups.

In addition to creating appropriate structures, Burns notes:

It's also important that each group has something which is clearly related to the car, rather just say your delivery performance against your works order due dates must be high. For it to work in Formula 1 everyone has to be able to relate their activities to the performance of the car.

While individuals such as Patrick Head have experience in all the component areas of the car, which they bring to bear when making trade-offs between different aspects of the car, many of those coming up have tended to have been specialists in one particular area, most notably aerodynamics. He said:

One of the problems created by this growth is that you see some people who were very capable in one particular area, such as aerodynamics, being headhunted to be a chief designer or technical director in another team, completely wrong for the individual and the company.

Technology transfer

It has perhaps been one of the myths of Formula 1 that much of the technology from the sport finds its way into normal road cars. There are very few past examples of this, with perhaps the paddle shift gear system which is now employed on a number of high-performance cars being one of the more visible examples. In fact there are probably more examples of the technology moving the other way; some road cars had traction control systems well before they were used in Formula 1. Williams used a highly developed version of the DAF variomatic belt-based transmission system (known as Continuously Variable Transmission or CVT) in the Williams FW15C in 1993, but the system was banned before it was raced. Renault's Tuned Mass Damper system was also based on a concept which had been applied in the Citroen 2CV!

However, with the car manufacturers becoming more heavily involved in Formula 1 there is a greater emphasis on creating broader value by seeking technology transfer that can be passed through to road-car manufacturing. One way that this is occurring is through the development of new technologies such as Kinetic Energy Recovery Systems (KERS), which is being introduced in 2009. For Honda's Ross Brawn, this provides a number of important benefits which are more to do with learning, ideas and processes than specific products:

For the KERS system the team at Honda that are developing our motor generator unit and control system for the race car have never had the budget, support and targets that we are giving them through the Formula 1 programme. In the normal economics of a road-car programme the balance between cost, performance and timing is different; it has different limits and objectives. For us, we can put in the support, we can put in the backing, we can put in the resources, and they're achieving things now that a year, eighteen months ago they didn't think they could achieve in terms of performance of the unit, in terms of weight of the unit, in terms of size of the unit. A road car cannot afford to have a Formula 1 system in it, that's a fact. We can justify different technologies, different materials and the economics for us are different, we are making a relatively small number of systems. But the people who are involved in that project will be the people that move into the road-car side with the 'can do' mentality that's come from the Formula 1 programme.

A similar situation is found at Toyota, as described by John Howett:

We have around twenty-five engineers based in our fundamental research company, which is outside of Toyota itself and they are working with our engineers on new materials technology. So even if we're not deploying it there are many discussions around how we use these technologies. We also have a machining activity in Japan with casting and machine shop. There's information transfer on the technology used, how to save money, how to make things quicker, and the alternative processes; so there is a constant interchange at all levels. Some of it's not exciting but it very often adds value to the business, either ours or theirs.

For BMW its involvement in Formula 1 is also a lot more than just a marketing programme; it is also looking to create value for the core business, through technology transfer. According to Mario Theissen, Team Principal, BMW Sauber:

It has to create technology transfer and that is why we set up the organisation in a way which is different from any other Formula 1 team. We have a dedicated Formula 1 foundry, dedicated Formula 1 parts manufacturing plant and these two units are not run by BMW motorsport but by the respective departments who do the road car parts in Munich. So both the foundry and parts machining create new technologies and processes on their premises and we are the customer.

What they learn working on Formula 1 they take immediately over to the road car. So we have real synergy, not in the way that you use any individual part of a Formula 1 engine or car but, you learn so much about technology and you speed up this learning process in a way that you couldn't do without Formula 1. Now it's becoming really interesting with the KERS system for next year. We are dealing with it on the power train side, which is in Munich, and we are now seeing that through the pressure, the time pressure and the weight constraints of Formula 1; we are achieving technology leaps within months. What we will have on the car on the grid next year in March [2009] is not available yet and the hybrid guys from road-car development are knocking at our door because they see the rapid progress we make in Formula 1. We can take higher risks, we need a shorter lifetime, we can take the risk of failure which is very different from a road-car project, so we are paving the way now and that will be very significant.

Technology transfer also works in a vertical, as well as a horizontal way in moving between Formula 1 and other motorsport series, as outlined by Peter Digby of transmission manufacturer Xtrac. It started out producing a new gearbox used in the demanding sport of rallycross which it found met a need in Formula 1:

We found that our rallying parts fitted straight into Formula 1 because although one has a lot more horsepower it's the torque demands that really matter, so in the late eighties our transverse Rally package at the time was able to go straight into Formula 1. After this, Formula 1 began to advance faster and some of that technology has now trickled down to our other formulas. So, what was our standard Formula 1 gear in 1995 became our standard touring car gear in 2000. So, there was a lot of trickle-down of components, actual hardware as well as technology.

He draws an interesting contrast between motor racing and tennis; as the surplus from the All England Club, which runs Wimbledon, goes to the Lawn Tennis Association to support smaller tournaments and clubs within the UK:

Formula 1 does not take cheques and write them out to lower levels of the sport as I believe happens at Wimbledon, as much of the Wimbledon income goes into grass-roots tennis in the UK. That doesn't happen in motorsport, but what does occur, for example, is the F1 teams going off and developing expensive semi-automatic gearboxes or Kinetic Energy Recovery Systems that can later be installed on a normal car in racing or even road cars for a fraction of the price.

In Formula 1 there have certainly been a number of notable innovations over the last fifty or so years. Here we pick a number of particular examples to consider some of the general principles of innovating within Formula 1. The Ford DFV engine in 1968; the six-wheel Tyrrell of 1976; the 'pit stop' Brabham of 1982; Ferrari's paddle gear change; the active suspension Williams of 1992; the all-conquering Ferrari F2004 of 2004 and most recently the tuned mass damper of the Renault R25.

Changing the face of Formula 1: Ford DFV engine

The Ford DFV engine was a disruptive innovation in Formula 1. It changed the way in which Formula 1 cars were designed and effectively further shifted the basis of competitive advantage away from the engine to the chassis and aerodynamic aspects of the car. In many ways it was this engine that created the regional cluster of expertise in the UK, known as Motorsport Valley; now the core competence needed was focused on chassis and aerodynamics rather than engine design. Its contribution to Formula 1 and the motorsport industry more generally is highly significant.

The basic concept of the Ford DFV was that it replaced the need to construct a full chassis along the entire length of the car. The DFV was part of the car and was attached to the chassis behind the driver with the rear suspension and gearbox attached to the back of the engine, as illustrated earlier in Figure 2. This created a significant increase in the power-to-weight ratio of the racing car.

As an innovation the Ford DFV was a joint development between Cosworth Engineering which developed the engine, and Formula 1 constructor Lotus, which designed its type 49 car around the engine, allowing it to be attached to the rear of the chassis. The Ford Motor Company sponsored the project with a capital investment of £100,000, and after this the engine was also known as the Ford Cosworth with the famous Ford oval logo carried on its cam covers. One of the main catalysts for the innovation was a change in regulation. In November 1963 the FIA announced that from 1 January 1966 Formula 1 engines would either be normally aspirated 3.0 litres or 1.5 litre turbo charged. Prior to this point the normally aspirated 1.5 litre engine had dominated, most notably with that produced by Coventry Climax and used by successful teams such as Cooper and Lotus. However, Coventry Climax decided that the development costs of a new 3.0 litre engine would be too high for it to bear; it announced its withdrawal from Formula 1 at the end of the 1965 season. Colin Chapman of Lotus approached Keith Duckworth of Cosworth to see if he could design and build a new 3.0 litre engine. Chapman then sought support from Ford, which he received from Walter Hayes (the £100,000 referred to above), who was responsible for Ford's motorsport activities. Duckworth developed a novel layout for the combustion chamber using four valves per cylinder. At the same time Ford had also commissioned a smaller four-cylinder Formula 2 engine using the same layout. The Formula 1 engine effectively doubled up two four-cylinder blocks into a V8 formation. It was therefore given the name 'DFV' for Double Four Valve. The car and

engine were developed during 1966 and made their first appearance
at the Dutch Grand Prix at Zandvoort on 4 June 1967. It won the first
race and went on to dominate the rest of the season. While Lotus and
Cosworth were delighted with the situation Ford's Walter Hayes was
not so sure:

*Almost at once I began to think that we might destroy the sport. I
realised that we had to widen the market for the DFV engine, so that
other teams could have access to it.*[35]

In 1968 the Ford DFV, which had been instigated by Colin Chapman
of Lotus, became available to other teams for the sum of around
£7,500 per unit. This started a tradition in Cosworth in building
customer engines. In 2004 Cosworth was still supplying 'customer'
engines to Minardi and Jordan, although the supply contract by then
ran into millions of dollars per annum.

However, as has frequently been the case, while Chapman was
the innovator he was not fully able to capture all the benefits of the
innovation. Hayes' decision to make the innovative engine available
to other teams ensured that while Ford dominated Formula 1 through
the late 1960s and early 1970s, Lotus, although it enjoyed some success, did not.

Four isn't enough: the six-wheeled Tyrrell P34

Tyrrell Racing was one of the most successful Formula 1 constructors
of the early 1970s (it was later sold to British American Tobacco as
the formation 'base' for the BAR Honda F1 team). However, its success, which had been based partly on the Ford DFV engine, had waned
and Technical Director, Derek Gardner, was looking for a new way
forward:

*In about 1974 it was becoming apparent that the Ford engine
had lost its edge, it was still producing the same horsepower that
it always had, or a little more even, but with the success of the
Ferrari, the possible success of engines like Matra or anybody else
who came along with a Flat 12, V12 or 12 cylinder whatever,
you're going to be hopelessly out-classed ... I wanted to make a big
breakthrough.*

Gardner's idea was a radical one that had started in the late 1960s, when he had worked with Lotus on a series of cars for the Indianapolis 500:

So I thought about the six-wheel car and looked at it in a totally different light to the way I had as a potential Indianapolis car. I thought if I could reduce the front track and keep it behind this 150 cm [maximum body height stipulated by the Formula 1 regulations] *then I'm going to take out all those wheels and their resistance, but above all I would take out the lift generated by a wheel revolving on a track.*

Although Ken Tyrrell had his reservations he decided to give Gardner the opportunity to develop his ideas:

It was Derek's idea [the six-wheel car]; *Derek had wanted to do it the year before* [1974] *but I didn't think that we were long enough established as manufacturers to go to something so radical. But he finally convinced me that we ought to try it, so we grafted four front wheels onto our existing car and created the six wheeler. We decided to show that car* [to the press], *we explained this was an experimental car which we were going to test, and if it was any good we would race it.*

A key aspect of the development of the six-wheel concept was the input of tyre manufacturer Goodyear, which at that time supplied all the Formula 1 teams with tyres. Gardner shared his ideas with Goodyear, which responded to the challenge by creating a tyre with a 10-inch width and a 16-inch diameter. The introduction of the six-wheel P34 temporarily restored the fortunes of Tyrrell racing, as can be seen from Figure 15.

However, despite a promising performance in 1976, when Tyrrell finished in third place in the Constructors' Championship, 1977 proved to be a different story, with the P34 becoming uncompetitive relative to conventional cars. The reasons for this appear to have been due not to any fundamental aspect of the concept, but to the speed of development of specific components that were supplied by external suppliers to Tyrrell. Ken Tyrrell said:

It became difficult to get big enough brakes to fit inside small front wheels. Because everyone else was using a standard front tyre, it

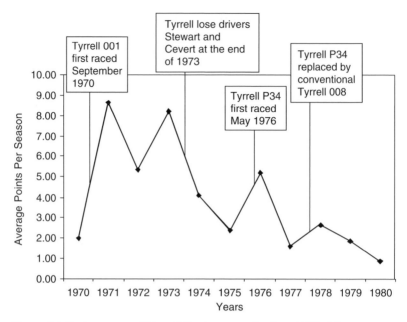

Figure 15 Performance of Tyrrell Racing organisation, 1970–80

became politically difficult for Goodyear to develop the small tyre for us. The car became too heavy with our attempts to put bigger brakes in it and at the end of the second year we had to abandon it.

Derek Gardner commented:

Where I think we went wrong was that Goodyear were supplying most of the teams with rubber, they were only supplying one team with very small front wheels. Therefore, the development of the tyres which are continually going on, it meant that almost with its first race the development of the front tyres went back – they just didn't develop as fast as everyone else. Whereas the rear tyres were being developed with the existing front tyres, so in effect you're having to de-tune the back of the car to stay with the front which was, really, not what it was all about.

As a result, Tyrrell returned to using a conventional chassis with the Ford DFV engine. Derek Gardner left Tyrrell to return to industry and it wasn't until he had retired and became involved with the Formula 1

Thoroughbred Racing Series, which race historic Formula 1 cars, that he was able to work with the six-wheel car once more.

Innovating the whole system: the Brabham pit-stop car

Pit stops have been a feature of Formula 1 for many years. But contrary to popular belief, they were not introduced by regulation to liven up the racing. Contemporary pit stops were created by the innovative Brabham BT50 or pit-stop car. The point of the pit-stop car was that this was not just a technical innovation, but an innovative race strategy which enabled a lighter, more nimble car to outpace the opposition to the extent that it would be able to enter the pits, stop, refuel, fit new wheels and tyres, return to the circuit and still be in front. It is a classic case of problem-solving and lateral thinking to win the race. Gordon Murray, former Technical Director of Brabham and McLaren Formula 1 teams, said:

I was the one who introduced pit stops in Grand Prix racing by designing a half-tank car – to get the advantage of the lower weight, the lower centre of gravity. But it wasn't just pit stops; it was a plan that allowed you to achieve advantage through a faster, lighter car and a pit stop. It's just pure mathematics; you just draw a graph of the race – you draw the car's weight, the centre of gravity and the benefit per lap as a curve and then you take a chunk, a negative curve out of the middle bit where you lose say 26 seconds slowing down and coming into the pits and refuelling and if the total equation's better, then you do it.

But Gordon Murray's idea created other problems, such as tyre temperature. The performance of a Formula 1 car is very susceptible to changes in the condition of the tyres. When a race is started the tyres are relatively cool and performance is only optimised as they warm up to operating temperature. The challenge with the pit-stop car was that this problem was multiplied one, two or even three times in a race. So its success was also dependent on the tyres being able to get to their optimum temperature as soon as possible. Gordon Murray said:

We developed these wooden ovens with gas heaters in them to heat the tyres up so the driver didn't lose the time and smacked those on at the last minute with the fuel.

One surprise for Murray was that the other teams were relatively slow to respond to Brabham's innovative approach:

In the first four or five races the turbo chargers kept failing, I said to Bernie [Ecclestone – then Brabham Team Principal], well that's it, we started in Austria, we only had four races left to end the year, everybody's going to turn up at Brazil with a pit-stop car. But no – Williams had it – but it was a kit that could be put on the car – it wasn't integrated into the design of the car.

Politics and innovating: the Ferrari paddle-shift

Perhaps of all the innovations in Formula 1 the paddle-shift gear change is the most recognisable innovation that found its way into road-going, high-performance cars. The paddle shift utilises a semi-automatic gearbox where the driver does not operate the clutch but selects gears by a pair of 'paddles' located left and right on the steering wheel; pulling one side towards the driver changes up a gear and pulling the other towards the driver changes down.

It was developed by John Barnard, who was trying to find a way to improve the performance of the turbo-charged Ferrari Formula 1 car. However, the problem with this innovative idea was that it meant that the car had to be either designed as a paddle-shift car or a conventional gear-shift car; there was no possibility of producing a competitive car which combined these two features. Barnard said:

There was a massive amount of politics around the whole paddle-shift concept. It actually happened at the time when Enzo Ferrari died. Vittorio Ghidella, who was running Fiat Auto at the time, came into Ferrari to take over Enzo Ferrari's mantle. Towards the end of 1988 I was designing the 1989 car, which was a more developed version of the 1988 test car, but I was designing it such that it would not take a manual gear shift; you could only have a paddle-shift gearbox in it, which was a pretty big commitment to make. Ghidella was so nervous of the fact that it wouldn't work, that he insisted that they built a manual version alongside it. I resisted heavily, because I knew that we didn't have the capacity to do that properly, but they did it and modified the car to put the manual version in and Mansell [driver Nigel Mansell] ran it for a few laps at Fiorano [Ferrari's dedicated test track] *and said 'Forget it, give me the paddle shift again'. So that was a diversion caused literally by politics by the head guy at Fiat. I had to literally lay my contract on the line to be able to do it. My contract said that I had overall technical authority on all the cars and the race team and I used that. I put my contract on the line such that if it didn't work or there were unseen problems with it, then, effectively I go and commit hari-kari. So that was how it was done, which puts a lot of pressure on that you really don't need when you've got enough technical pressure as well.*

Barnard went ahead with the paddle change on the elegant Ferrari 640, which won its maiden Grand Prix on 26 March 1989 at the Brazilian Grand Prix in Rio de Janeiro. However, the 640 suffered from reliability problems and despite also winning Grand Prix in Hungary and Portugal that year, Ferrari finished third in the Constructors' World Championship. The paddle-shift gearbox was quickly imitated by many other designers and is now a standard feature of a Formula 1 car. It is also used on some of the higher-performance Ferrari, Alfa Romeo and Subaru cars, as well being a common feature on many videogame steering wheels!

The gizmo car: Williams FW14B

The Williams FW14B won the first five races of 1992, with Nigel Mansell at the wheel; a record which even survived the dominance of Ferrari and Michael Schumacher in 2002 and 2004.

The FW14B was a highly innovative car in that it incorporated many of the leading-edge ideas of the day. Its designer, Patrick Head, had incorporated semi-automatic gearboxes, drive-by-wire technology and Williams' own active suspension system. The significance of these ideas was that many of them had been initially developed by other teams such as the carbon-composite monocoque (McLaren and Lotus), semi-automatic gearbox (Ferrari) and active suspension (Lotus). The source of advantage was therefore not one particular innovation, but the way in which they were all brought together, as summarised by David Williams, who was General Manager at WilliamsF1 at the time:

I think we actually were better able to exploit the technology that was available and that led to a technology revolution. We were better able to exploit it to the full, before the others caught up. It wasn't just one thing but a combination of ten things, each one giving you another 200/300th of a second; if you add them up you a get a couple of seconds of advantage.

The Williams car was so successful that many questioned whether this was a case of technology taking over Formula 1 and whether the skills of the driver were becoming replaced by the technology in the car. This led to further regulations to remove many of these so-called driver-aids from the cars.

The total package: Ferrari F2004

In recent years, Ferrari has dominated the Formula 1 Championships, with cars such as the Championship-winning F2004. So, what innovations have been applied to make these cars so competitively outstanding? Ross Brawn, former Technical Director, Ferrari, said:

Ferrari doesn't have an individual feature, perhaps it never has had, but our innovation is an integration of the whole. Our efforts have always been to make everything as good as it can be, but to work together as a complete package.

Ferrari's innovation is in process and mindset rather than in the technology itself. Since the Ford DFV engine was first raced in 1967 it shifted the dominant design of a Formula 1 car to the chassis, with the engine simply being bolted into the rear of the car (instead of its conventional position in the front). This approach enabled many teams to be Grand Prix winners and developed into a situation where engines were invariably 'outsourced' from engine partners; and, even where the engines are 'in-house', these can easily be made at a different site, perhaps in a different country, as is the case with Renault F1.

However, when he joined Ferrari, Technical Director Ross Brawn wanted to maximise the unique characteristics of Ferrari – having their chassis and engine design in one location, in the small town of Maranello near Modena, in Northern Italy. He said:

When I left Benetton we were using a Renault engine but so were Williams and there was always a conflict about what sort of engine they wanted and what sort of engine we wanted. I really felt that if we could get into a situation where the engine was completely integrated into the car then that must be the best situation. So one of the things that was very important to myself and Rory [Chief Designer Rory Byrne] was to have someone here who understood that and luckily Paolo Martinelli [former Ferrari Engine Director] very quickly appreciated our ideas and was completely receptive to the idea of a fully integrated engine as part of the car package.

One of the key ways in which they achieved this was by maximising the integration between the engine and the other systems of the car, as outlined by their former Engine Director Paolo Martinelli:

I think the integration of the work [between chassis and engine] has been a continuous process and is ongoing, so I think year by year, we are continuing in this direction. I think it was very important that there was trust from the top management and the direction given from the top, from Mr Montezemolo [President] and from Jean Todt.

We do have some cross-functional areas; for example, electronics. We do not have electronics for the chassis and a separate group for the engine and gearbox, they cover the whole car and they help us to integrate the designs between chassis and engine. It is the same for metallurgy, they cover the whole car. Within each area we have experts who also work together, for example, in the area of CFD [Computational Fluid Dynamics] where someone in the chassis group may be working on design of the airbox and someone in the engine group is working on the flow of gases in the engine, they may often share ideas and calculations.

The tuned mass damper: Renault R25

In 2005 Renault introduced the concept of the 'Tuned Mass Damper' (TMD) to Formula 1. Interestingly, applications of the concept of the mass damper have been around for some time and can be found in objects such as the domestic washing machine and the Citroen 2CV. As with most great innovations the concept of the mass damper is ingeniously simple. Dampers absorb vibration and by locating a tuneable damper – the damper is adjustable to absorb particular frequencies – in the body of the car, Renault was able to both create a performance advantage and develop an innovation which was difficult for the competition to imitate quickly. The value of the tuned mass damper is that it cancels out the natural vibration of the tyres, which is transmitted through the chassis of the car, thereby increasing the adhesion of the tyres and reducing wear.

Renault had exclusive use of the TMD during 2005, as the other teams had not been able to quickly recognise the system or develop a response. However, into 2006 it was believed that a number of other teams had developed their own interpretations of the Renault system. Controversially, the FIA made the decision to ban mass dampers half-way through 2006, at a time when Renault was leading the World Championship. Despite the ban, Renault was able to secure both the Drivers' and Constructors' titles in that year. Interestingly, following the ban both McLaren and Ferrari developed damping systems which were smaller and integrated with the suspension systems, and there-fore, less likely to fall into the category of a moveable aerodynamic device – which was the basis for the ban by the FIA.

The 'J' damper (apparently a random letter used by McLaren) uses a spinning mass inside the device to absorb the vibrations from the tyres, thereby producing a similar beneficial effect as the tuned mass damper.[36]

The drive for innovation

So what makes successful innovation in Formula 1 possible? One of the most gifted and influential designers over the last thirty years is John Barnard. Many of his ideas form the basis of the conventional Formula 1 car today. He summarised some of his ideas around being innovative in design:

If it's a really innovative project then that means that I can't be 100 per cent sure that it's going to work. So the one thing I always try to do when I'm either sitting down to design something, or I've got an idea in my head, is to have a back-up solution. I would generally try and think as I'm doing it 'Okay if it doesn't work what do I do?' so that I'm ready for that catastrophic event that there is something that we haven't foreseen that is so bad there is no other way to go but dump it. I tend to approach things like that, because you're not

*going to get too many chances to be very innovative in any business
and you have to recognise that everything is going to have some sort
of problem. That problem is either fixable in a fairly short space of
time, hopefully, or it's so big that you've got to think of another direction. Effectively, don't get caught, be ready for the unimaginable,
that your brainwave idea doesn't work.*

Underlining Barnard's approach is the fact that truly innovative thinking has to be methodical, structured and above all have the total commitment of those behind it. He continued,

*Give it a bit of time. Get to understand more about what you're try-
ing to bring this innovative idea into, what sort of field you're coming
into and understand more of the problems, and strength of character
really. Most times I would say eight out of ten people will rubbish
an innovative idea. Carbon monocoques and all the rest of it all got
rubbished by people in the business, paddle shift, all the rest of it, all
got rubbished. 'Why, what's the point? It'll hit something, be a cloud
of black dust!' Be ready for that and don't let it put you off, because
it's very easy to be steered away from it by someone you think should
know what they're talking about.*

10 | *Transforming: breaking out of the old ways*

There is no silver bullet to achieving success at Honda Formula 1, no switches that can be turned. We have to make sure that we are progressing all the time and that next year's car is better than this year's and the year after that is better than the year before and over a period we will achieve our ambitions.

Ross Brawn, Team Principal,
Honda Racing F1 team

Change is all-pervasive in Formula 1, whether it is the hundreds of small design changes made to a car during the course of a year, or the fact that the individuals employed within Formula 1 are likely to work for eight different teams during the course of their careers.[37] The teams themselves have an average lifetime of less than six years (115 constructor teams since 1950!) and are frequently either dissolved or acquired by other teams, creating a constant state of flux.

There are many explanations for the constant pace of change that pervades Formula 1. Not least is the incessant search for technological advantage. As a consequence, many radical ideas have disrupted the evolution of the Formula 1 car. These have included such developments as gas turbines, four-wheel drive and six-wheel cars.

In Formula 1 regulation not only responds to and tempers technological advances, it also causes change. There regulation can be a contentious issue and often the focus of political manoeuvring by the teams to try to ensure that changes benefit their own situation and disadvantage their competitors. The pressures for regulation can be grouped around three key areas: safety, competitive racing and cost reduction.

The safety imperative

The imperative of safety within the regulations of Formula 1 has steadily emerged since the 1960s when fatalities were all too frequent and a small number of drivers, such as Jackie Stewart, were outspoken in their criticism of safety standards. In 1978 Professor Sid Watkins was appointed as Grand Prix Surgeon, with the remit to develop overall medical standards at Grand Prix circuits. The efforts of Professor Watkins and his colleagues undoubtedly improved the situation, particularly in terms of the care that drivers received when injured on track.[38] However, more urgent pressure for radical change was created in 1994, following the serious accident that befell Rubens Barrichello in his Jordan during the Friday practice and the deaths of drivers Roland Ratzenberger and three times World Champion Ayrton Senna, in three separate accidents at the San Marino Grand Prix weekend at Imola in San Marino, Italy.

By 1994 there had been a period of eleven years without a single fatality, and many of those working within Formula 1 had never experienced the loss of a driver at a Grand Prix event. There was universal shock within the Formula 1 community, among the Formula 1 fans, but also beyond, among the public at large. Senna's death had been covered by live television broadcasts and there was widespread condemnation of safety levels within the sport, from the press, governments, sponsors and even the Vatican.

Max Mosley, FIA President, stated at that time that the only acceptable safety objective was zero fatalities and zero serious injuries. Mosley established the FIA Safety Committee, chaired by Sid Watkins, to explore how this objective could be achieved. Since then, safety regulations have covered many areas from the construction and testing of the cars, to the equipment worn by the drivers and the design of the circuits to protect both drivers and spectators. As the racing car designers constantly strive for enhanced performance, so must the regulators respond to meet increased speeds with appropriate measures to ensure the safety of all those involved.

But within the regulatory body a new imperative has developed, one which seeks to keep Formula 1 in touch with changes in the broader global environment and also to address the increasing problem of cost inflation, relative to the entertainment value of the sport. The FIA's Tony Purnell has been giving serious consideration to these areas. In Purnell's view a key part of the challenge is to keep Formula 1 relevant to the environmental agenda, to reduce costs, and also improve the show:

I would certainly like to make the races more entertaining, you know, because there's something wrong if the TV is dribbling away and the Formula 1 sizzle is sensational but the beef not that great.

Destroying competitive advantage

From the perspective of competitive racing the regulations seek to minimise any areas of competitive advantage a team may develop in order to maximise the competition on the track. There have been various regulations passed over the years in order to try to reduce the technological advantage of particular cars. However, it is interesting to note that invariably these regulations lag behind the innovations. This is perhaps not surprising, in that a regulation can only be drafted once the source of advantage is more widely understood or 'codified', thus enabling the regulation to effectively remove it. For example, it took a number of years before the principles of ground-effect aerodynamics were fully disseminated around the Formula 1 paddock. It was only when these concepts were fully understood that regulations were changed banning ground-effects, in order to prevent continually increasing cornering speeds, which were considered too fast and potentially dangerous at that time. There have also been situations where cars have been banned on their first race, or even beforehand. In 1978 Brabham designer Gordon Murray developed the Brabham 'fan-car', which used a mechanical fan to enhance the ground effect which other cars were achieving aerodynamically. However, the fan created a dust cloud behind the car as it raced around the track and it was banned on safety grounds, after winning its first Grand Prix at Anderstorp in Sweden. Another example was the Continuously Variable Transmission (CVT) system developed by Williams in the early 1990s. This system removed the need to change gear, with a belt and pulley system ensuring that the wheel speed was matched to the track conditions, the engine running constantly at maximum power. The system was based on technology used on the DAF road car, which had been developed by Van Doorne Transmission. The car appeared at a test session at Silverstone in 1993 driven by then Williams test driver David Coulthard. It was rumoured that a number of competitors had identified the huge potential of the system during the test, and somehow regulations were drawn up banning the use of CVT by the end of the year. Therefore, despite all the time and cash Williams had invested, it was never able to race the system in a Grand Prix.

Reducing costs

Regulation has also been used to reduce costs by stipulating certain standardised components to be used and reducing the usage of certain items. For example, in 2004 a regulation was passed which stipulated that each driver could only use one engine during a race weekend (in 2008 an engine must last two races or the team faces penalties should replacement of an engine be required) the intention being to prevent cost escalation by reducing the number of engines used over the course of a season. The impact of this change was significant to the engine builders. They now had to change their specifications regarding the lifetime of engines, resulting in many components having to be redesigned in order to cope with this change. As observed by Cosworth Racing's former Commercial Director, Bernard Ferguson, while the objective of the regulation was to cut costs, that was not necessarily the outcome:

The biggest cost for an engine manufacturer is obsolescence, so for us, the less change the better.

In addition to the changes created by the competition on the track, many changes were also created by the commercial demands of Formula 1. As discussed in Chapter 6, until the 1970s Formula 1 teams were either funded by car manufacturers or by private individuals, such as Rob Walker who funded his racing activities from the wealth created by his family's Johnnie Walker whisky business. Walker successfully ran his own team with cars purchased from Lotus and Cooper using top-class drivers such as Stirling Moss and Jack Brabham. When car sponsorship was introduced the teams needed to develop marketing and sales operations in order to both recruit and manage sponsors. As was noted earlier, during the 1970s, 1980s and early 1990s much of this sponsorship came from the tobacco companies who, due to increased legislation on tobacco advertising, had fewer and fewer alternatives to promote their products. In the

1990s Formula 1 enjoyed huge growth, both in terms of the television exposure and viewing figures, which ultimately attracted the car manufacturers back on a far larger scale than had been the case for many years.

The effect on Formula 1 teams was that they were transformed from micro-businesses – in 1971 the Brabham team employed seven full-time people[39] whereas the Championship-winning Tyrrell team had nineteen[40] – to medium-sized enterprises. Some today employ over 1,000 people. These factors have combined to create an organisational landscape which is continually changing and placing new challenges on those teams who seek to compete in Formula 1. While at one level it looks a particularly challenging environment, Sir Frank Williams has no illusions as to how well protected the Formula 1 world can be:

Many people say if you went into the real world you'd be a billionaire. I think it's quite the reverse. Formula 1 is a protected environment, outside it's a lot more cut throat. Look at the retail world, I don't think we'd last ten minutes outside.

For sure, the priorities of a small team struggling to stay alive against better-funded competitors are very clear. Several years ago we asked Paul Stoddart, who owned and ran the Minardi team that was eventually sold to Red Bull and renamed Toro Rosso, what made his situation different from that of the larger teams:

It sounds a simple answer but it's one word, survival. That is our biggest challenge and simply put we're competing on less than 10 per cent of the budget yet expected to consistently produce 96–98 per cent of the performance.

So how do the different teams deal with the constant pressure for change and what are some of the factors that explain how some are able to adapt whereas others do not? One perspective on organisational change is that organisations find it relatively easy to change incrementally – or in small steps – because such change fits with their dominant paradigm or mindset.[41] In the context of Formula 1 the pace of incremental change is probably far higher than in the average organisation, because of the flexible, problem-solving and informal basis on which they operate. This is illustrated in Figure 16.

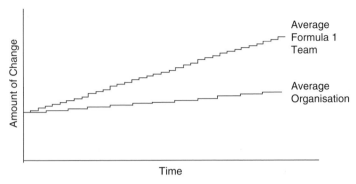

Figure 16 Comparative rates of incremental change

However, even though change is pervasive and impressive in Formula 1, it is nonetheless incremental change; it occurs in discrete steps within a dominant mindset and therefore produces relatively predictable outcomes. Incremental change in the context of Formula 1 would cover aspects such as changing sponsors and technology partners, adapting to new regulations, bringing in new people, systems, and so forth. The rate of change will also vary by team. For the smaller teams issues such as partnerships can change even race by race, presenting them with a very different problem when compared to Ferrari or McLaren as examples whose major partners would be retained on three- or five-year contracts.

As an organisational type we suggest that the flexible and responsive Formula 1 teams are able to deal with higher levels of incremental change than their counterparts in other kinds of industries. However, the challenge comes when they have to achieve more radical steps in performance improvement, which require fundamental changes in mindset, rather than continuous improvement within the existing organisational framework.

These radical changes are required when the competitive landscape is changing faster than the organisation's ability to change with it. If an organisation fails to respond to these changes it is unlikely to survive in the longer term.

As indicated in Appendix B, fifty-two teams have entered and not survived long-term in the Formula 1 arena. Many were just not capable of responding to the ever-changing landscape within the sport. Perhaps one of the most disastrous recent attempts was Lola cars in

1997. Established by former quantity surveyor Eric Broadley in 1957, Lola became a highly successful manufacturer of racing cars, at one time dominating the CART/Champ Cars series in the US, and winning the Indianapolis 500 in 1978 with Al Unser. It had a number of forays into Formula 1, first with a Broadley-designed car in 1962 and then in 1974 designing and building cars for Graham Hill's Embassy-Hill team. After several projects during the late 1980s, it attempted to re-enter under its own name in 1997. The outcome was that the major sponsor it had anticipated failed to materialise and while the cars arrived for the opening race at Melbourne in Australia, it was unable to take part. Lola racing folded with debts of $9 million in 1997, also forcing the parent company into administration.[14] While Lola has subsequently been turned around by new Chairman Martin Birrane, its 1997 entry into Formula 1 remains a dark period in the company's history.

We can discern three distinctive types of change situation in Formula 1. These are situations where teams have either failed to adapt to the changing competitive conditions of Formula 1 (Type 1 in Figure 17), where they have over-reacted or over-anticipated environmental change and therefore been unable to fully exploit the benefits of their transformation (Type 2 in Figure 17) or where they have been able to undertake a transformational change to re-establish their competitive position (Type 3 in Figure 17).

We consider three cases of highly successful teams which have responded in differing ways to the pressure for change and exhibit the three types illustrated in Figure 17. Each case has been used to draw out some of the principles illustrated in Figure 17 and we now expand these in further detail in order to clarify their characteristics.

For Type 1 we consider Tyrrell Racing. The team operated as a constructor from 1970 to 1998, competing in a total of 418 Grand Prix, winning 23 of these and taking the Constructors' Championship in 1971. For Type 2 we consider the Brabham Formula 1 team. It operated as a constructor from 1962 to 1992, competing in a total of 399 Grand Prix, winning 35 of these and 2 Constructors' Championships, in 1966 and 1967. Finally, for Type 3 we consider Ferrari. Competing in Formula 1 since 1950, Ferrari is the most successful team in the history of Formula 1. To the end of the 2007 season Ferrari had competed in a total of 768 races, with 201 wins and a total of 15 Constructors'

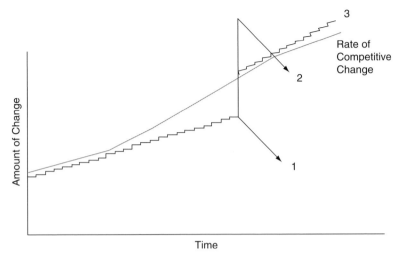

Figure 17 Differing patterns of change in Formula 1

Championships in 1961, 1964, 1975–77, 1979, 1982–83, 1999–2004 and 2007. We now review each in turn and then consider some of the issues these three case studies raise.

Tyrrell Racing (Type 1)

Figure 18 shows the success of Tyrrell Racing during the period from 1970 through to 1998. Tyrrell enjoyed a particularly successful period as a Formula 1 team, but eventually succumbed to an environment which was changing faster than its ability to adapt.

Interestingly, it was never Ken Tyrrell's intention to become a Formula 1 Constructor. Ken was a naturally gifted race team manager and talent spotter in the early 1960s, who ran his own team in the smaller Formula 3 category, with cars provided by Cooper. In 1964 he had signed the up-and-coming young driver Jackie Stewart to drive for his team. In order to improve their performance he negotiated with French aerospace and performance engineering conglomerate Matra to build a specialist chassis for the car. This it did and the relationship eventually moved into Formula 1, with Tyrrell running a Matra chassis with a Cosworth engine to win the 1969 World Drivers' Championship title for Jackie Stewart and also the Constructors' title

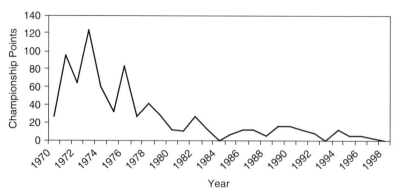

Figure 18 Tyrrell Racing, 1970–98

for Matra. However, Matra's desire to develop its own engine led to a parting of the ways, as Ken Tyrrell outlined:

Matra came to us and said if you want to use our car in 1970 then you have to use our engine. So we tried the engine. We put it in the car and took it to Albi in the South of France [North-East of Toulouse], *it made a very nice noise, but it actually didn't go very fast, so we made the decision to stay with the Ford DFV. We tried to buy a car from the established people – Lotus Brabham, McLaren, etc, but nobody would sell us a car. Fortunately March Engineering* [FIA President Max Mosley was one of the founders] *had just formed and they were prepared to build cars for anyone. So we had a car to go racing in 1970, but it was a bit of a lump, and the writing was on the wall. If we wanted to stay in Formula 1* [and be competitive] *we were going to have to build a car ourselves. I'd met Derek Gardner at Matra and I asked him whether or not he'd like to design a Formula 1 car, he said, 'Yes he would' and that's how it all started. If Matra had stayed with the DFV we would have been with Matra now, we didn't want to become a Constructor, but we had no choice.*

In the early 1970s the Tyrrell team had dominated Formula 1. With world champion driver Jackie Stewart, designer Derek Gardner and with funding from the Elf petroleum company, Ken Tyrrell had put together a winning team, until Stewart's retirement in 1973, and the untimely death of the talented Frenchman François Cevert, who was being groomed as Stewart's successor. During the mid-1970s Tyrrell was a strong midfield team, which was still winning Grand Prix and was also technologically quite innovative; in 1976 it surprised the Formula 1 community with its radical P34 six-wheel car. In 1991 it produced the first 'high nose' Formula 1 car, a design feature that was adopted by the other teams and became the dominant nose feature in Formula 1. But the real problem for Tyrrell was the changing business of Formula 1.

During the late 1980s and into the 1990s all the teams were developing highly professional marketing departments, in order to secure the range of funds needed to operate in the long term, allowing them to build up the technological infrastructure in areas such as dedicated wind tunnels, which cost tens of millions of pounds in capital cost. Many had also secured strong relationships with manufacturers to supply them with engines. Most of the teams were run as profitable businesses with state-of-the-art factories. Tyrrell, on the other hand, still operated from the original woodyard site at Ockham in Surrey, where he had started his motorsport activities in the 1960s. It was this site that had hosted the Championship-winning cars of the early 1970s and so held a great deal of the history of the team, but it was nonetheless a fairly basic facility, as former employee Jo Ramirez commented:

I had asked Ken about a job and he said to call in at the factory. Don't forget, the team had just won the World Championship in 1971. I couldn't believe it when I arrived in the woodyard for the first time. I remember thinking 'They did all that – from here? Impossible!' But it was the people rather than the place. I quickly discovered the fantastic atmosphere, and working with someone like Roger Hill, I learned so much. It was an incredible team, a very close team. If someone had a problem, then everyone would stop what they were doing and get into it. Nobody needed to say the word; everyone was there for you. And that was because of Ken and the way he worked.[40]

Some of the key problems the team faced in the 1990s were summarised by Mark Gallagher, who became Head of Marketing at Tyrrell, and who had gained his initial experience with the team in 1994. (Latterly he also worked for Jordan F1 and is now Team Principal of Team Ireland's A1 GP team.)

We got the job at Tyrrell by being blunt about their situation. That entailed telling Ken and Bob [Ken's son, who was Managing Director] *that a media survey viewed their team as being like a family shop, one that hadn't moved on ... The sport had moved on in many respects and the fact was that we had to find a way of raising the team's profile.*

In 1995 Nokia had become a major sponsor of the team after supporting Finnish driver Mika Salo, but this still didn't resolve the situation. He continued:

Nokia had been sold the deal that Tyrrell could go from a low ranking towards the top and that all they needed was money. Nokia gave them quite a big cheque, believing this would be the answer. The difficulty was that the selling of Tyrrell was always being done on rediscovering past glories. We've won three Championships with Jackie Stewart, okay, twenty years have gone by, but we still know the magic ingredient. But that was wrong, because they didn't have the infrastructure, the development facilities or the manufacturer behind them.[40]

The Tyrrell team won its last Grand Prix at Detroit, in 1983, which was also the 132nd and last win for the Ford Cosworth DFV engine. The years that followed became a constant struggle for cash and resources and the team was purchased by BAR at the end of 1997. The original plan had been for Ken to run the team as Tyrrell Racing in 1998 with it being renamed BAR in 1999. However, due to differences over the choice of drivers, Ken resigned from the team at the end of February 1998. The final race of a Tyrrell car took place at Suzuka, Japan in November 1998 without the presence of the founder of the team. Ken Tyrrell passed away on 25 August 2001. He left a legacy of the values of the team owner of the 1960s and 1970s who undoubtedly played a major role in the history and development of Formula 1; but as an example of a Type 1 in Figure 17, was unable to adjust to change.

Brabham (Type 2)

Founded by Jack Brabham with fellow Australian designer Rob Tauranac in 1962, Brabham was one of a number of teams founded

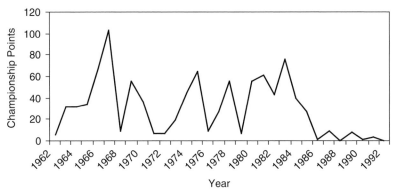

Figure 19 Brabham, 1962–92

by drivers to support their racing activities but which eventually became a successful constructor in its own right. Figure 19 shows the performance of the team from the period 1962 through to 1992.

In contrast to Tyrrell, which enjoyed success almost immediately as a constructor, it took Brabham a few seasons to establish and build up the performance of the team. However, once this had been achieved it became a successful operator, using a series of different engine suppliers such as Coventry Climax, Repco and Ford Cosworth. In 1966, at the age of forty, Brabham became the only driver to win the Drivers' World Championship in a car bearing his own name – the Brabham BT3 (the model number using the first letter of the two partners' surnames). This was followed by a further World Championship for both the Constructors' Cup and the Drivers' award, but this time with New Zealander Denny Hulme at the wheel. At the end of 1970 Brabham retired from driving, having sold his share of the team to Tauranac a year earlier and departed for Australia, to take up farming and a number of other business ventures. Interestingly, following Brabham's departure, chief mechanic Ron Dennis and his number two Neil Trundell also left, to set up Rondel Racing. Dennis went on to create a series of racing organisations, that eventually metamorphosed into McLaren International in 1982.

Tauranac found the commercial pressures of running the team, as well as designing and overseeing the construction of the cars, an unsustainable burden to bear. In the autumn of 1970 he sold the company to Bernie Ecclestone while he became joint Managing Director, with responsibility for car design and engineering. This situation remained until early in 1972 when Tauranac left the company and Ecclestone assumed full control.

Ecclestone set about restructuring the Brabham operation. He sacked four of the five-man design team and promoted the remaining designer, Gordon Murray, a 24-year-old South African, to chief designer. Ecclestone had a very direct style for running the team. Keith Greene, who became team manager of the new operation, described how he resolved the growing friction between drivers Graham Hill and Carlos Reutemann, as both believed the other was being supplied with superior engines:

Bernie said, 'Right, I'm not going to have any more arguments with these drivers. What we are going to do now is decide their engines for the year, OK?' So he got the drivers to alternately call out heads or tails while he flipped a coin and that decided who would have which engines for the year. Once the draw was finished he said: 'I don't want to hear any more about engines.' And he was gone and there were no further complaints.[39]

Ecclestone set about making some other changes to the operation. He had both the workshops and cars painted white, and redesigned the layout of the factory. Former Brabham employee Nick Goozée commented on the changes:

We found the changes, which were introduced quickly, a little over the top, but, in fact, we were not an efficient company. We were very basic in some of our methods, which had been fine in the sixties but once Bernie bought Brabham change was both inevitable and necessary.[39]

In the early 1970s the Brabham budget was around £100,000 per annum and the company employed seven full-time people. It was a very demanding time for all those involved, but the new team at Brabham had the sense that this was a new beginning with new opportunities, as outlined by Chief Designer Gordon Murray:

Bernie gave me the opportunity to be first of all Chief Designer and then Technical Director. And that was good and bad. The good thing was, and the reason the performance started to climb, that he had the trust in me to do a brand new car. He said to me: 'I'm tired of all these bits and pieces, I want a completely new Formula 1 car, we need a clear head, a clean sheet of paper. And that's why we started climbing and we led the first race in fact, with the new car and won in 1974 for the first time.

But things were very stretched and while Brabham's operation could be described in today's terms as an agile organisation, in that it was both lean and flexible, it also placed a great deal of strain on the individuals working within it:

The bad part was that he fired everybody and made me Chief Designer and, at the time, I was pretty hard headed about doing everything myself. I couldn't delegate, I wanted to draw the whole car, draw the gearbox, the body and the aerodynamics, everything. And I went far too long without any help. In fact I was on my own, running Brabham, designing and doing the truck spares and organising everything until 1978; that was far too long, by then people had an engineer on each car as well as a technical director, I was Technical Director and I was also engineering both cars, in the same race.

In addition to the organisational strains that Brabham was enduring, the competitive situation was also changing. Brabham, like most of the British-based Formula 1 constructors, was using a Ford DFV V8 engine. In 1975 Ferrari, which designed and built its own engines, was beginning a renaissance that was seeing a new kind of engine dominate the circuits – the Ferrari 'Flat 12'. The engine used four more cylinders than the DFV, and while it was heavier, the extra power it provided made it dominant on many circuits in the Grand Prix series. Ecclestone and Murray were very quick to respond to this new development and began to look around for an alternative engine to the Ford, which could provide the performance levels being enjoyed by Ferrari. Midway through 1975 they reached agreement with one of Ferrari's historic rivals, Alfa Romeo, to build them a twelve-cylinder engine similar to that currently being used by Ferrari. However, this meant that Murray had to begin work on designing a radically new car and engine combination, the Brabham BT45, midway through the 1975 season:

The BT45 was a completely new car. Well obviously it was a flat-twelve engine, it was a non-structural engine, so you couldn't use the current structure, so it was a total rethink. I had six months to design and build a flat-twelve Alfa car for the beginning of the 1976 season. And I was still halfway through the 1975 season, travelling to every race, every test, engineering both cars and running the company, and I was just about dead, basically.

In Murray's view, Brabham's desire to change radically at this point cost it the 1975 World Championship:

If we'd stuck with the [Ford] DFV, in retrospect, and developed the BT44 theme [the 1975 car], we would probably have matched Ferrari. The new team had only been together for three years and we were very understaffed, underfunded and we were learning to work together. I was running it like a really tight, small family.

Brabham had some success with the Alfa Romeo engine, but it took far longer to develop into a competitive package than it had anticipated:

We had no way of judging what sort of engine Alfa would make – we just assumed that it would be a reasonably good engine. The engine was very big, very heavy and incredibly thirsty. It didn't work, basically, it took most of the practice sessions to get the thing to run, let alone race, at the first Grand Prix.

While the technical team at Brabham was struggling to develop the Alfa Romeo engine, a new innovation was being developed by Lotus, which was to revolutionise the basis of Formula 1 car design, this time by making use of the airflow under the car to create a low-pressure area. The car was effectively sucked onto the track. This innovation, which became known as ground-effect aerodynamics, provided the cars with hugely increased downforce. The problem for Brabham was that this development was impractical when using a 'flat twelve' engine layout, because it meant that there wasn't the same capacity for airflow under the car as with the Ford DFV 'V' formation engines. This is shown in Figure 20.

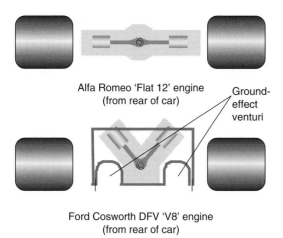

Alfa Romeo 'Flat 12' engine
(from rear of car)

Ground-effect
venturi

Ford Cosworth DFV 'V8' engine
(from rear of car)

Figure 20 Car profile for ground-effect aerodynamics

Murray therefore had to face the problem of again radically redesigning the Brabham car:

I'd said to Bernie, we're just about getting up there again, we've shot ourselves in the foot by going with Alfa, we're just starting to climb up again and now this ground effect, and he said 'What's ground effect?' Bernie's essentially non-technical and I got up and drew this thing, and I said I can't get past the engine – right where the venturi diffuser [the shaped underside of the car that creates the area of additional performance] *wants to start expanding, we've got a twelve-cylinder engine sticking out there and exhaust pipes. So he said 'Well, what are we going to do?' We sat there racking our brains, thinking how else can we do this – you know, we've got to have a ground-effect car. How can you have ground effect or downforce with a flat-twelve engine? The fan-car* [another radical design where the mechanically operated fan assisted ground-effect performance] *bought us time to go back to Alfa and say – we need a V12 engine.*

In fact, Alfa Romeo was able to respond more quickly than Ferrari to this new development, and provided a new V12 engine for Brabham to start to race in 1979. By this time everyone was returning to the Ford DFV as the ideal engine to use with ground-effect aerodynamics.

Brabham bowed to the inevitable and switched to the Ford DFV at the Canadian Grand Prix in September 1979.

The fortunes of the Brabham team took a marked upturn in 1981, when driver Nelson Piquet secured the Drivers' World Championship title by a margin of one point, in the ground-effect car with the Ford DFV engine. In 1982 it switched from the normally aspirated Ford DFV to a turbo-charged four-cylinder BMW engine. Renault had entered Formula 1 with a turbo engine in 1978, and won its first Grand Prix in 1979. With the banning of ground-effect skirts in 1982 Brabham was able to emulate Renault and Ferrari and switch to a turbo-charged engine supplied by BMW partway through 1982. However, the BMW engine, while hugely powerful, suffered from reliability problems.

In 1983 these problems were resolved and, when combined with Gordon Murray's revolutionary 'pit-stop' car (as discussed in Chapter 9 on Innovating), Brabham was able to win its fourth and final World Drivers' Championship. Brazilian Nelson Piquet took the Drivers' Championship for Brabham BMW in 1983, with Brabham also coming third in the Constructors' Championship.

This was the last positive highlight in the history of Brabham. With Ecclestone increasingly involved with the Formula One Constructors' Association (FOCA), and also becoming central to the negotiation of television and advertising rights for the Formula 1 series as a whole, Brabham was left more and more to its own devices. Nelson Piquet, who had given the team many victories, quit at the end of 1985, being unable to agree terms with Ecclestone for the 1986 season. In 1987 a dispirited Gordon Murray left to join the McLaren team, with whom he enjoyed a successful period as Technical Director, as well as going on to develop a series of high-performance McLaren road cars.

During 1987 Brabham only managed eighth place in the Constructors' Championship. In 1988 it did not submit an entry to compete in the World Championship and Bernie Ecclestone sold Brabham and its holding company, Motor Racing Developments, to Alfa Romeo. Alfa intended to use the team as a basis for a production car racing project. Later in 1988, Brabham was again sold, this time to a Swiss financier Joachim Lüthi.[39] However, the team was kept afloat with support from Japanese sponsor Nippon Shinpan, and in March 1990 was purchased by the Middlebridge Group of Japan.

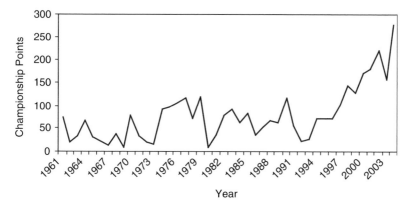

Figure 21 Ferrari, 1961–2004

Brabham did manage to keep going up to 1992, with the Italian female driver Giovanna Amati. It also introduced driver Damon Hill to Formula 1. Hill finished eleventh at the Hungarian Grand Prix of 1992, Brabham's final race. Hill went on to become World Champion in 1996 driving for Williams.

In 1993 the FIA declared that Brabham would not be allowed to enter the World Championship in 1994 unless all its debts were settled, a demand it was unable to meet. This brought to an end the journey of a team that had been the first Championship winner for an owner-driver, had produced many highly innovative and striking cars, and also provided the basis by which Bernie Ecclestone became President of FOCA and subsequently a Vice-President of the FIA. While the company disappeared, many loyal Brabham employees such as Herbie Blash and Charlie Whiting took on key roles with the Formula One Administration, in fact, so much in evidence were the former employees of Brabham that they became known in Formula 1 circles as 'BOBs' or Brabham Old Boys.

Ferrari (Type 3)

Founded by Enzo Ferrari in 1929, Ferrari is the oldest Formula 1 team by some margin. It is the only team that has been in Formula 1 since its inception and at the end of 2008 was the most successful team in the history of Formula 1. Figure 21 shows the performance of the team from the period 1961 through to 2004, which is examined in this section of the chapter.

In 2004 Ferrari won its sixth successive World Constructors' Championship title, the first time this had happened since the award began in 1958. Furthermore, driver Michael Schumacher won his fifth successive Drivers' World Championship, the first time a driver had achieved such a concentrated dominance. His previous World Championships for the Benetton team in 1994 and 1995 also meant that he surpassed Juan Manuel Fangio's record of five World Championships with a total of seven, making him the most successful World Champion since Formula 1 began in 1950. However, this success had not come without controversy. At the Austrian Grand Prix of 2002 Ferrari was accused of unsporting behaviour, when its second driver, Rubens Barrichello, who had dominated the race, moved over on the last corner to allow Michael Schumacher to win, thereby maximising Schumacher's World Championship points. While there was a furore in the press, the Ferrari management remained stoical about its approach. After all, this success had been a long time coming – its 1999 Constructors' Championship title had been their first for sixteen years, during which the honours had been dominated by the British-based Williams, McLaren and Benetton teams. Ferrari's focus had always been to secure the Drivers' Championship, and Schumacher's title in 2000 had been Ferrari's first since Jody Scheckter in 1979; a gap of twenty-one years.

Scuderia Ferrari

In 1929 Enzo Ferrari, a former driver with the 'works' Alfa Romeo Grand Prix team, created Scuderia Ferrari (SF) based in Modena, between Parma and Bologna in North Eastern Italy. SF prepared Alfa Romeo cars for competition by private enthusiasts; in 1932 Alfa Romeo outsourced all of its racing activity to SF. The partnership between SF and Alfa Romeo was a very successful one, winning 144 out of the 225 races up to 1937. Following the Second World War, Alfa Romeo split with SF and Enzo Ferrari went on to build his first car at his new factory in Maranello, some 10 km from Modena. The Ferrari 125 made its debut in May 1947.

A key feature of the 125 was the Ferrari supercharged twelve-cylinder engine, the first in a long line of *dodici cilindri* to feature in

Ferrari cars. The 125 was entered into the first season of Formula 1 in 1950, which was won by Alfa Romeo. In 1952 Ferrari secured its first World Drivers' Championship (the Constructors' Championship did not start until 1958) for Alberto Ascari. Ascari went on to win a further Championship in 1953 and this was followed up by Mike Hawthorn in 1958. Around this time the red Italian cars of Ferrari, Alfa Romeo and Maserati were beginning to be outpaced by the smaller, lightweight Coopers and Lotuses whose designs focused on maximising mechanical grip through better weight distribution and improved suspensions. This was in contrast to the philosophy at Ferrari, where the engine was always the starting point of car design and the search for enhanced performance.

Enzo Ferrari had a rather enigmatic approach to running his company. After the death of his son Dino he very rarely left the Modena area, and hardly ever attended a race, preferring instead to spend his time either in the factory or at the Ferrari test facilities. He relied on the Italian media – which had always reflected Italy's strong interest in Ferrari – and his closest advisors for information. This often created a highly political atmosphere in the team.

Ferrari initially resisted the trend being pioneered by the British constructors, whom he referred to as '*assemblatori*' or '*garagistes*'. He defended the engine layout of the Ferrari with the analogy that the 'horse' had always pulled, not pushed, the cart (although he later denied having made this statement). Not an engineer himself, the designers who Ferrari employed up to 1980 (Alberto Massimino, Gioachino Colombo, Carlo Chiti and Mauro Forghieri) had first learnt their trade as engine designers, and so the design of a new car would always start with the engine. Ferrari himself often referred to '*the song of the twelve*', underlining the distinctive high-pitched note of the Ferrari power unit.

However, by 1960 the dominance of the British cars was clear, and Ferrari had to build a lighter rear-engined car, which it did using a highly effective V6 engine. The Dino 156 (1.5 litre, V6) or 'shark nose' dominated 1961 and gave Ferrari a further Drivers' title (for American Phil Hill) and Constructors' World Championship title. However, the advances made in chassis construction by other teams had meant that it was increasingly uncompetitive and, in 1964, the Ferrari 158 was launched with a similar monocoque-type chassis to the Lotus 25 of 1962.

Also in 1964 Ferrari first tried out the 'Flat 12' engine developed by Mauro Forghieri. Originally commissioned for an aircraft application, the Flat 12 was designed to fit into the wing of an aircraft. However, it was powerful, relatively light and its flat profile gave it a low centre of gravity, which would help in improving mechanical grip. It was this twelve-cylinder unit that was seen to be the future for Ferrari.

Merging with Fiat

In the late 1960s Ferrari merged with Italian automotive manufacturer Fiat. This was, in effect, a benign acquisition, with Fiat acquiring 40 per cent of the equity in Ferrari, thereby providing a huge injection of cash to support research and development. This allowed the construction of a private Grand Prix circuit at Fiorano adjacent to the SF factory in Maranello. The technical team used this facility to engage in a period of intensive development focusing on the 'Flat 12' engine.

The new ownership and influence from Fiat meant increased resources, but also increased pressure for results. In the early 1970s Formula 1 was dominated by the Ford DFV engine (see Chapter 9). Built by Cosworth Engineering near Northampton and funded by the Ford Motor Company, the DFV was Formula 1's first widely available purpose-built engine; it was light, powerful and relatively inexpensive. In 1968 the engines were available for £7,500 per unit and were fully capable of winning a Grand Prix. This enabled the British constructors, who specialised in chassis design, to become increasingly competitive. In 1971 and 1973 every Grand Prix was won by a car using a DFV engine. Its impact was that it made the cars both very light and very powerful; at a time when tyre technology was relatively primitive, this left the designers searching for other ways to increase grip. The answer came from aerodynamics with aircraft-type 'wings' being used to create downforce (negative lift), described technically as aerodynamic grip, allowing the cars to both enter and exit corners at vastly increased speeds.

1970s renaissance

During this time Enzo Ferrari had been suffering from ill health. Now in his 70s, he made the decision to appoint a team manager to run the day-to-day activities of the Formula 1 team. Luca di Montezemolo was a 25-year-old lawyer who was also connected to Fiat's Agnelli dynasty. In addition, Mauro Forghieri had been recalled to Ferrari in 1973, as Technical Director. In 1975 the fruits of Montezemolo's team building, Forghieri's creative ideas and the intensive testing at Fiorano were exemplified in the new 312T which featured a wide low body with a powerful 'flat 12' twelve-cylinder engine and a revolutionary transverse (sideways mounted) gearbox which improved the balance of the car, making it handle extremely well. While the new car was not ready until the season had already started, driver Niki Lauda, with the support of teammate Clay Regazzoni, was able to easily secure both the Drivers' and Constructors' World Championships.

The Ferraris dominated the 1975 season. With their elegant styling, handling and the power advantage of the engine, they were in a class of their own. Ferrari success continued, winning in 1976 (Constructors' Championship), 1977 (Drivers' and Constructors' Championships), and 1979 (Drivers' and Constructors' Championships). But perhaps its greatest moment was in the 1979 season when Ferrari finished first and second at the Italian Grand Prix at Monza. This sent the fanatical Italian fans, or *tifosi,* and the Italian press into a complete frenzy.

By 1980 the 312T5 car was outclassed by the competition. New innovations in aerodynamic design brought the 'ground-effect' revolution, pioneered by Lotus and quickly adopted by Williams (see Chapter 9). While the Ferrari's engine was one of the most powerful, it was a 'flat 12' meaning that the cylinders were horizontal to the ground, creating a low and wide barrier, which gave little opportunity to create the ground effect achieved with the slimmer V8 DFV engines (see Figure 20).

In 1979, as engine supplier to Brabham, Alfa Romeo had launched a V12 engine to replace its flat 12 for this very reason. No such initiative had been taken at Ferrari, which had concentrated on a longer-term project to develop a V6 turbo-charged engine. *Autosport* correspondent Nigel Roebuck commented on this change of fortune:

Maranello's flat 12, still a magnificent racing engine, is incompatible with modern chassis. Villeneuve and Scheckter were competing in yesterday's cars.[43]

The lowest point came in the Canadian Grand Prix, when the reigning World Champion, Jody Scheckter, failed to qualify his Ferrari for the race, the equivalent of Italy failing to qualify for the soccer World Cup. Once again the full wrath of the Italian press descended on the team.

The Ferrari GTO

In the mid-1980s more and more investment was poured into the Italian facilities, but to no effect on performance. A key problem was that new developments in aerodynamics and the use of composite materials had all emerged from the UK's Motorsport Valley.

In 1984, British designer Harvey Postlethwaite became the first non-Italian Technical Director of Ferrari and in 1986 British designer John Barnard was recruited to the top technical role. Barnard was responsible for the introduction of the carbon-composite chassis into Formula 1 in 1981; this material created a lighter and stronger chassis than the aluminium monocoques which had previously been used. It is now accepted as an essential and central part of Formula 1 design.

Barnard was not, however, prepared to move to Italy as he felt that his technical team and network of contacts in the UK would be essential to his success in the role of Technical Director. Surprisingly Enzo Ferrari, now eighty-eight years of age, allowed him to establish a design and manufacturing facility near Guildford in Surrey. Barnard said:

Through intermediaries, Enzo Ferrari contacted me and the outcome was that I didn't want to go to Italy, but he wanted me so he said, "Okay, do you want to set something up in England?' and given that opportunity I said 'Yes'. So we started what was called 'GTO' which stood for Guildford Technical Office. Ferrari was at that time [1986] fundamentally an engine company and the chassis was always second place. Enzo saw what was going on in the British side of Formula 1 with the introduction of composites and so on, so he wanted to give the chassis side a boost.

The fact that Barnard was defining the technical direction of Ferrari meant that he became increasingly involved in activities at both sites. The geographical separation between the car and engine departments led to the development of various 'factions' within Ferrari, making Barnard's job increasingly difficult. In 1987, on arrival at Maranello, he became famous for ordering a ban on the consumption of wine at the midday canteen:

When I went racing and testing with them in '87, in the middle of the day out come the tables, out come the white tablecloths, and a bottle of Lambrusco or something on the table, and they all sit down and tuck in. You know, pasta, a glass of wine, that's what they tended to do for their lunch. Marco Piccinini, Enzo's right-hand man said 'What did you do at McLaren?' I said, 'Well we'd have a few sandwiches and a cup of tea and get on with it', you don't stop, you just have a quick snack and then you were eating at 6 o'clock in the evening or something like that because it's all going on and you've got to get ready for qualifying and so on. 'Yes,' he said, 'I thought so.' He said, 'Do you want to change the way they do this? Because it's up to you if you want to change this ... we can ...' and I said 'Well yes I think we should Marco, you can't sit down in the middle of the day, it's completely unrealistic, if you've got work to do on the car, you've got to be keen ...' 'Right' he said 'Well leave it to me ...' and of course the next thing you know 'John Barnard bans wine', it was a classic, and Marco climbs in there and said 'Mr Barnard he doesn't want the glass of wine ... sorry but what can I do, he's the boss' and I thought 'Right, I'll watch you Mr!' but at the end of the day it's what needed to happen. It was probably things like that, that Enzo saw were fundamentally wrong with the team, but he didn't know how to change them.

Enzo Ferrari's death in 1988 created a vacuum which for a number of years was filled by a series of executives from the Fiat organisation. It was written into the contract between Fiat and Ferrari that on Enzo's death, Fiat's original stake would be increased to 90 per cent. This greater investment led to attempts to run Ferrari as a formal subsidiary of the Fiat group.

Barnard became frustrated with the interference and politics of the situation and left to join Benetton in 1989. Ferrari had recruited World Champion Alain Prost to drive for it in 1990, but while the GTO-designed 1990 car was highly competitive (an example of that year's Ferrari 641 was displayed in New York's Museum of Modern

Art), the organisation was falling apart and in 1991 Prost was actually fired by the Ferrari management for criticising the car and, thereby, the sacred name of Ferrari. Former driver Patrick Tambay commented on the situation:

No-one's in charge anymore. When the Old Man was alive the buck stopped with him. Maybe he took some curious decisions – but at least he took them. I'm not saying that Ferrari will never win again, but the fabric of what the name meant has gone. There are so many layers of management, so many bosses reporting to bosses, until ultimately it gets to Gianni Agnelli [Chairman of Fiat].[42]

Transforming the Prancing Horse

At the end of 1991, Agnelli appointed Luca di Montezemolo as CEO, with a mandate to do whatever was needed to take Ferrari back to the top. Since leaving Ferrari in 1976 Montezemolo had taken on a range of high-profile management roles, including running Italy's hosting of the Soccer World Cup in 1990. Di Montezemolo accepted the role on the basis that Ferrari and in particular, the racing operation, was independent of Fiat. Montezemolo understood he was about to embark on something different:

I have not been in the Fiat management stream for ten years. Maranello is another world and has to be treated as such.[45]

In an article in *Autosport*, he described the situation as follows:

After I arrived last December [1991] *I spent five months working to understand the situation. To understand the manpower, to understand the potential of the car. Once I had absorbed all this I decided to approach the whole situation in a completely different manner. Ferrari had become an inflexible monolith of a company, which was no good for racing. As a result I decided to divide it into three small departments: future developments and special projects in the UK under John Barnard; the engine department in Maranello under Paolo Massai; and finally the Scuderia Ferrari under Harvey Postlethwaite, which is the place where we build the cars and manage the team.*

I also wanted to build up a strong relationship between our UK facility and Italy in order to take full advantage of the Formula 1 'Silicon Valley' in England for chassis development and specialist sub-contractors while still harnessing the huge potential of Maranello.[46]

When asked why he was repeating the 'GTO' initiative that Enzo Ferrari had set up with Barnard and which had ultimately ended with Barnard leaving and taking the facility with him, Montezemolo had a very clear response:

I think that the GTO concept of Enzo Ferrari was a super idea. Unfortunately, at the time Ferrari was very old and the situation was managed in a bad way. But the fundamental idea was very good. For me the approach is slightly different. First of all, I am in charge of the company with full powers, so I can take a decision without anyone else taking a parallel initiative. I take my responsibilities and I want the people in the company to follow my ideas. If they follow, I am very happy. If they don't then there are many other doors, many possibilities available to them outside Ferrari.

My objective is to create a smaller racing department which contains less bureaucracy. Of course there will be a lot of discussion between the engine and chassis departments. In Maranello we have a huge organisation geared to building cars, but I want to take advantage of the UK facilities, and for a worldwide company like Ferrari it is certainly not a scandal to have an affiliate in the UK. If you want to make pasta, then you have to be in Parma; I want to make a sophisticated Formula 1 project, so I want to be involved in England. Then it is up to me to put everything together.[46]

In August 1992 John Barnard signed a five-year contract with Ferrari to design and develop its new cars. In an effort to avoid a 'them and us' situation between the UK and Italy a number of Italian technical people were recruited to work for Barnard in the UK. The re-established UK operation was called Ferrari Design and Development (FDD) and was a Ferrari-owned subsidiary.

At the launch of the 1992 car, Luca di Montezemolo broke with tradition, and introduced a new numbering system based on the year a car would be racing, an approach which has been followed from 1992 up to the Championship-winning F2004. Prior to this the numbering of many Ferrari cars had been based on the characteristics of the engine – the 312 of 1971 representing 3.0 litre 12 cylinders; the 126C4 of 1984 representing a 120° 'V' angle with 6 cylinders, and C standing for 'Compression' or turbo-charging. Montezemolo said:

At Ferrari we have always devoted and will continue to devote, great attention to racing; racing is part of the history, the culture and the traditions of this company. We live in a country in which, especially in recent times, people have yelled and complained a bit too much. We hope that the only noise around here will be our engine as it sets new lap records at Fiorano. We are looking for a revival here, and with an eye to the future we have tried to put together a group which combines young engineers, many of them with the highest qualifications, and people whose enthusiasm and abilities will make a notable contribution. We have a lot of work to do; we have a lot of ground to make up on the opposition. We have code-named the new car F92A to demonstrate that we are turning a new page in our history.[45]

When asked about drivers in 1992, he also gave some further indication of his thinking:

The main priority is the new organisation. We are lucky because it is a big challenge to offer a driver the chance to help re-establish Ferrari to a competitive level. I want a driver who is motivated and prepared to work with us. Motivation is everything in a driver, as Niki Lauda reminds us![46]

In addition to the structural changes, di Montezemolo had also brought in some familiar faces from Ferrari's successful period in the mid-1970s: driver Niki Lauda acted as a consultant to the team and Sante Ghedini took on the role of team manager. With an Englishman heading up design di Montezemolo followed this up with the appointment of a Frenchman, Jean Todt, to handle the overall management of the team. Todt had no experience in Formula 1 but had been in motorsport management for many years and had recently led a successful rally and Group C Sportscar programme at Peugeot with 1982

World Champion Keke Rosberg at the wheel. Driver Gerhard Bergher commented on Todt's team building skills:

I was able to bring some links in the chain to Ferrari, but it took Todt to join them together. Ferrari is now working as a team for the first time. He has made a huge difference.[46]

Chief Mechanic Nigel Stepney joined Ferrari in 1993, but his first impressions were not positive:

When I joined Ferrari at the beginning of 1993, it was like being thrown into the lion's den. I was in a non-position, regarded as John Barnard's spy and not allowed to take any responsibility.

However, he recalled the arrival of Jean Todt as a turning point in the team:

It was like Julius Caesar every day. People getting sacked and leaving every five minutes. You never knew who was boss – not until Jean Todt arrived, took control of the situation and instilled organisation, stability and loyalty into the team.[40]

The physical separation between design and development in Guildford and the racing operation in Maranello led to increased problems and, in early 1997, Barnard and Ferrari parted company for the second time. This opened the way for Ferrari to recruit not only driver Michael Schumacher but also a number of the key individuals in the Benetton technical team, which had helped him to his world titles in 1994 and 1995. The arrival of Schumacher provided new impetus for the team, as Nigel Stepney recounted:

Once Schumacher arrived, everyone started putting us under incredible pressure. We weren't quite ready as we still needed key people, but at some point you just have to go for it and get the best driver around. He was the icing on the cake and it sent out signals that we were serious again.[40]

Todt and di Montezemolo also chose not to make a direct replacement for the role of technical supremo who would both lead the design of the car and the management of the technical activity. They split the role between a Chief Designer, Rory Byrne, who had overall responsibility for designing the car, and Ross Brawn who managed the entire technical operation. These were roles which both had had when working with Schumacher at Benetton. However, on leaving Ferrari, Barnard had purchased the entire FDD operation from them. As most of the existing staff remained working for Barnard, this meant that Byrne and Brawn faced the task of building up a new design department from scratch – around fifty people, this time based in Italy. The engine department continued to develop Ferrari's engines, but in line with new technologies and regulatory requirements, these were now lighter V10s to compete with the Renault and Mercedes engines, rather than the beloved, but now dated Ferrari *dodici cilindri*.

As part of its recruitment in 1996 of Michael Schumacher, Ferrari entered into a commercial partnership with tobacco giant Phillip Morris to expose its Marlboro brand on the Ferrari cars. In a special arrangement Philip Morris, rather than Ferrari, paid Schumacher's salary, and also made a significant contribution to Ferrari's annual operating budget. However, there was one price to pay which was too high for many long-term Ferrari *aficionados*, the blood-red Ferrari of old was now replaced by a bright orange red, because it was more closely matched to the Marlboro colour scheme. Most importantly, it was more effective on television than the original Ferrari red.

In addition to Marlboro, Ferrari also entered into a long-term partnership with Shell, to provide both financial and technical support to the team. This was a departure for Ferrari which had previously always worked with Italian petroleum giant Agip. With these kinds of arrangements Ferrari led a trend from just selling space on cars to long-term commercial arrangements, with coordinated marketing strategies enabling commercial partners to maximise the benefits of their investments.

To many, the team now revolved around Schumacher, in contrast to past decades when drivers were honoured just to work for Ferrari. Jean Alesi, a former Ferrari driver, commented on this change in attitude at Ferrari:

Schumacher does whatever he wants, and they do whatever he says.[44]

Enzo Ferrari had famously rejected a number of top-class drivers because they wanted too much money, such as Jackie Stewart in 1970 and Ayrton Senna in 1986, whose wage demands Enzo described as '*imaginativo!*'[44]

This rejuvenated team provided the basis for Michael Schumacher's dominance of Formula 1. In 1997, Ferrari's fiftieth anniversary, there was great anticipation that would be its year, but the team fell just short, finishing second in the Constructors' Championship with the Barnard-developed Ferrari. As Nigel Stepney recounts:

1997 was a great disappointment for the team as we so nearly won the Championship, we felt we had the right way of working; we just had to keep at it and not panic.[40]

Ferrari's competitiveness continued to improve and in 1999 it won the Constructors' World Championship – although the Drivers' World Championship went to Mika Hakkinen in a McLaren-Mercedes. Stepney recalls:

It was a very stressful year; we lost Michael Schumacher after he broke his leg at Silverstone. Then we made mistakes such as the pit stop at the Nurburgring. But although we paid the price in one respect, we gained from the experiences. We realised that as a team, we had to pace ourselves, to switch off and recharge our batteries sometimes.[40]

In 2000 Ferrari secured both World Championship titles, a feat it repeated for the following four years. It was at this point that it felt it had truly returned to the glory of the mid-1970s.

Transforming performance in Formula 1 teams

Figure 17 outlines three conceptual responses to the need for transformation. The first is illustrated in the case study on Tyrrell Racing. Here we see the difficulty of an organisational mindset which is no longer consistent with the basis for superior performance in Formula 1. As the name suggests Tyrrell Racing was just that, an excellent racing organisation which was unable to keep up with the escalating demands of technology and commercial part-nerships needed to succeed as a constructor. What was required was for Tyrrell Racing to become a true Formula 1 business and perhaps this was something that Ken Tyrrell and his management team would have felt was going too far beyond their original ideals in establishing the business.

The case study on Brabham illustrates a different set of issues. In many ways Brabham had made some of the transformations needed to align itself to succeed in the 1970s and 1980s. A key problem seemed to be that it was too fast to react, as was the case with the flat-12 engine, but also that its lean and agile organisation lacked the resources to enable it to fully exploit its creative ideas. It had the vision and the innovation, but lacked the ability to integrate these ideas into a coherent whole. It undoubtedly got the success it deserved in the early 1980s, but was unable to sustain the managerial focus needed to really turn the organisation into a major Grand Prix player, in the way that Williams, McLaren and Ferrari have.

Ferrari provides the example of the transformational organisation that not only achieves the changes needed but is able to integrate these elements into a high-performance organisation which for a period of five years left the competition well behind and the regulators searching for ways to reduce its advantage, in the interests of more entertaining racing. Ferrari took almost ten years to achieve this turnaround. This type of transformation underlines the difficulty in being able to both create the level of change needed to effect a transition, but also to provide the resources and commitment to achieve the level of integra-tion, that has underpinned Ferrari's success during the first part of the twenty-first century.

Changing the way Formula 1 teams operate to deliver enhanced performance is a key imperative for senior management. No-one knows this better than Christian Horner, Team Principal of Red Bull Racing. He took over the organisation shortly after Red Bull's acqui-sition of Jaguar Racing from the Ford Motor Company and has the job of moving the team up the grid:

The initial observation that I made upon joining Red Bull Racing was that previously there had been a large corporate entity trying to run a corner shop. Formula 1 and mainstream automotive industry are two very different things. You have to be very reactive within

Formula 1, moving to the demands of the business and at the end of the day you have got eighteen weekends that you are judged upon. Many of the fundamental areas were quite sound but the team lacked technical direction, technical leadership and so basically we focused from a very early point on addressing the technical structure.

Horner's recognition of the need for technical direction meant that a top-line technical director needed to be recruited to the team; one who not only had the breadth of technical skills necessary, but one whose very presence would motivate and inspire existing staff and encourage new talent to move to the team. Perhaps surprisingly, in Formula 1, this was not the work of a moment:

Through the first twenty-four months we went through a process of identifying the key individuals and recruiting them into the company, obviously Adrian Newey being the most significant as Chief Technical Officer. Recruiting Adrian was a key appointment for us. One of the later key appointments was Geoff Willis who had recently been at Honda and BAR as Technical Manager. This allowed Adrian to continue to focus on the strategic direction of performance technologies, with Geoff being very much the facilitator to make it happen within the team.

Recruiting Adrian Newey from McLaren was only the start of the process for Red Bull Racing. What then had to follow was putting the right infrastructure in place, to allow the technical team to deliver the performance needed:

We've really invested heavily in the technical infrastructure, and then the operational structure as well in manufacturing and the trackside operation. So in many ways we kept what was working efficiently from the old Jaguar regime, and had a bit of a clearout across the technical and operational groups, to put in a focused and disciplined structure with clear technical direction. We've also spent a lot of time investing in the tools you need to get the job done, in the wind tunnel, in CFD, in various other dynometers and simulation tools, so we really have started to move the team into the twenty-first century.

Transforming performance in Formula 1 partners

In addition to creating changes for itself and the teams within it, a Formula 1 team can also provide a mechanism for organisational change for its partners. ING bank entered Formula 1 on a clear marketing platform; however, it found that its involvement was having such an energising impact on its employees that there was an opportunity to utilise this energy in a positive way to deliver organisational change. Isabelle M. Conner, Chief Marketing Officer for ING Group's Corporate Communications and Affairs division, who led the entry into Formula 1, has been given the responsibility for this initiative. She told us:

Formula 1 has proven to be more than just a platform for global brand visibility; it is a catalyst to advance change within the organisation. For example, in our new global advertising campaign we use a Formula 1 metaphor: in F1 the driver's job is made easier by all the professionals supporting him; similarly, at ING we believe that consumers who are saving and investing for their future should benefit from an easier financial services experience. And we are committed to making the changes within our organisation to make that happen. That's ING's new positioning, 'Easier'. We want to make financial services easier for consumers and F1 can help us explain that complex things don't have to be complicated when you have the right team working with you.

As we said at the outset of this chapter, change is pervasive in Formula 1. By examining three distinctive types of change, which have encompassed success and failure of Formula 1 teams, we have attempted to illustrate how sometimes radical changes are required when the competitive landscape is changing faster than the organisation's ability to change with it.

Plate 9a Drivers Robert Kubica (BMW Sauber) and Fernando Alonso (Renault) chatting in front of the BMW Sauber motorhome.
Source: the authors

Plate 9b Lewis Hamilton, McLaren-Mercedes driver, heading back to his hotel after a long day of testing and qualifying for Sunday's race.
Source: the authors

Plate 10a The rows of race transporters as seen in the reflection of the McLaren-Mercedes motorhomes' frontage.
Source: the authors

Plate 10b The Ferrari motorhomes that accompany the team to all European races.
Source: the authors

Plate 11 The BMW Sauber race transporter carries an important message that typifies the effort of all teams competing in Formula 1.
Source: the authors

Plate 12 Mechanics making adjustments to the Renault F1 car in the pit- lane garage.
Source: the authors

Plate 13 Ferrari driver and 2007 World Champion Kimi Raikkonen in the midst of a media scrum. The cap of 2005 and 2006 World Drivers' Champion Fernando Alonso (Renault F1) can be seen at left also engulfed by cameras and reporters.
Source: the authors

Plate 14 The antennae reaching high above the paddock from the teams' transporters, beam telemetry data from cars to motorhomes and also to team headquarters.
Source: the authors

Plate 15 Only 334 hours to go: an FW30 monocoque is stripped down in the race bay at WilliamsF1 headquarters. All the major assemblies will be serviced or replaced before the next event.
Source: Williams F1

11 | *Achieving and sustaining performance*

It's difficult when you're winning to keep the team at the top, because if you're winning you can get a bit arrogant. But it's also difficult when you're losing and what you need to do is change.

Flavio Briatore, Managing Director,
Renault F1 Team

The focus of this book is organisational performance – the nature of performance and how it is achieved 'at the limit'. Organisational performance relates to the extent to which an organisation achieves its stated objectives. Of course such objectives can be wide-ranging, potentially conflicting and also emphasising the needs of different stakeholders. In business the performance criteria tend to focus on financial variables, such as profitability, cash flow and shareholder value. However, with the development of tools such as the balanced scorecard[47] there is a greater awareness of the need to complement financial performance with other performance criteria such as the delivery of customer needs, the efficiency and effectiveness of internal processes and the ability to learn and grow.

In Formula 1, performance is measured ultimately by winning races and accumulating points in the Drivers' and Constructors' Championships. We have also seen that performance is measured in other ways within the team as in their quest for speed and efficiency of a pit stop; or by a team's partner in terms of an increase in brand recognition.

A further aspect of performance often exemplified in Formula 1 is the differing timescales upon which performance is considered; the tension between short- and long-term performance. In every race of the World Championship a team is under careful scrutiny as to how well it performs: a bad weekend and they are written off as 'no-hopers', a good result and they suddenly have the Championship in the bag.

Managing Director of Renault F1 team, Flavio Briatore, also recog-
nises that further pressure is brought to bear by the incredibly small
margins that mean the difference between success and failure:

*The line between good and bad is very thin; in one second you have
now fourteen to fifteen cars.*

Similarly, even within a race weekend there may be varying timescales
being considered in terms of optimising performance. At the pre-
qualifying practice sessions the smaller teams will often focus on
achieving a fast time in order to impress their sponsors, while the
leading teams will focus on preparing their cars for the following day
and therefore are less concerned with any immediate impact on the
timesheets.

When a new technical director is appointed to a team at the start
of the season – as was the case with Ross Brawn who moved from
Ferrari to Honda at the beginning of 2008 (he took 2007 as a sab-
batical year to recharge himself after leaving Ferrari) – there are
different timescales considered when bearing in mind performance.
Throughout 2008 Honda made no secret of the fact that its focus was
the development of the 2009 car, which would incorporate the new
hybrid-based KERS technology. While elements of the press were sug-
gesting that Brawn's arrival at Honda would have an immediate and
positive impact on the performance of Jenson Button, Brawn himself
was in no doubt that this was the first year of a three-year project, and
only at the end of those three years would he know whether or not he
had been successful in turning around the fortunes of the team:

*I've been asked how long will it take me to turn it around. To me
it's initially a three-year programme. If after three years we are not
showing that we can really compete at the top then we have failed.
For me, three years is the time to understand, to structure, to build,
and mentally I've set myself out a three-year programme.*

So what is performance in Formula 1? Interviewed in 2004 Jordan F1
Principal Eddie Jordan saw his role as focusing on two key areas:

*I have two very great responsibilities that are linked to performance.
One is performance on the track, but the other one is performance*

on the balance sheet and that is not always the concern of the major teams.

Also in 2004, Minardi's Commercial Director Paul Jordan did not see the measure of performance purely in terms of what happens on the track:

If you look at success in terms of what we achieve with what we have, then we're right up there with all the big teams.

In 2008 things had changed significantly: with the demise of Super Aguri in May, forced into receivership by a lack of funding, there were no really small teams fighting to survive on a race-by-race basis. The larger, manufacturer teams had differing performance criteria and agendas. For Ross Brawn, building Honda into a more successful racing organisation meant also building its political as well as technical capabilities:

You're building everything, not just the engineering, but building the team, the people, the relationships, the understanding of all the people of what needs to be done. The political side of Formula 1 is also important; working with the authorities, working with the decision-makers, and working with the other teams. I've come from a team that was very adept politically and was able to work well with the authorities. Ferrari never criticised the FIA in public and that was a principle. You had your arguments with the FIA behind closed doors. There is no value in challenging the FIA through the media. You need to build up the relationship and hopefully the respect so you can go to the FIA and say 'I think you've got this wrong' and they will listen and consider your views. Confrontation rarely works.

Do budgets explain racing performance?

In Figure 22, we see that budgets of Formula 1 teams have steadily increased over the nine-year period between 2000 and 2008. We see also that there is a 'top team' figure of around the $400 million mark, and that the smaller teams drop down to a level around $100 million.

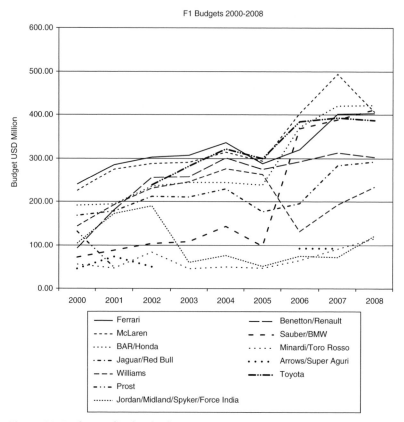

Figure 22 Budgets of individual teams, 2000–08

These figures also emphasise the marked distinction between the 'works': manufacturer-owned teams where the lowest budget is Renault at $303 million, in 2008, and the independent or 'private' teams of Williams and Force India. The one exception to this is Red Bull Racing, whose support from the Red Bull drinks organisation takes it close to the manufacturer scale of budget.

So is performance in Formula 1 simply a matter of budget? In this case the most successful teams would be those who are able to bring in the biggest budget. To some extent this is true. The larger budgets are normally associated with the highest performers, but not always, as illustrated in Figure 23. In 2007 we can see that Ferrari was the highest performing team and also the recipients of the highest budget. Force India (formerly known as Jordan F1, Midland F1 and Spyker)

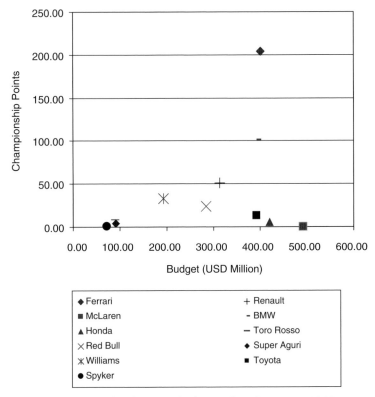

Figure 23 Relationship between budget and performance, 2007

was the weakest performer but was struggling with the lowest budget. In between these two points we see McLaren, Honda and Toyota as the exceptions to the rule in that they enjoy large budgets but none of them has been able to translate this into the equivalent level of performance. In McLaren's case this was due to losing all its constructors' points for 2007, as a result of a ruling by the FIA relating to the 'Spygate' episode. In the case of both Toyota and Honda it appears that the resources available to the team are not being translated into competitive performance.

If we consider the relationship between budget and performance, over time, we can represent this as an index in terms of the proportion of championship points gained over the proportion of the total budget. A figure greater than 1 indicates that the team are capturing

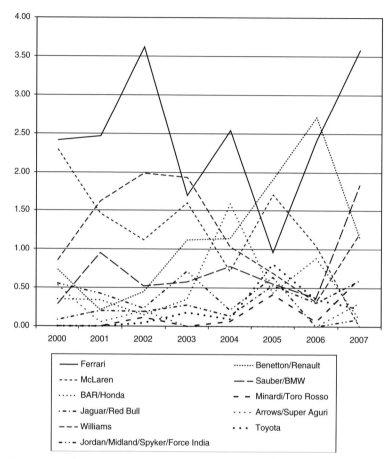

Figure 24 Value for money in Formula 1: share of points v. share of budget, 2000–07

a greater share of the race performance than its proportionate budget suggests. This is shown in Figure 24.

One of the problems in the current structure of Formula 1 is that it is, understandably, geared to the winners, the top teams. Tony Purnell describes this as a 'celebration of unfairness':

I describe Formula 1 as a celebration of unfairness: if you win you get more money, you get more TV. Everything's stacked in your favour and frankly you don't have to be so very good to continue winning, in business terms. But if you're down the bottom it is an awesome struggle. As you look up the stack everything is against you doing well. This is because all sorts of wheeler-dealer types and the top teams have bought advantage. You know, the best team gets the best garage, the best drivers, the best engineers. This has gone to such extremes that they are horrified that cars don't get out of the way for them. It doesn't just stop on the track; the position with the motorhomes is the best team get the best position. It's absolutely stacked up to favour the top teams. The important thing here is that the TV revenues and the extra sponsorship you command give you a huge advantage if you're in the top three, because money buys success in this game. So it's a bit odd in that way. It is not a remotely even playing field.

So what are the different levels of performance within Formula 1 and is it a different set of performance criteria that are needed at the back of the grid as compared to the front? We consider three categories of performance within Formula 1: the qualifiers, the winners and the champions.

The qualifiers: they made it to the race

For the qualifiers the focus is on survival. The critical measure is being able to attend and compete in Formula 1. If they can sustain this, then they have achieved a great deal, but history suggests that it is particularly difficult to sustain this kind of level; therefore, the qualifiers come and go.

In 2004, a team such as the now defunct Minardi would only have had 10–15 per cent of the budget of the top teams, yet its performance levels, based on lap times, were around 96–97 per cent. This means that it needed to operate at a different level; it figured out the minimum resources needed to sustain activities and worked back to achieve this. In contrast, the front-running teams were and are today focusing on the extra investment needed to win and retain their star drivers. Paul Stoddart, former Team Principal and owner of the Minardi team, said:

We get so much more out of each dollar we spend. We look to spend obviously the least amount possible, we look to get the maximum value for every dollar and we do things differently.

He went on to say that every opportunity Minardi had to raise money it did. This was even to the extent of finding mineral water companies to provide free product and refrigerators at the Grand Prix, so that the pit crew could quench their thirst without the team having to spend the money to do so.

One of the key assets that the qualifiers have is that they can provide a route in for new untried drivers. For Eddie Jordan this became an important part of his role in Formula 1:

I think when you get the image and reputation as being a so-called 'talent scout', or someone who is prepared to take new drivers on they come to you rather than they go to somewhere else first. It's something that you earn, it's a reputation.

Jordan most famously gave Michael Schumacher his first drive in Formula 1 and promptly lost him to the Benetton team, as a result of which Ron Dennis, McLaren Team Principal, commiserated with Jordan by saying: '*Welcome to the Piranha Club!*'[14]

For these teams, bringing on new drivers can be beneficial but it also carries a lot of risks. Inexperienced drivers can be very expensive and costs can quickly escalate after a few major accidents. It is therefore important that they are able to coach and mentor their new talent. Eddie Jordan said:

You see the guys who are being really good in Formula 3, it takes them a bit longer to be really proficient or to be kind to the car and the car should be smooth, it's no different to any sport or anything that you do, it's about a rhythm isn't it, and you get into a rhythm, whatever it is whether it's swimming it's the style, 'Oh, it's not like that, it's smooth it's power, it's motion and it's structure and that's what I'm always trying to give them, not a high technology.

In addition to drivers, there is also the opportunity to bring on other staff in both the commercial and technical areas of Formula 1. Eddie Jordan went on:

We are the 'University of Formula 1'. We are a kindergarten if you want to be cruel and a university if you want to be kind. We made at least five of the top designers, we employed Sam Michael [now Williams'

Technical Director], *Mike Gascoyne* [now Force India's Technical Director], *people like that.*

This category of teams is also able to bring in its own kind of sponsors, who perhaps would not wish to spend the amounts of money to work with a top team, but who would still derive business benefits from involvement in Formula 1. Eddie Jordan again:

Jordan has its own niche in the little market, people who like it a little bit blasé, a little bit vibrant, a little bit rock and roll, and a mixture of all of those things but a very serious person.

For other teams the focus is very much on moving on from being a qualifier to a winner. For Red Bull Racing's Christian Horner the key to achieving this is time and also changes in regulations which often serve to even out the competitive landscape. We asked Horner what is stopping Red Bull from winning races today. He said:

I guess we're still quite a young organisation; we still need time to mature as the groups are working, you know, getting that harmony together. We probably work on a budget that's 50 per cent of the likes of Toyota, Honda, McLaren, probably Ferrari, but that will not stop us from achieving our goals. We will just have to be smarter and work harder.

Time will tell whether Red Bull move to the winner's category. Due to its strong corporate backing it may be able to sustain the push to become winners for longer than some other qualifiers.

The winners: they get on to the podium

In very simplistic terms, in the 1970s all a team needed was the money to buy a couple of Cosworth engines, basic premises, a few skilled and dedicated workers and the ability to build a reasonable chassis, and it could go racing. This was epitomised in 1974 by Lord Hesketh's privately funded Hesketh Racing, which eventually beat the Ferraris into second and third place at the Dutch Grand Prix at Zandvoort on 22 June 1975. Hesketh Racing also introduced driver James Hunt (World Champion for McLaren in 1976) to Formula 1 as well as designer Dr Harvey Postlethwaite, who went on to design cars for Ferrari, Sauber, Tyrrell and Honda.

Things changed in later years with the influx of the automotive manufacturers. The basis for success was provided by an equity stake purchased by a manufacturer in a team: for example, Renault purchased the Benetton team, McLaren is now partly owned by Daimler Chrysler, and BMW acquired the Sauber F1 team.

The unpredictable nature of Grand Prix racing has meant that some teams have been able to make a one-time only visit to the top of the podium. These may have been due to rain – for example the Stewart Grand Prix team secured its one and only victory at the Nurburgring in September 1999 when drivers Johnny Herbert and Rubens Barrichello (who finished third) made the right decision in changing to wet weather tyres when a downpour started. Or victory may have been due to massive levels of attrition. Olivier Panis won the Monaco Grand Prix at Monte Carlo in 1996 in a Ligier Honda, but at the end of the race there were only four cars remaining out of the twenty-one that started the race.

The Jordan team may have slipped down Formula 1's pecking order before it was sold, but over the years it had won a total of four Grand Prix, which certainly puts it above the 'one-win wonders' – which up to 2008 included Stewart, Ligier, Penske, Eagle, Shadow and Porsche (in 1961).

For BMW's Mario Theissen, whose team won its first Grand Prix in 2008, this fits within a very clear strategy for success, which was set out in 2006:

We are here to win. We set a very clear plan three years ago, which caused me some headache at that time. We wanted to be in the points in the first year [2006], on the podium in the second [2007], win races in the third [2008], which is this year, and fight for the Championship from 2009 onwards. That's the clear schedule.

Another perspective for considering the category of winners is to reflect on why these teams are not champions. Many of these organisations, such as McLaren and Renault (formerly Benetton), were at one time champions, so why are they no longer in that situation? Former CEO of Ferrari Jean Todt offers one explanation that we alluded to earlier:

The final result in F1 is very much the combination of all the details. And if one detail does not work, you fail, that's why it is so difficult.

So these teams are not in a position to put all of these details together; why is this? Again Jean Todt, when he ran the Ferrari team:

One of our strengths is stability, but stability could be a disaster if you have bad people. If you have a bad, stable organisation, it is a disaster, so stability is good if you have the right people at the right time.

So in one sense, the winners are those with the potential to be champions, but various details have not yet come together. They are 'champions in waiting'. They just need a special influence that will enable the team to take the important step together towards being champions. This may be achieved by bringing in new individuals, such as a driver; or perhaps by bringing together new technologies; or obtaining new partners to create the high performance needed. What matters is finding some way to help bring the organisation together as one cohesive team. As Alex Burns at WilliamsF1 said:

We have to keep that sense of belonging. There are people who've been here fifteen or twenty years who are saying, 'We've lost the sense of belonging, we've lost that connection with the product because it's got so big.' We have to make it happen again, to build that connection even though we're a lot bigger.

What is interesting is that all of these factors are related to the process of integrating. Winners are organisations that have not yet integrated into champions.

The champions: they won and kept on winning

So what makes a Formula 1 team a World Championship winner? Fundamentally the World Championship team is one that is able to bring together all of the many factors which create a winning performance and then repeat this again and again; in other words, sustain their competitive advantage.

For Jean Todt the answer to creating a Championship-winning team is very simple:

We don't take things for granted because we know it can be very fragile. We are living convinced that we will be beaten tomorrow ... After we win a race and the champagne has been drunk, we stay one and a half hours together making the debriefing or talking about what did not work.

This view is echoed by Todt's replacement at Ferrari, Stefano Domenicali, who believes that the concept of 'dynamic stability' is a key element in sustained winning:

We say that there is dynamic stability. What does this mean? It means that we have a set of values and principles that are the common ground for our company. This gives us two areas to focus on: one, to ensure these values and principles are understood throughout the organisation, and two, that everyone is applying these in the way they work day by day.

So part of being a Championship-winning team is believing that you're not! It is constantly trying to find ways to win the next race; just because you won the last doesn't mean a thing. Ross Brawn when at Ferrari told us:

I think complacency is the thing that we're aware of. Most of our people realise that what we're doing is not normal. The results we're achieving are not normal and they're coming about because we having a very special period and it's very fragile as well. We talk far more about our failings than we do about our successes.

12 | *Twelve business lessons from Formula 1 motor racing*

In the first edition of this book we distilled ten lessons from Formula 1 that might be applicable in part or in whole to organisations in other industries. Since then we have had opportunities to discuss and test these concepts during our speaking and teaching engagements, with a large number of businesses representing different industries and countries. Our judgement is that they are as well-received, germane and on-target today as when they were first written. We have decided to stick with the same ten lessons in this second edition. However, our ongoing research has revealed two further ones that we believe are fundamental to long-term success.

These lessons are the underpinning of our performance framework shown in Figure 6. In the framework we explain organisational performance as a function of individuals, teams and partners coming together; and by integrating, innovating and transforming these elements in changing competitive situations, sustainable performance can be achieved.

These lessons are not instant panaceas that every organisation should necessarily adopt, but they do offer insights that will help business leaders who are trying to galvanise their organisations into becoming more performance-focused, flexible, innovative and above all, more competitive.

The first five lessons, open communication, no-blame culture, building on the informal network, and alignment of goals and focus, are all central to the integration needed to make the organisation work as a team. The following four, making quick decisions, looking for gains at the boundaries, being realistic and never believing in your success, relate to the processes of innovating and transforming. The tenth lesson, of dispersed leadership at all levels, relates to all three processes and provides the basis by which organisations are able to move fluidly between them, thereby delivering high performance in a complex and dynamic environment. We have added two

223

additional lessons at the end of the list based on our more recent research.

Lesson 1. Maintain open and constant communication

During our research one concept was voiced by virtually all the individuals we interviewed; that is, the importance of maintaining an open flow of communication involving everyone in the organisation. This communication takes place both formally and informally, on a small and large scale, in person and virtually.

Lesson 2. Isolate the problem not the person: the no-blame culture

Here we pick up on WilliamsF1's Dickie Stanford's comment that when something has gone wrong, the focus must be put on resolving the problem in a systemic sense, rather than blaming the person. This is difficult to achieve in practice. In many instances when a team falls into difficult times it goes through a period of blame to explain the failure. It is the ability to break out of this blame culture which often signifies a period of further success. This can be stimulated by improved performance, but to be sustained it has to be underpinned by a work environment that allows failures to be shared and openly discussed by all.

Lesson 3. Build the organisation around informal processes, networks and relationships

Across all of the teams we found a common emphasis on building from the expertise and relationships of the people within the organisation, and the partners allied to the business. This approach enables the structure to emerge from these relationships, rather than imposing a 'theoretical' organisation which is populated by rigid, specified roles and job descriptions that do not relate to the pressurised world that Formula 1 teams inhabit.

Perhaps we could criticise those teams who do not have ready-to-hand organisational charts or detailed job descriptions. Clearly these are important aspects of modern organisational life. But in a situation where there is real commitment and passion from employees, the lack of such management tools illustrates how the organisation becomes 'empowered' by removing layers of potentially needless bureaucracy.

In reality, we know that organisation charts rarely reflect how people in the business actually work together or relate to one another in terms of getting tasks completed. The Formula 1 organisation is an emergent structure that is designed to optimise and facilitate the potential of individuals and their relationships, rather than determining and micro-managing such interactions. The conclusion that we reach is that it is only through effectively supporting these interactions and relationships that performance can be truly optimised.

In business management there is a mantra that structure drives strategy which in turn drives performance. In Formula 1, people and their relationships drive the structure which in turn drives performance. Perhaps surprisingly for its strong technology orientation, Formula 1 is a very people-driven business.

Lesson 4. Alignment of goals between individuals, teams and partners

There are two parts to the issue of alignment. One is commonality of goals towards which teams and sub-teams in the organisation are striving. The other is the connection between the individuals' actions and the end result. Perhaps this is best illustrated in the way that Frank Williams constantly asks the question when signing cheques: *'How will it make the car go faster?'* against which all can measure the value of their specific contributions on a day-to-day basis. From the Formula 1 team partner's perspective the question may be different: *'Will it help us sell more product?'* It is the continual alignment of these factors that helps to optimise business processes in Formula 1 teams.

Lesson 5. Focus, focus, focus

The rigour of a nineteen- or twenty-race season puts a heightened premium on getting the right job done at the right time. It seems quite a basic concept, given the industry's often changing regulatory constraints, budgetary limitations under which many teams operate, and very tight deadlines. Formula 1 teams must focus on the tasks at hand in order to be on the grid with an improved car, week after week. Even in this context, we have seen examples of where successful teams have lost their focus, lost their edge and ultimately paid a very high price: perhaps most famously through McLaren's departure into high-performance, limited edition roadcars in the early 1990s (the McLaren F1). Likewise, drivers who are facing great demands on their time have to learn to focus on what truly matters, which in the end is performance on the track.

Lesson 6. Make quick decisions and learn from the results

Seeing the opportunity, being decisive and then learning from the result of one's actions is central to continual improvement of performance in this fast-paced environment. These ideas fit closely with the concept of the learning organisation, where continual experimentation and learning provide the basis by which firms move forward. Formula 1 teams have to continually learn from their mistakes otherwise they soon fall off the pace, and lose the interest of their sponsors.

But to work it also requires a culture where individuals are not constrained from trying something, and where failure does not undermine their position or credibility in the organisation.

Lesson 7. The real gains come at the boundaries

The real performance gains occur at the margins, at the boundaries between the various interfaces, whether these are component areas of the car, between partner organisations or between different teams and sub-teams. These are the gains that are particularly difficult to achieve and sustain, but they are the ones that will make the difference in performance, if all other areas are working effectively. When teams are operating at the top of their game, their focus moves from building up particular specialist competence, to integrating the whole system and ensuring that it operates to the maximum. In order to deliver the best racing package, barriers between functional departments must be eliminated so that communication between and across them can be clear, constant and directed towards achieving their common goals.

Lesson 8. Be realistic about what can be achieved

Continual change is necessary in order to keep pace with competitors' strategic actions and customers' ever-changing demands. However, change fatigue is not an unusual problem in organisations today. One of the important lessons that can be drawn from the recent success of Ferrari is that change in organisations has to take place within realistic constraints, otherwise the development process may fall apart. Setting high, but realistic goals and keeping everyone apprised of progress against those goals is a key factor in driving the change process forward.

Lesson 9. Never believe you can keep winning

The Icarus paradox[48] considers the problem of success blinding the organisation to future threats. In the case of Ferrari, the trick appears to be to refuse to believe that you are inherently capable of being consistently successful. Always assume each win is your last victory and, therefore, you will continually search for those extra tenths of seconds that will sustain you at the top. There is not a better time to challenge one's processes and methods, or business strategy for that matter, than when leading the industry. The really hard part is maintaining the pressure and urgency to do so while retaining the energy and motivation that is so important for the team. That is one reason why Ferrari has been able to build such a formidable record in recent years.

Lesson 10. Leaders exist at all levels of the organisation

Due to the fast pace of this industry, employees throughout Formula 1 teams are empowered to make decisions, drive processes and take risks. We have witnessed people at all levels within Formula 1 organisations stepping up to be accountable and to lead their colleagues when it is their time to take responsibility.

This means that the more senior roles are concerned with problem-solving and connecting up different parts of the organisation, rather than coaching or directing. At times this can be problematic particularly where big egos are not in short supply, but the lesson here is to recognise that in the most successful teams people are prepared to put their heads above the parapet and lead their project or initiative. Also, in these contexts, the drivers are not prima donnas but real catalysts for the team, encouraging everyone to play their part to achieve performance at the limit.

Lesson 11: Measure everything

Formula 1 is first and foremost an engineering-based industry. In that context, the delivery of the key product, a fast Formula 1 car, is entirely contingent on design, manufacture and refinement using the latest in software, telemetry and computer capacity, to measure *everything*. Measurement comes into play at the factory, in the pit lane, on the track and also, as we have seen, in the physiological readings of the drivers. Like all people in business, Formula 1 teams have to determine what useful information can be drawn out of the massive amount of data that is captured. They must apply reasonable thinking to utilise that information, to make strategic and tactical decisions. In turn, those decisions need to evolve, usually very quickly, into actionable tasks. Once delivered, the impacts of those tasks are measured, and the process starts over again. Recording of input and measurement of output goes beyond the teams themselves, and is the primary process by which sponsors determine whether their investment in the sport provides the returns they are seeking.

When a business is using scorecards of some sort or re-engineering techniques, it is embracing a model of measurement, evaluation, and action in the organisation, just as Formula 1 teams do.

Lesson 12: At the edge, not over it

This may be an obvious statement, but conflict within an organisation can undo all of the strong efforts and goodwill that has been built to that point. Given the competitive nature of the individuals in Formula 1 and the fact that they operate within a media fishbowl, it is not uncommon that dirty laundry is aired in public. Whether it is an employee disgruntled because he was passed up for promotion who then shares insider information with a competitor, or two drivers on the same team who cannot seem to get along, the impact of their attitudes and actions most certainly infect the organisation's culture and eventually performance in a negative way.

Organisations that have a culture where people feel free to share their thoughts with peers and bosses without reprisal, where managers are in touch with their employees' aspirations and development needs, and that foster teamwork as a guiding value are less prone to find themselves operating with internal conflict situations that get out of hand.

Appendix A: Grand Prix Champions 1950–2008

Year	Drivers' Cup	Car/Engine	Constructors' Cup
1950	Giuseppe Farina	Alfa Romeo	
1951	Juan Manuel Fangio	Alfa Romeo	
1952	Alberto Ascari	Ferrari	
1953	Alberto Ascari	Ferrari	
1954	Juan Manuel Fangio	Maserati	
1955	Juan Manuel Fangio	Mercedes-Benz	
1956	Juan Manuel Fangio	Lancia-Ferrari	
1957	Juan Manuel Fangio	Maserati	
1958	Mike Hawthorn	Ferrari	Vanwall
1959	Jack Brabham	Cooper/Climax	Cooper/Climax
1960	Jack Brabham	Cooper/Climax	Cooper/Climax
1961	Phil Hill	Ferrari	Ferrari
1962	Graham Hill	BRM	BRM
1963	Jim Clark	Lotus/Climax	Lotus/Climax
1964	John Surtees	Ferrari	Ferrari
1965	Jim Clark	Lotus/Climax	Lotus/Climax
1966	Jack Brabham	Brabham/Repco	Brabham/Repco
1967	Denny Hulme	Brabham/Repco	Brabham/Repco
1968	Graham Hill	Lotus/Ford	Lotus/Ford
1969	Jackie Stewart	Matra/Ford	Matra/Ford
1970	Jochen Rindt	Lotus/Ford	Lotus/Ford
1971	Jackie Stewart	Tyrrell/Ford	Tyrrell/Ford
1972	Emerson Fittipaldi	Lotus/Ford	Lotus/Ford
1973	Jackie Stewart	Tyrrell/Ford	Lotus/Ford
1974	Emerson Fittipaldi	McLaren/Ford	McLaren/Ford
1975	Niki Lauda	Ferrari	Ferrari
1976	James Hunt	McLaren/Ford	Ferrari
1977	Niki Lauda	Ferrari	Ferrari
1978	Mario Andretti	Lotus/Ford	Lotus/Ford

(*cont.*)

Year	Driver' Cup	Car/Engine	Constructors' Cup
1979	Jody Scheckter	Ferrari	Ferrari
1980	Alan Jones	Williams/Ford	Williams/Ford
1981	Nelson Piquet	Brabham/Ford	Williams/Ford
1982	Keke Rosberg	Williams/Ford	Ferrari
1983	Nelson Piquet	Brabham/BMW	Ferrari
1984	Niki Lauda	McLaren/Porsche	McLaren/Porsche
1985	Alain Prost	McLaren/Porsche	McLaren/Porsche
1986	Alain Prost	McLaren/Porsche	Williams/Honda
1987	Nelson Piquet	Williams/Honda	Williams/Honda
1988	Ayrton Senna	McLaren/Honda	McLaren/Honda
1989	Alain Prost	McLaren/Honda	McLaren/Honda
1990	Ayrton Senna	McLaren/Honda	McLaren/Honda
1991	Ayrton Senna	McLaren/Honda	McLaren/Honda
1992	Nigel Mansell	Williams/Renault	Williams/Renault
1993	Alain Prost	Williams/Renault	Williams/Renault
1994	Michael Schumacher	Benetton/Ford	Williams/Renault
1995	Michael Schumacher	Benetton/Renault	Benetton/Renault
1996	Damon Hill	Williams/Renault	Williams/Renault
1997	Jacques Villeneuve	Williams/Renault	Williams/Renault
1998	Mika Hakkinen	McLaren/Mercedes	McLaren/Mercedes
1999	Mika Hakkinen	McLaren/Mercedes	Ferrari
2000	Michael Schumacher	Ferrari	Ferrari
2001	Michael Schumacher	Ferrari	Ferrari
2002	Michael Schumacher	Ferrari	Ferrari
2003	Michael Schumacher	Ferrari	Ferrari
2004	Michael Schumacher	Ferrari	Ferrari
2005	Fernando Alonso	Renault	Renault
2006	Fernando Alonso	Renault	Renault
2007	Kimi Raikkonen	Ferrari	Ferrari
2008	Lewis Hamilton	McLaren/Mercedes	Ferrari

Note: The Constructors' Championship is based on the cumulative points gained by a team during the season. Currently each team is limited to entering two cars and drivers per race.

Appendix B: Grand Prix Graveyard 1950–2008

(Adapted from '*The Piranha Club*', *Timothy Collings*, *Virgin Books*, 2001: p. 278)

	Team	Lifespan	Formula 1 races
1.	AGS	1986–1991	48
2.	Alfa Romeo	1950–1985	112
3.	Arrows	1977–2002	382
4.	ATS	1977–1984	99
5.	BAR	1999–2005	117
6.	Benetton	1986–2001	260
7.	Brabham	1962–1992	394
8.	BRM	1951–1977	197
9.	Cooper	1950–1969	129
10.	Dallara	1988–1992	78
11.	Eagle	1966–1969	26
12.	Ensign	1973–1982	99
13.	Fittipaldi	1975–1982	104
14.	Forti	1995–1996	23
15.	Gordini	1950–1956	40
16.	Hesketh	1974–1978	52
17.	Honda	1964–1968	35
18.	Jaguar	2000–2004	85
19.	Jordan	1991–2004	250
20.	Lancia	1954–1955	4
21.	Larrousse	1992–1994	48
22.	Ligier	1976–1996	326
23.	Lola	1962–1997	139
24.	Lotus	1958–1994	491
25.	March	1970–1992	230
26.	Maserati	1950–1960	69
27.	Matra	1967–1972	60

(*cont.*)

	Team	Lifespan	Formula 1 races
28.	Mercedes	1954–1955	12
29.	Midland	2005–2006	18
30.	Minardi	1985–2005	340
31.	Onyx	1989–1990	17
32.	Osella	1980–1990	132
33.	Pacific	1994–1995	22
34.	Parnelli	1974–1976	16
35.	Penske	1974–1976	30
36.	Porsche	1958–1964	31
37.	Prost	1997–2001	83
38.	Renault	1977–1985	123
39.	Rial	1988–1989	20
40.	Shadow	1973–1980	104
41.	Simtex	1994–1995	21
42.	Spyker	2007	17
43.	Stewart	1997–1999	49
44.	Super Aguri	2006–2008	39
45.	Surtees	1970–1978	118
46.	Talbot	1950–1951	13
47.	Tecno	1972–1973	11
48.	Theodore	1978–1983	34
49.	Tyrrell	1970–1998	418
50.	Vanwall	1954–1960	28
51.	Wolf	1977–1979	47
52.	Zakspeed	1985–1989	54

Appendix C: Interview respondents

	Name	Organisation	Position at time of interview
1	Sir John Allison	Jaguar Racing	Operations Director
2	John Barnard	McLaren (1981– 1986) Ferrari (1986– 1990; 1992–1997) Benetton (1991) Arrows (1997)	Former Technical Director
3	Ross Brawn	Honda Racing F1	Team Principal; former Technical Director Ferrari
4	Flavio Briatore	Renault F1 Team	Managing Director
5	Martin Brundle		Former Formula 1 Driver and now Driver Manager and Commentator
6	Alex Burns	WilliamsF1	Chief Operating Officer
7	Luca Colajanni	Ferrari	Motorsport Press Officer
8	Isabelle M. Conner	ING	Chief Marketing Officer
9	Peter Digby	Managing Director	Xtrac Limited
10	Stefano Domenicali	Ferrari	Racing Management General Director
11	Bernie Ecclestone	Formula One Administration	President
12	Paul Edwards	Edwards Hospitality Services	Managing Director
13	Bernard Ferguson	Cosworth Racing	Commercial Director
14	Scott Garrett	WilliamsF1	Head of Marketing

(*cont.*)

	Name	Organisation	Position at time of interview
15	Patrick Head	WilliamsF1	Director of Engineering
16	Aki Hintsa MD	McLaren Racing	Team Physician
17	John Hogan		Freelance Marketing Consultant
18	Christian Horner	Red Bull Racing	Team Principal
19	John Howett	Toyota F1	President
20	Eddie Jordan	Jordan F1	Founder and CEO
21	Paul Jordan	Minardi	Commercial Director
22	Heikki Kovalainen	McLaren-Mercedes	Driver
23	Paolo Martinelli	Ferrari	Engine Director
24	John Mardle	Renault	Operations Director
25	Felipe Massa	Ferrari	Driver
26	Max Mosley	FIA	President
27	Ian Phillips	Red Bull Racing	Director of Business Affairs
28	Raoul Pinnelll	Shell	Chairman, International Brands
29	Tony Purnell	FIA	Technical Consultant to FIA and former CEO of Ford's Premier Performance Division
30	David Richards	BAR	Team Principal, currently Chairman of Prodrive and Aston Martin
31	David Robertson	Formula Management Ltd	Business Manager for Kimi Raikkonen and Jenson Button
32	Nico Rosberg	WilliamsF1	Driver
33	Dickie Stanford	WilliamsF1	Test Team Manager
34	Sir Jackie Stewart	Jaguar Racing (2000–2004)	World Drivers' Champion in 1969, 1971 and 1973
		Stewart Grand Prix (1996–1999)	Director, Jaguar Racing

(*cont.*)

	Name	Organisation	Position at time of interview
35	Paul Stoddart	Minardi	Owner and Team Principal
36	Pat Symonds	Renault F1 Team	Executive Director of Engineering
37	Jean Todt	Ferrari	CEO
38	David Tremayne		Formula 1 Journalist
39	John Walton	Minardi	Sporting Director
40	Mark Webber	Red Bull Racing	Driver
41	Sir Frank Williams	WilliamsF1	Team Principal
42	Jim Wright	Toro Rosso	Head of Sponsorship
43	Hiroshi Yasukawa	Bridgestone	Director of Motorsport

Further to the above we have also utilised transcripts from a series of research interviews conducted by the first author to explore the nature of performance in Formula 1:

Gordon Murray	Brabham (1972–1986) McLaren (1987–1989)	Former Technical Director
Ken Tyrrell	Tyrrell	Founder and Team Principal
Derek Gardner	Tyrrell (1971–1977)	Former Technical Director
David Williams	WilliamsF1 (1992–1998)	General Manager

References

1. Fédération Internationale de l'Automobile, the sport's governing body.
2. *MotorSport* vol. 83, no. 13, p. 59.
3. Peters, T. J. and Waterman, R. H., Jr. (1982) *In Search of Excellence: Lessons from America's Best-Run Companies*. New York: Harper & Row.
4. Collins, J. C. and Porras, J. I. (1994) *Built to Last: Successful Habits of Visionary Companies*. New York: HarperBusiness.
5. D'Aveni, R. (1994) *Hypercompetition: Managing the Dynamics of Strategic Maneuvering*. New York: Free Press.
6. Brown, S. L. and Eisenhardt, K. M. (1998) *Competing on the Edge: Strategy as Structured Chaos*. Boston, MA: Harvard Business School Press.
7. 2008 'Dennis doubts BMW can keep up'. autosport.com/news 7 April.
8. *Financial Times* (2008) 'The Business of Sport, Formula One', 23 May, pp. 40–1.
9. *Initiatives Sports Futures* (2008) 9 January.
10. *MotorSport* vol. 83, no. 13, p. 57.
11. *Financial Times* (2008) 'The Business of Sport, Formula One', 23 May, p. 5.
12. Herzberg, F., Mausner, B., and Snyderman, B. B. (1959) *The Motivation to Work*. New York: Wiley.
13. *F1* magazine (2004) July p. 48.
14. Collings, T. (2002) *The Piranha Club*. London: Virgin Books.
15. Hotten, R. (1998) *Formula 1: The Business of Winning*. London: Orion Business.
16. *International Herald Tribune* (2008) 'The art (and science) of making a Formula One champion', 6 June.
17. Hughes, M. *Autosport* (2002) 'Seats of Power', 28 November, p. 39.
18. *F1 Racing* (2004) February p. 43.
19. *F1 Racing* (2008) 'Britain expects', July, p. 78.
20. 2008 'Kimi could quit at end of 2009 season' www.planet-f1.com 5 June.

21. Katzenbach, J.R. and Smith, D.K. (1994) *The Wisdom of Teams: Creating the High Performance Organization*. London: Harper-Business.

22. *Hoshin* ensures that everyone in the organisation is working toward the same end. The plan is hierarchical, cascading down through the organisation and to key business-process owners. Ownership of the supporting strategies is clearly identified with measures at the appropriate level or process owner within the organisation.

23. Gilson, C., Pratt, M., Roberts, K. and Weymes, E. (2000) *Peak Performance: Inspirational Business Lessons from the World's Top Sports Organizations*. New York: Texere.

24. (2007) 'Todt, Raikkonen, Massa and Montezemolo talk' www.pitpass. com. 29 October.

25. *International Herald Tribune* (2008), 9 May.

26. *Autosport* (1998) 'Price of success'. 15 January, pp. 38–41.

27. *Autosport* (2002) 'Winning isn't everything'. 28 November, pp. 40–41.

28. Saxenian, A. (1994) *Regional Advantage: Culture and Competition in Silicon Valley and Route 128*. Cambridge, MA: Harvard University Press.

29. (2007) 'F1nvestor: There's no 'I' in Team ...' www.pitpass.com. 28 November.

30. *MotorSport* (2008) August, p. 21.

31. *F1 Racing* (2008) 'Mark Webber'. July, p. 115.

32. *Financial Times* (2008) 'BMW join Formula One's big boys'. 26/27 April.

33. Tichy, N.M. and Cohen, E. (1997) *The Leadership Engine: Winning Companies Build Leaders at Every Level*. New York: HarperBusiness.

34. Mintzberg, H. (2001) 'Managing Exceptionally'. *Organization Science*, vol. 12, no. 6, pp. 759–71.

35. Robson, G. (1999) *Cosworth: The Search for Power*. Yeovil, Somerset: Haynes Publishing.

36. Scarborough, C. (2008). Autosport.com Journal, vol. 14, no. 9, 7 May.

37. Henry, N. and Pinch, S. (2002) 'Spatializing Knowledge: Placing the Knowledge Community of Motor Sports Valley'. In Huff, A. S. and Jenkins, M. (eds.), *Mapping Strategic Knowledge*, pp. 136–69. London: Sage.

38. Watkins, S. (1996) *Life at the Limit: Triumph and Tragedy in Formula One*. London: Macmillan.

39. Lovell, T. (2003) *Bernie's Game*. London: Metro Publishing.

40. *Formula 1* (2001) 'Ferrari's Nigel Stepney: The Man Who Can'. April, pp. 69–71.

41. Johnson, G. (1988) 'Rethinking Incrementalism'. *Strategic Management Journal*, pp. 75–91.
42. Hamilton, M. (2002) *Ken Tyrrell: The Authorised Biography*. London: HarperCollins.
43. *Autosport* (1980) 'Seasonal Survey', December.
44. *Autosport* (1998) 'The Day the Magic Died'. 13 August, pp. 32–7.
45. *Autosport* (1992) 13 February, p. 5.
46. *Autosport* (1992) 'The Man Who's Rebuilding Ferrari'. 10 September, pp. 28–30.
47. Kaplan R.S. & Norton D.P. (1996) *The Balanced Scorecard: Translating Strategy into Action*. Boston, MA: Harvard Business School Press.
48. Miller, D. (1990) *The Icarus Paradox*. New York: HarperBusiness.
49. Wright, P. (2001) *Formula 1 Technology*. Warrendale, PA: Society of Automotive Engineers.

Sources

List of published sources used in the research undertaken for this book:

Websites

autosport.com
thefia.com
formula1.com
grandprix.com
pitpass.com
ten-tenths.com

Secondary works

Autosport
Eurobusiness
F1 Racing
MotorSport

Index